TO MA·

Best w·

 Nick Tuffney

Building Six

A True Story

JACQUELINE HOMEWOOD

Text Jacqueline Homewood

Design Grade Design and Adeline Media, London

First print July, 2020

TABLE OF CONTENTS

PROLOGUE

This is a story that needs to be told. It is about a four- year nightmare during which an innocent man was locked in one of the most brutal prisons in the world.

It is about injustice, corruption and the sickening descent from apparent security into the darkest chaos.

My name is Nicholas Tuffney, and while I am thankful that I survived, the cost to my physical and mental health, my independence, my personal happiness, has been devastating. Many I know were not lucky enough to make it out alive. This book is for them. Above all, its purpose is to shine a hard, unblinking light on Panamá's rotten justice system, a human rights travesty that the British and American governments would rather ignore, even when one of its citizens is incarcerated.

In 2010, I was a successful businessman with prized British and American passports. I had grown up in Kent, moved to Florida in my 30s and worked hard to establish a supply company trading in a wide variety of goods. After marrying a Panamanian woman, I went on to invest heavily in that country. My interest went far beyond making a profit. I built houses there and founded a charity, which procured and donated equipment to medical centres in the remote

Darién region. Many of the people I met there were good and genuine, struggling against hardship unimaginable to comfortable Westerners, and I felt a compulsion to help improve their lot.

My marriage disintegrated when my wife, Laura, had an affair with a colleague. The events that followed were pitched between terror and

1

farce. I was accused by her family of corrupting minors – by witchcraft. I went from being an affable rich guy who liked a beer to a demonic gringo who practised sorcery in the jungle: a character assassination broadcast on national TV.

I was first admitted to Panamá City's central detention centre, Ancón , which is a windowless shithole once used to house the enemies of Panamanian dictator General Manuel Noriega. There, I was stripped and humiliated before being given a beating by fellow inmates that robbed me of several teeth. At one point, I had a seizure and collapsed, and was briefly kept in a hospital chained to a bed that had, ironically, been supplied by my own charity. A police guard with a machine gun kept watch in case I somehow slipped my bonds and tried to hobble to freedom. The next stop was the police station in the Darién town of La Palma, where I was chained for 24 hours a day like a Victorian circus attraction to rusty iron bars outside the walls of its prison. The building was so decrepit that it had been condemned by the state three years earlier and supposedly closed. There was nowhere for me to sit or lie down and my food, such as it was, came in a filthy trough. More than a month later, my health broken, I was finally transported to Panamá City's inaccurately named La Joya prison – it means 'the jewel' in Spanish.

La Joya has earned its place among the world's 10 most feared prisons. It is a stinking, teeming, violent, vermin- infested, drunken, drug-addled glimpse of hell. Inmates belonging to rival gangs regularly kill each other. A fellow prisoner who made the mistake of stealing someone else's cocaine was hacked to death with a machete during my stay.

It was still better than being kept on display in the main street of La Palma.

In La Joya's Building Six, a block reserved for foreigners, I saw people degraded but I also marvelled at their resilience in the face of endemic neglect and cruelty. Corruption drove the system and the inmates were ingenious about bending the rules – all of which were negotiable for cash – to suit their own ends. It resulted in a micro-economy of pop-up businesses selling everything, from the medicines impossible to obtain through official channels to freshly baked cakes. The richest and craftiest survived – somehow. The poorest and weakest went to the wall.

Corrupt Panamanian police

Something positive did emerge from my time inside: I met the extraordinary Cambridge and Harvard-educated Dr Arthur Porter, who has inspired me to persist with this book. Once an advisor to the Canadian prime minister, he was accused of taking kickbacks from the construction of a new hospital in Montreal. It was his misfortune to be in Panamá when Interpol agents caught up with him. He claimed innocence. All I can report is that he tended to many sick prisoners as best he could when no one in authority gave a damn. He also gave me a sense of purpose that helped to make La Joya bearable.

Many times, I felt suicidal despair. (Suicide in La Joya is commonplace.) The fear that I would be trapped, forgotten, until the day I succumbed to infection or disease, made me consider giving up the struggle. The ever-present danger, despite my attempts to befriend protectors, of being knifed by a blade fashioned from a sardine tin was not exactly uplifting either. Murder of another inmate barely registered as an offence. Despite, or maybe because of the challenges, Arthur and I quietly built a bond. Together, we gathered covert video evidence of the day-to-day horrors of prison life. We vowed that whoever got out first would expose those horrors to the eyes of the world. I'm sad to report that Arthur died of cancer in 2015, while still officially in custody. It therefore falls to me to make good on our promise, now that I have the strength to do so.

When my own case finally reached court in 2014 (on the eighth attempt after multiple suspicious cancellations), it was dismissed. My accusers didn't even bother to turn up. Why would they, when their star witnesses had already admitted they had been bribed to come up with their allegations against me?

They have to date faced no consequences for perjuring themselves and lying. I, by contrast, am now barred from Panamá for life because I was (wrongly) imprisoned by the state and it is therefore impossible for me to return there to find my beloved son, Jason. In 2010, Laura took him - without warning or consultation – to Panamá from our house in Miami. I have not seen him since. Though I have tried repeatedly to make contact, Laura has thwarted every attempt by either having me arrested or blocking me in court.

To have missed watching my son grow from a child of six into a young man is the worst loss of all. God knows what poison he has been fed against me. Does he believe that I abandoned him? I yearn to see him again so that I can explain how hard I fought for him. The other casualties – the water-side house in Miami, the plantation and property in Panamá – mean far less to me, but it would be wrong to say they mean nothing. I was, after all, someone who defined himself in terms of hard work and achievement.

I marvel, with hindsight, at my naivety about my ex-wife. I guess I saw what I wanted to: namely, that she was stunning and I was smitten. I longed for a happy family life with our son, so I chose to ignore signs that I was less of a love-match than a ticket to American citizenship. My wealth, way behind the billionaire bracket though it was, must have seemed intoxicating to a girl who'd grown up in a tin-walled jungle shack.

Nuevo Paritilla village, Darién

My focus now is to expose the evils of Panamá's prison system – and the complacency of the British and American embassies when one of their citizens is thrown in jail and kept there without trial. Whatever platitudes they spout, the embarrassment of damaging possible trade deals always out- weighs the welfare of the individual.

The UK government produces a reassuring 33-page 'prisoner pack' for British nationals who happen to find themselves in La Joya, or one of its sister institutions. There are sections on the number of consular visits you can expect and the standard of medical care you will receive. Yes, it is careful to emphasise that conditions are poor, but the reality I experienced of malnutrition and neglect makes it read like an Enid Blyton book by comparison.

Panamá has the highest rate of pre-trial detention, per capita, in the world. In 2014, the year I was released, more than 60 per cent of the prison population had not yet been sentenced. According to Juan-Carlos Arauz, president of the National College of Lawyers, there is effectively no limit to how long someone can be detained before trial. The unlucky ones, with no strings to pull, family to support them or money for lawyers – and let's not forget the money for bribes – might be incarcerated for year upon endless year.

The truth is that if I ended up in jail for 16 months, so could you. This isn't just some entertaining thriller. It reflects how vulnerable we are when we leave the comfort of home and how fragile our so-called human rights turn out to be when no one cares about applying them. I was innocent. It made no difference. I was locked away on the flimsiest and most absurd charge.

The evidence I gathered with Arthur, using an HD camera wristwatch he arranged to have smuggled inside La Joya, amounts to more than 600 hours of uncut video footage. I have put it all on a website with pictures, documents and blog posts to provide irrefutable proof of what thousands suffer in that hell-hole called Panamá. Some of the scenes are hard to watch. Believe me, they were harder to live. I urge you to take a look if you are planning a vacation to this God-forsaken country.

It remains important to me that the injustice I suffered is acknowledged. I try to apply Christian standards of generosity, but I find it difficult to forgive Laura and her family for the callous way in which I was manipulated. They stripped me of my dignity, as well as my son and the assets I had sweated to acquire. They also made no distinction when it came to collateral damage, which meant that my friend, employee, translator and right-hand-man, Angel, was also hauled into their drag net.

Perhaps the best I can hope for is that officials in the British government will finally have the courage to confront Panamá. I won't, as the saying goes, hold my breath.

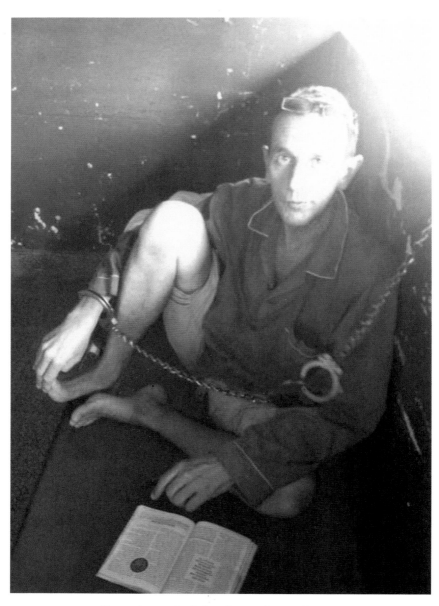

Chained up in La Palma Prison, Darién Provence

La Palma Prison, Darién Provence

1

WELCOME TO MIAMI

I moved to the States with something to prove. I was 33 and had already done well back in the UK, but I wanted the excitement and the challenge of setting up an American arm of our family business. It really mattered to me that I should repay the trust implicit in the £10,000 seed money I had been given for this new venture.

The thought that all my optimistic plans would be destroyed in a Panamanian jail was not one that occurred to me. Tuffney by name, tough by nature. We prided ourselves on sticking at things until they worked.

I grew up in a boisterous home where my four brothers - including my stepbrother – and I picked up the message that anything was possible if you put in the hours. After my parents divorced, when I was around 10, my mother set up a wholesale paper and stationery company, Dominion, in Kent with her new partner, and it became very successful. We boys lived with her simply because being bounced from house to house in shared custody proved too disruptive, but we maintained a good relationship with our dad.

Simon and I were twins and the youngest, born in 1963; Kevin and Roger were our big brothers. There was terrible grief inflicted on us as a family when Kevin died in a motorcycle accident at the age of only 17. I think it drew Simon and me even closer together. Of course, being typical British males, we expressed our bond in the form of banter and practical jokes that became increasingly elaborate as we grew older.

One day, as I was leaving for work, I found that Simon had barricaded my front door with cement blocks. After escaping via the side gate, I discovered that the wheels had been removed from my car and it had been left on blocks. I think the neighbours suspected that I was involved in some kind of gangland vendetta!

Among my pranks was buying a 'Virgin Revenge kit' that was on sale in Hamleys. (Appropriate that it should have come from a toyshop considering how childish our behaviour was.) The contents included a pre-printed label for the neck of a milk bottle, with the following request for the milkman: 'six extra pints and a yogurt please'. There was also a surprisingly effective letter on official looking paper, stating that his property was on an ancient burial ground, and by order of the local council, a special excavation was to take place in a week's time.

Possibly, things went too far when my friends and I captured Simon, bound his legs to an office chair, stripped him down to his boxers, put a waste bin over his head and wheeled him onto the high street. I think he's forgiven me, but I feel that if the opportunity arises, he will kick off the pranks again, even though they've lain dormant for 20 years. I left school when I was 15 and began to work at McDonald's in Maidstone, even though, legally, I was too young to be employed. This was during a period when there were very few branches in the UK, perhaps 20 or so, and fast food was considered excitingly exotic. I started in the kitchens, earning my first golden star, was then promoted to floor manager and eventually progressed through the ranks until I was being sent to work with branches in the States, in Queens, New York and Chicago, which was the only McDonald's in the world that sold wine with your meal. The company liked me so much that they gave me the responsibility of opening their new Chatham branch in Medway.

In some ways I wish I'd stayed with McDonald's because the prospects were excellent, but in my early 20s I decided to try something new. My dad was working for a company that sold immersion heaters and elements, and he suggested I start up my own little business, buying stock from him. I did exactly that, and it grew well enough to allow me to buy my first house when I was 24, having already married.

My first wife and I had two sons and a daughter together but, maybe because we were so young when we met, we grew apart. After eight years, the marriage was definitely foundering, and I moved out. Remembering my own experience as a youngster, I decided it wasn't fair to pull the children between two homes so that they were constantly having to readjust to their surroundings and adapt to different routines. Kids need familiar anchors to keep them feeling secure. By the mid-90s I had decided to move to the United States, although I had mixed feelings because of the inevitable difficulty of seeing the children so often. My wife and I divorced before I left.

We already had family connections in America, which made the prospect of starting a branch of Dominion out there a tiny bit less daunting. But daunting it still was. On the positive side, I could make decisions without having to consult squabbling family co-directors. On the negative side, if things tanked, the blame was squarely on me.

My uncle was a director for the airline Pan Am, and one of his professional partners was a guy called Vincent, who lived in Florida. We'd been there for family holidays and I got along with him extremely well. It was natural to ask if he could give me guidance and local information when I came to America to establish Dominion Business USA Inc. Not only did he say yes, he invited me to lodge with him and his wife, Franny, in their house near Fort Lauderdale, about half an hour from Miami.

The thought of lazing in the warm tropical waters of

With (centre) Vincent and (right) Mark, an employee of United Stationers

Miami Beach flitted through my head, but I never got the chance. I was far too busy.

My proud pioneer outpost of Dominion began in Vincent's back bedroom. I had a telephone, a desk squeezed into a corner and three boxes of business cards. It was a shame that I also had a severe case of the tropical sweats, not the most enticing way to attract customers, while my body adjusted to the intense heat and humidity of the climate.

My first deal was with a large stationery wholesaler that off-loaded a consignment of dud pens on me, nine out of 10 of them so shrivelled that they contained no ink. Other suppliers were so eager that they overwhelmed me with catalogues: I had to stack them head-high in my cramped office. I was in a state of high anxiety about working my way through the current consignment of 500 catalogues before the next 1,000 for 1997 were on the press ready for delivery. For two months, I sold nothing at all. A complete zero.

The pressure I felt to be successful made me panicky and nervous, so it's not surprising that nobody wanted to buy from me.

In total, the first 18 months were a real struggle. I had to learn to sell in American and to 'speak American', because the vocabulary as well as the accent was different. I remember running from one potential client to another, looking like a wet rag, and having conversations consisting of what sounded like gibberish. They would be asking about erasers and stick pens and correction fluid and I would be thinking, *Does that means a rubber, Biros and Tipp-ex, or not?* I didn't want to make mistakes and look like a plonker.

I had to do something to supplement my meagre income, and for that reason I signed up as a film and TV extra for a year, finding a useful amount of casual work on sets. I enjoyed my time at the edges of show business. It was a buzz to be around the cavalcade of trailers and caravans that come with location filming, the lavish buffet meals served to the actors and crew, the chance to spot well-known faces. I even picked up some voice-over work for radio stations. My attempt at landing some slightly more serious acting jobs did not come to anything, however.

Eventually I was desperate enough to pay for a consultation with a hypnotist, in the hope that he would improve my confidence and help me to sell It cost me $50, which I thought at the time was money wasted. I have no idea what he said to me while I was in a trance, but something must have worked because my luck started to change after that half hour sitting in his chair listening to the sound of running water.

One of my earliest customers was Racal-Datacom, part of a British company with a massive facility in Fort Lauderdale. It so happened that I clicked with a girl called Donna who worked there, and when she placed their first order I was so delighted that I sent her a bunch of flowers. I think the order was for about $20 and the flowers cost about $40: not in itself a fantastic piece of business, but the cost-to-benefit ratio worked out very well. From that day onwards she promised to pass all her orders through me.

Another valuable contact was a woman called Rhonda, who worked for a liquor distribution company, William

M. Thies, that dealt with all the Heineken and Budweiser coming into the state of Florida. I don't want to sound like an ego-maniac, but I think she might have had the hots for me, despite being married to the head of Miami-Dade Fire Rescue. Her first order came through on my thermal fax machine without product codes or reference numbers and meant about as much to me as a Chinese menu. It took me days on end of browsing through lists of 700 different pens before I finally admitted that I needed more information. Although I felt like an idiot, I did at least learn the valuable lesson of swallowing my pride.

The important thing was that Rhonda placed her faith in me, and was a wonderful help when it came to spreading my name to other clients. Sometimes in business, just one lucky break can have a cascade effect of good fortune.

Rhonda's firefighter husband, Bob, was a great guy, by the way. When my children later came out to visit me, he arranged for us to board a fire truck and drive through Coral Springs with the lights flashing and the siren wailing, which was probably the highlight of their stay.

Considering my shaky start in Florida, the about-turn

Rhonda's husband Bob at his fire station with my boys

in my prospects was a huge relief. I was able to repair my dented confidence and start believing that I had made the right decision by moving to the United States. Dominion gained a reputation as a company on the rise and I found that unlike the Brits, who have a tendency to downplay success, the Americans were unembarrassed about applauding it. Their attitude was refreshing to me and filled me with even more conviction.

I was fascinated by the people I met in Miami, a melting pot of different cultures, and it was strange to realise that, in their eyes, I was just as interesting, with my quaint English accent and my experiences of growing up in Maidstone!

I was still operating as a one-man business, and it became genuinely hard for me to find enough hours in the day to complete basic admin tasks, let alone do the delivery driving, accounting and sales duties that were vital to keeping the business healthy. I'd get back to Vincent's place after a day on the road, when I had been in constant touch with clients on my mobile phone, and find my fax machine spewing out orders onto the floor. I filled out invoices by hand, tapped my own sums into the calculator and spent a lot of time at the typewriter with a bottle of corrector fluid handy.

I joined the British Chamber of Commerce, Fort Lauderdale, in order to network and met many influential businesspeople from the area. The orders kept coming. I realised that I needed some help.

I found warehouse premises in North Miami Beach and

My father joining in at a function held at Sir Freddy Laker's offices Fort Lauderdale

I started to take on some sales staff. One of them was a middle-aged Liverpudlian called Alexander Worthington, who sported a waxed handlebar moustache that wouldn't have looked out of place on a Wing Commander. He had an eccentric manner and a broad Scouse accent, so I had my doubts about how he would be received in Miami, but I'm always prepared to give people a shot. He needed a job and I agreed to pay him in commission. He turned out to be a brilliant salesman and the Americans lapped him up. His connections at the Chamber of Commerce helped to push me ever upwards, so that within a year I was promoted on to the board of directors.

Alexander managed to enlist Shaquille O'Neal, the legendary basketball player, as a client. Shaquille lived next to Oprah Winfrey on Star Island, where all the celebrities had houses. Then we got an account for Sony in South Beach, the Convention Centre on Miami Beach, British Airways, Virgin Atlantic, and eventually all the British embassies in South America through their consulate in Miami. Alexander was a money machine.

The best part was that the British Latin American embassies had an annual get-together at a different location each year, and it just so happened to be the turn of Fort Lauderdale. We were invited too. I remember our phalanx of private buses zooming down otherwise deserted streets as police outriders led us to the convention and feeling a thrill of importance. Each embassy had been allocated a table in the conference room of the Marriott Hotel, which gave us the perfect chance to meet the staff and offer our services. The conversation soon moved on from stationery to cover the many other items they wanted us to obtain for them.

The list started with Pimm's – apparently impossible to find in South America for ambassadorial functions – and also included Manchester's finest: Boddington's Bitter. We said yes to both. Then it was washing machines, fridge freezers, easels, TVs and even hurricane supplies for the British High Commission in Kingston, Jamaica. Nothing to do with office supplies, but we said we would get it for them and we did. Alexander pulled off an amazing stunt by securing the account for Nova South Eastern University, a massive institution in Fort Lauderdale, which was about to open a new campus in Panamá. We sent them 15 trailer-loads of stuff, from standard-issue stationery to electrical equipment such as multimedia projectors and monitors, which were worth more than $1 million to us. It was our biggest single contract to date.

Dominion was in great shape by then, with a fat cushion of money in the bank. Our wholesalers had subsidiaries in every state and through them we were able to expand into other areas outside of Florida. Three years after I'd moved gratefully into Vincent's back bedroom, I was able to secure my first proper office, a postage stamp-sized place on Hollywood Boulevard, Fort Lauderdale. In the office next door was a Jewish guy, David, and his wife, Hanna, who were running another start-up, CG Accounting, and I took them on as my accountants. The relief of handing over some of the sums to another person was sweet indeed.

I began to get a taste of how your path is smoothed once you have some influential friends. My step-brother (he went on to co-found the Sugardaddie.com dating site in 2002, which gained more than five million members) came over to work for me in Florida as a delivery driver, but it was quite a baptism of fire for him as a young guy in charge of a big truck on dauntingly unfamiliar highways and freeways.

One day he was sent to deliver to a well-known politician called Senator Kendrick Meek, who was a customer of ours out on the Palmetto, on the outskirts of Miami city. Jon parked the van and went in to leave his parcel, but when he came back the vehicle had disappeared. He was in a complete panic and ran back into Kendrick's offices, shouting that the van had been stolen. In fact, it had been towed away for a parking violation. It so happened that Kendrick was there and feeling helpful. He picked up the phone and promised to sort matters. Within a minute, the van was back in its original position... It may not be fair to get special treatment, but it can definitely be useful.

I made friends with a delightful elderly woman – the heiress to the Carters Little Liver Pills fortune – who took me under her wing and introduced me to many places that would otherwise have seemed out of bounds to a working- class lad-made-good. Every Sunday, I would be invited to the Coral Ridge Yacht Club in Fort Lauderdale, for a mimosa (a mixture of Champagne and orange juice, with a dash of

Grand Marnier) brunch. Then we would head over to her private box at the Royal Palm Beach polo club.

"Look at me, Mum and Dad," I wanted to shout. "I know what a chukka is now!"

In the spare time I managed to claw back from work, I loved to go game fishing for marlin and tuna, out through the Bay of Miami, under the Haulover Bridge and into the vast Atlantic. A friend, Willie, who I had met at the United Stationers wholesale company, where I purchased supplies on a daily basis, was also a keen fisherman. We would go out together when we could, and often talked about the exhilaration of chasing down big fish using neon fluorescent lures that were as large as dinner plates.

With Alexander at our new distribution centre in north Miami

By this point I felt financially secure enough to buy myself a stunning town house on 135th Street, North Miami Beach. It had a large deck at the back and so, of course, I had to have a brand-new Bahia walk-around boat with a centre consul. It turned out to have quite a few mechanical problems, but it was a beauty all the same. I used to step aboard, crank up my Mercury engine, unleash the mooring whips and set sail across the bay with Skippy, my rescue dog, proudly standing at the gunwale. I had that happy feeling that whatever I wanted I could afford.

Willie onboard baiting for a day's fishing

I was living the American Dream: the exact thing I had been searching for when I had arrived in Florida. I had a Range Rover in the drive and opulent furnishings in my home. It was flash by British standards, but it was a lot of fun.

The boat had a barbeque at the back, and almost every night I would go out to catch delicious snook, a species limited to individual fishermen and not commercially available in markets. When my mum and my kids visited, we would float past the homes of Oprah Winfrey, the Bee Gees and Sheena Easton, all overlooking the Bay, and catch ourselves a fresh supper, which we topped with a cauliflower sauce. It was quite an eye-opener to see what a famous rapper – whose name escapes me – was up to when we drifted past his place. He had a jazzed-up cigar boat moored outside and there were often strippers partying on his roof, to the sound of blaring music. If you cast your eyes in another direction, you might see manatees and dolphins swimming in the water, perhaps even sharks. Sometimes they used to pass right by the back of my house.

In fact, when the children came to stay, they would play by jumping off the roof of my boat, or from the dock, into the water. At least they did until they saw an five-foot shark on one of my fishing lines. That seemed to change their minds.

Within 800 yards of where I lived, near the Haulover Bridge, was Beer Can Island. When the tide went out it formed a sandbar, where boats would park for three hours while a massive party took place in the crystal-clear waters. Frankly, we'd get trashed, swim round and then head back once the water rose again. My dog, Skippy, used to love these spontaneous outings even more than I did. (She also loved Heineken.) She was a mutt who had belonged to the daughter of a neighbour. When they couldn't look after her anymore, I took her in, although it was my step-brother who really wanted her. She was ugly and scruffy, but she was a great companion and I loved her.

Every Sunday we would be out together on the water.

Sand Bar Haulover Bridge

Leaving Haulover Inlet

There was a particular weekend when I had my rods tied up like Houdini to the dock posts, with big reels at the ready, 250lb test lines and a huge fish head as bait. I was waiting for a super-size tarpon to pass by. All of a sudden one of the wheels started to spin at a terrific rate, making an enormous noise as the ratchet clicked in. It was unravelling like a cotton reel, and I knew there was something huge at the other end as the line was set to move only when there was over a 250lb pull. Skippy had her own ideas on how to land the catch, and sprang off the dock like Zebedee, into the water after the fish. As I was trying to reel it in, she was straggling on its back, chewing its dorsal fin as if *she* had caught it. That's what Heineken did to Skippy.

Fishing was my passion. Once I had passed under Haulover Bridge into the teal waters of the Atlantic Ocean, I was floating in a paradise where I could find mental refuge from the mundane stresses of the week. The peace and solitude were a soothing counterpoint to the frantic pace of running Dominion. As I developed the infrastructure, I could divert the office phones to my mobile and take the boat out in the afternoons. Sometimes I'd be out with seagulls calling overhead and a fish reeling out a line when a delivery enquiry came through, and I'd have to say the computers had gone down and I would call back. I can't help wondering if they believed me.

The boat gave me enormous pleasure, but it was also a headache. It caused the first serious altercation of my charmed Miami life. I spent good, hard-earned money on it, only to discover that it was a true lemon. The agent who had done the deal had offices at the end of the canal where I lived, which meant that all his boats had to pass my property, as did the potential buyers who were trying out their would-be purchases on an ocean-going test run.

I complained on numerous occasions about the boat's poor performance, but the agent had mysterious difficulty in doing anything to remedy the problems. Henry, my next-door neighbour, was a cameraman anchor at WSVN- 7 News and offered to do a bit of filming to help my case, but I had another option: protest in the British way.

I placed a big billboard sign with the agent's company details on top of the boat and then used cotton and Blue-Tac to attach hundreds of hanging lemons. This embarrassingly public show of discontent seemed to do the trick. Within 24 hours, my faulty boat was back in the workshop, being repaired. It was sad that this particular vessel was not destined to live out its days at the back of my house. The reason why will become clear later.

As a result of my widening business interests, I met a diverse cross-section of new people. One of the less refined characters was the buyer at the British High Commission from Kingston, Jamaica. We had built a good friendship over the phone, dating from my time in Fort Lauderdale. When she asked if she could stay with me while she was attending a seminar in Miami, I said yes, of course. I was expecting my important guest from the embassy to be quite prim and proper, like most government officials. Having sought a bit of help with the hosting and sight-seeing duties from my neighbour, Henry, I remember telling him he would have to mind his Ps and Qs.

My first surprise was her sheer, intimidating size when she came through those arrival doors at Miami International Airport. She was an extremely big mama, in bottle-bottom glasses. Henry was speechless.

On the second day after her seminars, I offered to take her back to MIA, and she casually asked if we could do some shopping on the way. I thought nothing of it, until she mentioned that what she was interested in buying was a vibrator and sex toys from a particular sex shop.

As someone who had never been inside one of those places, I was immediately nervous about the thought of adding it to our itinerary.

We pulled up outside a grimy-looking sleaze store on NE 167th Street. Maybe I could wait in the car? No, she wanted my advice. So I trailed behind her while she cast an expert eye over a selection of garish, rubbery dildos. She also did a fair bit of flopping them about and squeezing them. Not, trust me, a sight for the squeamish.

770 NE 167th St. Miami, FL 33162

After requesting her chosen model in black, she asked if there was a discount for buying two. Rarely had my preconceptions been so thoroughly overturned.

A rather better friend of mine was Rhonda, the person who had done so much to help me when I was starting out in Miami by using me for office supplies. She knew I was single and had been for years because work was my priority, and she decided to play Cupid by matching me with someone she considered suitable. I was not at all keen and had to be bludgeoned into accepting my blind date. "Remember, the customer's always right," said Rhonda.

The meeting point was to be the huge marina, Keystone Point, which stood at the end of my canal. (Rhonda's husband Bob also had a boat in storage there.)

Keystone Point Marina, North Miami, Florida

I had no clue at all who my date might be – I didn't even have a photograph for reference. My only information was that she was single and a hard worker.

The plan was to go out on Bob's boat to the sandbar, for a good barbeque and some beers. Sunday soon arrived and I was on the dock, nervous as a schoolboy on his first date. Bob and Rhonda were there at nine in the morning, as arranged. When my blind date came into view, I was knocked for six. "Mama Mia, she's as hot as a boiling tea pot," I remember muttering to Rhonda.

Trisha was a brunette in her early 30s, and she was drop- dead gorgeous. We had an immediate rapport and the chemistry between us was intoxicating. It seemed to me that we went together like gin and tonic. That day out on the sandbar, with the hot Floridian sun on our backs and the sizzle of mutual attraction in the air, was one of the best I ever experienced in Miami. I will always remember the boats, downing cervezas and the clouds of fragrant smoke hanging in the air from the barbeques.

On our return to Keystone, I was somewhat surprised and a little miffed by all the men, dressed in uniform beige dock shorts to show off their tans, who were giving Trisha an unusual amount of attention. I had a strong urge to tell all the dock mates who rushed over to 'assist us' that Trish was now taken – by me. I felt irrational jealousy bubble inside me, and I wanted to leave as quickly as possible so that I could outrun the emotion. That is, until I heard one of the eager helpers talk to her. "Hi boss, is there anything else you need?" *What?*

Trish owned this whole bloody marina. That was my first ever blind date and it happened to be with a millionaire princess. I had to pinch myself. It could not be true that she was lovely *and* rich! I had thought there was more chance of winning the lottery than of finding that combination.

Our relationship deepened over the following year. I wooed her with regular deliveries of flowers and other romantic gestures I had almost forgotten existed during the previous six or seven years, when there had been no room in my life for relationships. It was refreshing for me to talk to a woman without feeling like I was cultivating a business contact but, all the same, I now felt a pressure to keep up with her pay grade and social life. The mission was on to woo this gal.

Trish was a very astute businesswoman and could be ruthless when necessary.

Trish promoting her marina at the Miami international boat show, 2014

We reached a stage when I wanted to take her back to the UK and introduce her to my family. Trying not to burn through any more cash, I called in some of my credits with Sir Freddie Laker, the owner of Laker Airways, who owed my company some money. I asked if he could upgrade us on our flight from Fort Lauderdale to Gatwick. To my shame, when we boarded, we were put into economy class seats. I had been trying hard to impress this woman and show off a bit, but I looked – in American parlance – like a loser. Then, just before the plane took off, someone from the cabin crew came down the aisle and took us into First Class. The day, and possibly the relationship, was saved.

The trip to Britain was a success. Trish met my mum and my children, and they all seemed to like each other. We decided on the strength of how well it had gone that we were ready to become engaged.

I bought her a custom-made diamond ring from one of her nominated jewellers in Coral Gables – for the not inconsiderable sum of $10,000 – and made my proposal on one knee. Things were good for a couple of days, and then we went to her parents' palatial house on the waterway in Rio Vista, Fort Lauderdale, where we were going to be entertained on their super yacht. Halfway through the evening, Trisha's mother mentioned that her daughter was terribly upset. I went, perplexed, to find her on the top deck.

Rio Vista, Fort Lauderdale

Tears were streaming down her face. "The diamond was too small," she wailed in between sobs. *What?* It was news to me, and it forced me to re-think the whole engagement. I decided, with sadness, that it was over.

As far as I was concerned we had had a genuine connection, but maybe with hindsight there was something superficial about it. I can't help thinking that there is a fundamental difference between a British and American way of evaluating people. Americans want to know you, foremost, for who you are, how much you are worth and what you own. Fair enough, but the British are more interested in your emotions and values.

I'd been working so much that most of my relationships with Americans were based on business transactions rather than personal ties, so maybe my radar was a bit wonky and I had missed the warning signals that our priorities were at odds. I was naive, but that would be true about me at many points in this story, especially when it comes to women. I'm a good businessman, but as far as personal relationships go, I'm not quite so canny. I give too much too quickly, I don't stop to ask enough questions and I open myself up to being exploited.

And, to be honest, when Trish and I broke up my first thought was not that my world had ended; it was, *How on earth am I going to tell my mum we've split over something as silly as a ring?*

If only the maxim 'Once bitten, twice shy' applied to me.

2

A GIRL CALLED LAURA

My bachelor days of business and fishing resumed. By the first anniversary of my blind date with Trish, I was single again. Throughout, I had kept in close contact with my kids and my ex-wife back in the UK. We might not have been married any more but the bond we shared with our sons and daughter was unbreakably strong, and indeed remains so.

The kids came to Miami for their summer holidays, and I can safely say that they had a wonderful time in what to them was an exotic wonderland. We forged memories that I will cherish forever. For instance, the enjoyment and freedom of cruising down South Beach in a soft-top Mercedes 500SL convertible, the warm breeze blowing through our hair. I was proud to be the provider of such experiences, but most importantly it gave the children a spirit of positivity and the sense that anyone can make their dreams come true. To this day all my children are blessed with energy like a Duracell bunny.

Those days were certainly an improvement on going out to McDonald's or trying to dodge the British rain back home.

My children still talk about their initiation into making money the American way. They were eight and 10 years old. We set out really early on a Sunday morning as the sun came up over Fort Lauderdale, accompanied by their two best friends from the UK, in a van filled to the brim with discontinued office supplies. It was time for them to build their confidence by proving themselves as young businessmen in the making.

Upon arriving at the 'SwapShop' on Sunrise Boulevard, which was basically a huge car boot sale with over 1,000 pitches, the boys set up five foldaway wallpaper tables. Within an hour, we were good to go. What the youngsters didn't know was that I was going to leave it entirely up to them. They had to guess their prices and give the exact change in dollars.

I returned every so often, but stayed out of sight. They were loving it and the crowds were five-deep. When I did return, four hours later, their pockets were bulging with greenbacks.

It blew them away. Back home with their mum, they were living on a modest budget. Now they had $1,000 split four ways and were able to afford those Nike trainers they'd previously only dreamed of. Those hot, idyllic Florida days with the boys went too quickly.

After a long period when my head was buried in work, my Colombian friend Willie insisted it was time that I come up for air. He organised a blind double-date for me and him with a Venezuelan woman and her Panamanian friend, Laura. I have to say I was reluctant, but I knew he was right and eventually he wore me down.

We booked to go to Monty's, a bar and seafood restaurant, for sunset in South Beach. I did enjoy it, and although Laura – my date – didn't speak much English, the language gap was not so much of a problem. In fact it somehow made the night more fun.

I'll never forget what she was wearing. She was stunning in blue slacks and a white top, and I was smitten. I was talking Spanglish and Willie was the official translator for the bits we couldn't get across in sign language. Her English was as bad as my Spanish, but the night went really well.

I was captivated by her good looks, but our sense of humour also seemed to click from the start. We fell about laughing when we made silly mistakes while trying to converse, which the tequila made all the more hilarious.

As the night came to an end, Willie suggested that we should have another date on the following Sunday, but this time back at my place for a barbecue and a boat trip.

I wasn't sure at first, because once you take it to the next step then things quickly become more serious. After the first date you can always say bye-bye, adios, on your bike – but inviting her to my home was a different matter altogether. There was nothing about Laura herself at that stage which planted any doubts, in fact quite the contrary. I was just reluctant to get into any kind of relationship right then. I could see that she was really nice, and we enjoyed our time together, but I also had in mind my work and my business, and I felt that had to be the priority. I didn't want to jeopardize everything I'd built up by taking my eye off the ball, however much I liked her.

So I wasn't that keen to move to the next level, but Willie – who's a most persistent guy, like a boil on your bum – was pushing all the time, and eventually I gave in. At the same time, as the days went on, I suppose he didn't have to push that hard – I found I really couldn't get her out of my head.

But oh, how I wish I had pressed the stop button at that moment and saved myself so much grief later on.

That barbecue at my place was a typical Floridian Sunday afternoon, with a light sea breeze and perfect sunshine. We had some delicious blackened grouper on the grill, and I had my second round of Spanglish lessons, without the assistance of our translators. It was lovely, and so different from my normal monotonous days filled with phone calls, ordering and invoices.

Men always say how sexy Latina women are, and Laura certainly lived up to the hype.

My initial reluctance to become closer to her had nothing to do with Trisha, because I was over our breakup within a couple of months. It was more about how much time I could commit to a romance while the business was demanding so much from me. The disaster with

Trisha had, though, made me question whether I was suited to a relationship with an American. So when Laura came along, there was a voice of the back of my head suggesting that I might find more compassion from a Latina woman, and have more fun. What I hadn't factored in – but would eventually discover – was that all the fire and passion also came with a fiery temper.

I had to admit that Laura had brought something into my humdrum existence that I really enjoyed, and our relationship began to progress. By now, Willie was coming over every weekend and we would go fishing together. We'd have onions and steak, Latin style on the barbecue. I'd supply the beers, then we'd set sail and bring home the food. Not long after that, Willie met a Russian girl called Patti, whom he went on to marry and with whom he now has a daughter.

Laura moved in with me pretty quickly I suppose, after four months or so. I've always been a sucker for a sob story. Maybe I see myself as a knight in shining armour riding to the rescue. I had no way of knowing that this time I was heading directly into a catastrophe.

I heard through Willie that Laura had been living in a car. It was hardly surprisingly, therefore, that she was quite keen on the idea of moving in with me. Don't forget that before she came to the States, Laura had lived in the jungle in Darién, so she was blown away by my house and lifestyle. She had arrived in the US as a nanny in 2000 and overstayed her visa. Sometime after that, she was caught shoplifting, though I wouldn't learn that until years later.

Número de salida

691284817 08

Servicio de Inmigración
y Naturalización

I-94
Registro de salida

U.S. IMMIGRATION
060 MIAMI-IAP 1708

JUL 3 0 2000

ADMITTED *B-2*
UNTIL
29 Aug 2000

14. Apellido
Gallardo

15. Primer nombre
Laura

16. Fecha de nac. (día/mes/año)
03-08-76

17. Ciudadanía
Panamaria

I'm surprised she wasn't deported; instead she was put on a programme where she had to pay back the money and attend some kind of counselling course. Looking back, I wish they had kicked her out right then.

In reality, I didn't put up much resistance to her moving in with me and our relationship grew from there. When we met, she was working in a clothing factory out on the Palmetto, half an hour from where I lived. I found her culture and her manner very interesting and attractive. She was so completely different to any girl I had met before, and that's what drew me in. You hear a lot about Latin American girls being so compelling, and I suppose I just wanted to find out more about what made her tick.

When Laura did move in it was a big change for me – I'd been living alone for a long time since my divorce. I guess it was the end of the single life for Skippy and me. What struck me first about her was her naivety. She didn't know how to use a microwave, or indeed many other basic items around the house. She had no idea about credit cards and didn't seem to understand that there was a limit, and that you had to pay it back at some point.

But by God, she soon learnt how to use one!

After I let her have a Platinum American Express on the back of mine, with no credit limit, the first statement that came in showed that she had spent thousands and thousands of dollars. Each month, the statements were the same. I would say to her, "How the fuck do you expect me to pay for all that?" She of course would respond, "I don't know, Nick."

At one point, she bought a photo-shoot in downtown Miami using 'Glamour Models', so that she could send lots of glamorous pictures to the folks back home, saying, "Look at me now!"

Making herself attractive and grooming herself was her passion. She even spent $12,000 at the Beauty School of America learning how to do styling, make-up and all that jazz. She did complete the beauty course, but was unable to graduate and obtain a license since she lacked the credible documents – and she withheld from me why she had no diploma. I can't lie, she was a knockout and drop dead gorgeous when she dressed up, but it came at a price, as my Amex statements reminded me each month.

Did I mention the Gucci and Chanel handbags at $1,000 a pop on Amazon? Later, when I brought her to England and Paris, she would buy Louis Vuitton bags and all the designer gear she could lay her hands on. She was certainly an expensive ticket.

Once she got herself settled in, I gave Laura the very un-glamorous job of typing invoices for the firm, with help from a Spanish-to-English dictionary.

In February 2002, we got married at the back of my house. My other next-door neighbour Alex was a notary, and he said he would conduct the ceremony while my friend Henry, the TV cameraman, filmed our big day. What I didn't know at the time was that my mum and my daughter had been flown out for the wedding. They were hiding in the closet and jumped out to surprise me. It was a truly wonderful moment in a happy and lovely day.

We enjoyed the early part of our married life and, shortly before our second wedding anniversary, Laura became pregnant. I still remember every detail of Jason's birth, on August 29, 2004, as if it happened yesterday.

It was three in the morning. "Wake up, Nick!" Laura said. "Let's go! The baby's coming!" After eight hours of merry chaos in Jackson Memorial hospital, I heard my son's first cries.

I returned to the hospital full of warm feelings about becoming a dad again, but my reverie was quickly shattered when I glanced at the new baby's tiny wrist band. It stated his name as Jason Gallardo.

"What the fuck?" I shouted. "He is my son, he should have my last name."

Laura hesitated for a moment, looking sheepish: "I'm illegal," she blurted out.

The news hit me like a body blow. I'd come to America to make my way there, and had adopted US nationality. I'd even worried about getting a parking ticket a few weeks before getting my citizenship in case it got in the way.

Yet now, here I was harbouring – and married to – an illegal.

I promised from then on to spend every waking moment trying to legalise both Laura and Jason, but I was carrying a heavy burden. Later I was to discover, to my even greater shock, that Laura had registered our son with no mention of his father. It was only when I applied to the official registrar at the state capital of Tallahassee to have Jason's surname changed that I discovered this.

I thought this very suspicious. I managed to get the omission overturned in the end and had his name officially changed to Tuffney. Laura never gave me a proper reason for not entering my name on that document. Nor did she explain why, although Jason was born in the Jackson Memorial Hospital, she'd been attending a clinic called Oneida with her other illegal friends for her pre-natal care. Maybe the subterfuge was all linked to her illegal status.

I was none the wiser, as she'd told me during those absences that she'd been out socialising with her girlfriends. That certainly had the ring of truth at the time. There was a clique of them from Panamá, Venezuela and Colombia who would meet for Pinot Grigio, coffee and lunch.

I suppose I was guilty of being too engrossed in the business, and should have been more inquisitive about what was going on.

Jason's grandmother, my mum Jacqueline, and my eldest daughter, Charlotte, were ecstatic at the news of his birth, and flew in again from London to welcome him to the family. I never told them about our little 'immigration problem', but I should have done.

Laura asked whether she could do the same and bring in her relatives from Panamá at my expense. I agreed that it was the perfect time to see my wife's family, even though it meant putting a $5,000 deposit into each of their Panamanian banks in order for them to obtain visas, because the screening process required them to have accounts and funds in Panamá.

And so, in they came. Baby Jason was doted on, yet the families were doing very nicely out of their trips to Miami. I soon found myself giving away loan after loan in money. Eventually, the debts piled up.

I ignored them and lived my life. After all, it was 'picture perfect' in my eyes.

Since I was a little boy, I had always been taught to be honest and take other people at their word. "Innocent until proven guilty," was my mantra. At that time, I believed that Laura was the ideal girl. How could I have been so naive?

One of Laura's favourite phrases when she wanted to get something out of me was, "If you really love me, you'll give me..." followed by whatever it was she'd set her heart on that week, and it still haunts me to this day. She kept insisting on one thing in particular, and I eventually caved in, revising my property's titles into joint ownership only months into our marriage.

Laura would tell me stories of her home country, of how she had had to struggle in poverty, but adding that her family had worked hard and earned themselves middle class status, along with a host of business contacts. She made Darién sound like a jungle paradise. In my mind's eye I began to see a huge potential for investment, especially in teak and honey farming, plus the rental property market.

After giving birth to Jason, Laura produced a shopping list.

Number One: Liposuction and breast enhancement, which I did not agree that she needed – but at that stage, what Laura wanted, she pretty well got.

People have asked me whether my warning bells were beginning to ring, but they have to remember that I was head over heels in love with Laura and, later, with Jason. Everything else flowed from that genuine feeling of tenderness towards my family.

I couldn't turn around to her and say, for example, "No, your grandparents can't come up to visit." It just wasn't in my nature. The truth is that at that time I had more money than I knew what to do with. If I'd been living on a budget it would have been a very different story, but I always had a good chunk of cash in my pocket and in the bank account, so financial considerations didn't weigh too heavily on my mind. In any case, I've always liked to be generous and kind to people, and in some ways, that quality would stand me in good stead later on when I was in prison. It's just who I am. I would give money to someone else before I would spend it on myself. I simply wasn't in the mind-set of counting every dollar as it went out and then resenting it.

To my mind, things started to go wrong after we'd been married for a while, when Laura began working as a highly decorative extra on a soap opera produced by the giant Telemundo Spanish language station based in Miami.

With her portfolio tucked into her Gucci tote bag and a new Range Rover at her disposal, she had caught the eye of the show's producers. It was hardly Hollywood, but she would definitely settle for it. At least, she would for now.

When I reflect on our relationship, I realise there was a huge gulf between us, quite apart from the language barrier. Our cultures were so different. For example, she and her family were absolute believers in the power of witchcraft, and it's impossible to emphasise strongly enough how important that kind of thing is to Panamanians generally – as I was to discover to my cost years later.

These beliefs emerged in odd ways as I got to know her better. If you happened to place a broom the wrong way up outside the house, for example, Laura would go absolutely nuts and turn it back the right way up. Sometimes she would insert a lemon inside her bra to ward off evil spirits. When I first saw her do that I thought, *F****** hell, what's going on here?* Having a feather in the house was another thing that would drive her crazy, because it supposedly brought bad luck. She took these things very seriously, and so did her family and friends. On the surface she was a Christian, but it was a branch of Christianity that believed in speaking in tongues and that kind of weird shit.

Looking back now, I'm sure she had a plan to get the maximum out of me – and the US – while she could, because to her, meeting and getting married to me was like a massive windfall that would change her life. I accept I was blinded by love until it was way too late.

Her friends were encouraging her to send more and more money down to Panamá or to buy things down there so that she'd have a nest egg, which I suppose made me the plump golden goose! I was just pumping the money down to Panamá and not really suspecting anything. For instance, I bought her mother, Nora, a car, which they wrote off within a week and hadn't even paid to have insured.

Despite my growing misgivings, I kept on with the legal fight to have Laura and Jason accepted as American citizens, and finally it paid off. Without US passports, there was no way either of them could even take a holiday out of the country – the nearest we could get to Panamá was an occasional drive down to Key West along the spectacular overseas highway, on US Route 1 – but once I'd managed to secure them legal papers, we were able to travel abroad and make our first visit to Panamá together.

Finally, we were on our flight bound for Laura's country of birth. As the plane descended for landing, I expected from the glossy, in-flight magazines to see the sun sinking slowly into lush, steep-sided green valleys and for a whole new world to appear.

Of course, I knew it would be different from the towering skyline of downtown Miami, but the reality was something else entirely.

I pressed my nose up against the window like an excited child, but in truth the view near Tocumen airport was less than awe-inspiring. I could see an endless array of cluttered buildings, rusty tin roofs and piles of garbage dotting the landscape, and not much else.

Upon landing, we were greeted at the airport by Laura's older brother, Luis. The night was filled with the sound of blaring horns, cops with AK-47s and people yelling like mad men. It was so different from anywhere I'd ever been before. The beaches and mountain views I had imagined were nowhere to be found.

To my surprise, Luis's beaten-up sedan car rolled up at the kerb with more family members stuffed inside.

Where were we all going to sit? The answer was that six of us would be packed in like sardines. The trunk containing Laura's expensive designer luggage was precariously tied down with twine, and we set forth with bachata music blaring at 110DB. The windows were wound down, but as the air conditioning didn't work anyway, it just meant the warm, wet wind turned the car into a crowded mobile sauna.

We exchanged pleasantries and greetings with lots of fake smiles, but it was still awkward as I could only remember so many basic Spanish phrases from school. I was mainly limited to, "Gracias, amigo."

We probably drove no more than a kilometre before turning off onto a side road into a small community. The shacks cast a dark shadow over us, streetlights were flickering or non-existent, and groups of people huddled at street corners.

Welcome to Tocumen Roja. Only later did I discover that Roja meant 'the red zone'. In other words, a no-go area for anyone who wants to keep hold of their valuables – or their life – after dark.

The pavement soon gave way to a gravel road, packed with deep grimy potholes filled with water from the afternoon rains. Rubbish was stacked up on each side of the track, as high as the car. My mouth dropped open at the flimsiness of the wooden shacks they called homes.

I was awoken from my trance by the barking of stray dogs, to hear Luis telling me that we had arrived.

Entering the family home, my new mother-in-law, Nora, greeted me. At least now I could put a face to the recipient of my monthly transfers of cash. The 'middle-class lifestyle' Laura had mentioned was somehow absent.

Am I being tricked? I wondered.

I was, quite frankly, confused. The family seemed at first impression to be more likely to have criminal contacts than the business contacts Laura had claimed they had. Something didn't add up, but I chose to simply brush it off, blitz my new hosts with smiles and give them the benefit of the doubt.

What better way to break the ice than food? Nora, a fairly rotund woman, seemed to agree as she served some rough- tasting Panamanian home-brewed coffee. I sipped from the chipped cups and nibbled the partially stale bread she gave out. Diplomatically passing on the many condiments, I happened to notice the Nutella being piled onto the bread in thick dollops, and it occurred to me why it was the women here looked a little overweight.

However, when Nora opened a rusty fridge, I saw it was virtually empty. A mouse darted behind it as someone walked past.

Questions were popping into my head – where, for example, had all that Western Union money gone? However, yet again, I put it to one side – surely things would get better. The dark had fully set in as the family began to grow ravenous for dinner. It became clear that I'd have to cover the meal – however much that might cost. Chinese was the unanimous vote-winner. Luis and Nora took care of placing the order by phone, after handing around the well-worn menu to everyone. Luis returned an hour later, with what appeared to be enough food to last the next three or four days...

Then, in twos and threes, various members of the extended family began to turn up like flies for the Chinese banquet. I'd imagined I'd bought a set meal for six people, not 16. Another development was that, sitting at the table, we were joined by an army of ants, blazing a trail from the outside window to the leg of the table. They made rapid work of the food that had spilt onto the greasy, well-worn vinyl tablecloth.

When it was time for bed, the family dragged out a stained mattress and grimy sheets from the laundry basket. *I'm glad I won't be sleeping on that,* I thought.

How wrong I was.

I asked to use the toilet. I was probably aged three the last time I had used an outside loo, but here I was again. The chipped tiled floor with stained corking, dripping tank and missing toilet seat were enough to give me the shivers.

I rose enthusiastically on my first morning in Panamá, the first one awake. Before going outside for a morning smoke, I grabbed a pack of paracetamol from my flight bag; then I sat on the shabby, battered outside sofa outside on the porch, which had certainly seen better days, and bathed in the glorious rays of the morning sun.

Laura with some of her family members

Re-entering the house, I looked around and try to find something resembling toilet paper. Nothing was obvious so I grabbed the previous day's newspaper instead, which was surprisingly named the *Critica*. Above the din of a screaming rooster, I could now hear cockroaches scampering back like Dracula into the wooden furniture. Blaring Latin music coming from Luis's room completed the symphony.

How nice it was to be the guest of honour.

My first order of business was to arrange for a rental car to be dropped off and to hire a chauffeur, namely Luis, my new brother-in-law. I reasoned that he probably knew the ins and outs of the city, and from what I'd seen on the run in from the airport, I really didn't fancy my own chances at the wheel in Panamá City.

Soon, we were ready to roll – or so I thought.

Just as we were just about to set off for the day, I couldn't find the key to the hire car. As hard as I searched, after five hours I reluctantly gave up. Who knew how long it would take to get a replacement? I rang Avis and they told me a replacement key would cost $1,000. I was quick to agree, but Luis seemed to have other ideas.

To my horror, he dropped the bombshell that he'd filed a police report over the phone on my behalf, claiming that I had been carjacked. With that report, he assured me that I could make a fraudulent insurance claim.

Before I knew it, the police were at the front door. They wanted a statement, and I was cursing Luis in the back of my mind. These guys would not stop ringing for a statement. Finally, I insisted that Luis tell them that I'd left the country. What an idiot he was – but always a criminally minded one. If we kept going at this rate, I worried that I'd be in jail by Friday. The next day, Avis turned up with a replacement car and took the old rental away. I could get to work again, with Luis at the wheel and a full tank of gas. I agreed to pay him five times over the national wage for his services.

I'd seen details of a residential property for sale that interested me, and once we were on the road, I found that doing business in Panamá was easy.

Making some good connections in the city, I soon became a property owner of three new-builds going up in Brisas del Golf, an upmarket suburban development of villas

Houses in the Brisa del Golf

overlooking the Gulf of Panamá, well away from the dirt and squalor of the city centre. I headed back to the red zone, with contracts in hand, ready to study the heaps of pamphlets I'd collected.

The whole family was seated in the living room. Nora had put away her iron, which was her source of income at 25¢ an item. "Not much to sustain a family," I thought to myself. The father had passed away some years back, and the three boys seemed more like hustlers than businessmen. To complete the family, Alina, a teenage foster girl, helped Nora around the house. Dinner was some reheated Chinese leftovers.

Perhaps because they'd witnessed my earlier generosity in employing Luis, the other members of the family weren't slow to get in line. Sitting around the kitchen table as we swatted ants, everyone took their turn to state in broken English exactly what their needs were. They used paper scraps and a half-bitten pencil to help get the message across. I heard the family's rapid Spanish and all I could do was smile and nod my head, like one of those dogs you see in the back window of a car.

Everyone wanted at least $20 or $30 and I succumbed to their demands. Perhaps to keep the peace, I tolerated this abuse of generosity. I also filled their fridge with Coca Cola and ice cream on a regular basis. It seemed to be a fundamental truth not even up for debate that a rich gringo in town should be charitable.

Later, a power cut silenced the TV news. The whole house went suddenly dark and silent, finally killing off the din of Luis's music. After everyone had harassed him for a good hour to get the electric back on, he managed to somehow fix the issue with a wooden stick. The TV burst into life again with a shocker for everyone. 'Live Breaking News' flashed at the bottom of the screen, with a picture of my wife's brother, Henry. By this time, all the family had started gathering around the TV, and I was trying to get the drift of what was being said.

65

Laura told me Henry had been arrested after being caught in the middle of an armed robbery. What kind of life had I gotten myself into?

That night, Nora decided to conduct a bible-bashing session, in the hope of saving Henry from prison. I was in complete shock as these crazy fanatics started screaming, chanting and frantically waving their arms and bibles in the air.

By day three, I thought things surely couldn't get worse. I was wrong. I heard thumping at the door, and upon opening it, an attorney presented himself. He was representing Henry, he explained, and went on to say that he needed the help of the ex-president's ex-wife, Vivian Torrijos, whose connections could help get Henry out.

Then came the sting. Only with $3,000 could he work his magic. As soon as I heard those words come out of his mouth, I knew what was coming next: it was milking time for the cash cow yet again.

The five long days of our stay couldn't have ended soon enough for me. Despite my doubts about the criminal Gallardo clan, I was still happy with what I'd accomplished. Or was I? Banking arrangements made, I had located three new high-end properties. I went back to Miami with brochures and a smile. Oh well… The political and business contacts of the family were somewhat lacking, but progress had been made all the same.

I began to get excited about the new prospects in Panamá. It was definitely a challenge, especially since the country's reputation was in ruins. Poverty was rife, and people wanted to swoop in and make improvements, but on the other hand, it was a perfect location for business investment because values could only go up.

Of course, the place was littered with shady operators who hid money from their home countries and who would later be exposed in the Panamá Papers scandal. The infamous fraudster John Darwin, who faked his death in a canoe accident in the UK, also turned up in Panamá.

But I reckoned I could navigate these choppy waters. I had a stunning wife and a wonderful two-year-old son. Jason was turning into a charming, fun-loving boy, whose passion was joining me and Skippy on daily boat rides. Life was great and I had Panamá in my sights. I thought that the province of Darién, where Laura's family was originally from and whose people lived in the jungle, would be the

To go from having all these properties to calling a mattress and two five-gallon water buckets my sole possessions...

perfect place to begin an innovative tourism project, and that was the goal I'd set my heart on. The only drawback was the war in Colombia, with FARC rebels overflowing into Panamá. As long as the fighting stayed away, everything would be fine.

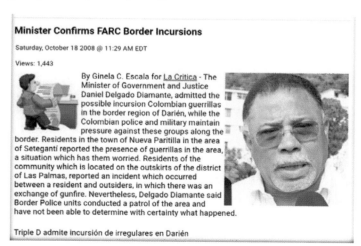

Minister Confirms FARC Border Incursions

Saturday, October 18 2008 @ 11:29 AM EDT

Views: 1,443

By Ginela C. Escala for La Critica - The Minister of Government and Justice Daniel Delgado Diamante, admitted the possible incursion Colombian guerrillas in the border region of Darién, while the Colombian police and military maintain pressure against these groups along the border. Residents in the town of Nueva Paritilla in the area of Setegantí reported the presence of guerrillas in the area, a situation which has them worried. Residents of the community which is located on the outskirts of the district of Las Palmas, reported an incident which occurred between a resident and outsiders, in which there was an exchange of gunfire. Nevertheless, Delgado Diamante said Border Police units conducted a patrol of the area and have not been able to determine with certainty what happened.

Triple D admite incursión de irregulares en Darién

My family's safety came first. Always. After becoming legal, Laura's attitude and sense of responsibility seemed to mature and we could finally travel the world together. She soon became the head of the snake, rather than its tail. Regardless, she was well aware of her new status and took full advantage. Was I being used by her? I'd get my answer, but not for some time.

A business plan that could rake in millions was my first priority. I decided to return to Panamá for a second look.

Even as I became more interested in investing in Panamá, our relationship began to slide inexorably toward the rocks.

Laura would throw full-on tantrums, like nothing I'd ever seen before. She made the more restrained British girls back home look like angels. Things were changing. She became more distant, and started to scare off my colleagues, including the neighbours. Even my beloved Skippy was locked in the downstairs bathroom daily by my wife.

My family thought she was OK, and they liked her Latin Style, thinking it was cool, but they didn't have to live with her. In fact, I think my family found Laura's tantrums a source of amusement sometimes. Like their father, my boys were always pranksters, but one time their tricks nearly caused Laura to leave me.

I had set up a Halloween surprise for my youngest, Ollie, by hiding a shop mannequin with long hair under the sheets of his bed, complete with a little fake blood. That night we watched some scary DVDs. At bedtime, he ran screaming from the room just as I had planned, but his terror soon turned to thoughts of revenge and, as they say, it's a dish best served cold.

He and his brother went to the Miami mall and purchased a skimpy pair of lady's panties. When I was away, they slid them down the side of the sofa. A few evenings later, we all gathered on the sofa to watch another movie on the big screen.

Suddenly, Ollie pulled out the planted lingerie from between the cushions.

"Dad, whose are these?" he asked innocently.

Laura immediately saw red, despite my furious denials. Within an hour, she'd packed her bags and was about to head off to a friend's house. Only then did Ollie break his silence and tell the truth.

After a while Laura began to get her feet under the table and exert a bit more control. She started blocking Willie from coming over at the weekend, and Henry next door from popping round for beers. It had previously always been open house at my place at the weekends, but she put a stop to that. The gates were starting to come down.

We were together eight years in all. It started off brilliantly, but as time wore on you could see her chiselling away, trying to recreate me in the image she wanted. That was when she became confident enough to say, "No let's do this, let's not do that," trying to grab the reins.

One thing that really upset me was when one of my key employees, Amos Laylay, a Fijian guy, was having a tough time financially and I wanted to help him out. I rented an apartment on South Beach for him, his wife and child. When Laura found out she said I shouldn't do it, but my reply was that the guy needed help, he was a good salesman who'd been loyal to me and worked bloody hard to bring in the dough. He was just finding life a bit challenging.

She was dead against my helping him, and perhaps for the first time, I had to tell her what was what and point out that she didn't run the business and that he worked for me, not her. It caused a huge row between us, because she hated the idea of me spending money on someone other than her and her family. I won that particular battle, but it marked the stage at which I started to realise I wasn't happy with our situation. Here she was, a factory worker, trying to tell me how to conduct the business I had been running long before we had ever met. At the same time she was beginning to neglect her own chores, wanting to employ cleaners to do the simplest tasks. The dynamic was changing, and not for the better.

As the years wore on, Laura felt more secure that she had her meal ticket in place and began to insist that small tasks were beneath her. It was an entitled attitude guaranteed to raise my hackles, because I came from a family who had earned what we had by putting in the necessary hard work. At the same time, she was blowing thousands of dollars on her eBay shopping sprees.

I realised too late that I was just a pawn in Laura's big chess game, positioned as a gringo surrounded by Latins. She wanted me to be controlled by her every whim, at her beck and call. Foolishly, I still believed in our marriage and scrambled to please her, but things were about to get drastically worse.

3

Nuevo Paritilla

Darién, or the Darién Gap as it is usually known, is one of the least explored, most inhospitable areas on Earth. It spans the borders of Panamá and neighbouring Colombia, changing from mountainous tropical jungle in the north to swampy marshland in the south. A hundred miles long at its greatest extent, it has claimed down the centuries the lives of many missionaries, explorers and would-be colonisers who thought they could conquer the terrain.

Even modern technology has been unable to drive a road through the region. The famed Pan-American Highway that runs from Alaska right down to the tip of Argentina stops here for 66 miles – hence the 'gap'. A mixture of environmental concerns and potentially explosive politics have combined with the logistical difficulty of crossing thousands of rivers and streams to thwart all attempts at a solution.

In Panamá's Darién Province, the population is sparse and includes indigenous tribes such as the Emberá-Wounaan, along with the Mestizo people of mixed Native American and European descent. Most of them are poor, and their priorities revolve around feeding their families and hustling for a buck. Canoes remain a chief means of transportation. They live in scattered villages or ramshackle towns such as the provincial capital of La Palma, which sits at the mouth of the Rio Tuira river where it empties into Panamá Bay on the Pacific

Ocean. A few miles from La Palma, the inter- American Highway runs out.

The words 'town' and 'village' when applied to Darién give a false impression of sound infrastructure, smooth roads and solid buildings. The reality is chaotic and often dangerous. There are long-standing tensions between the indigenous people and the authorities over land rights, justice is rough and the police can be selective in how they interpret the law.

Bearing all of the above in mind, it is fair to ask why I wanted to take a trip to my wife's homeland. Even the official advice from the British embassy's website was to stay away. The answer is that, in the same spirit that had taken me to Florida, I sensed opportunity and adventure. I was curious, too, to see where Laura had grown up.

For all the drawbacks, the other thing to say about Darién is that it is beautiful. The lush vegetation in a hundred different shades of green is a feast for the senses, and the ever-present calls of wild birds remind you how far you are from urban civilisation... unless a chunk of urban civilization in the shape of the Gallardo clan follows you there.

Laura had decided to invite all her relatives from Panamá City and a few neighbours along for our inaugural 2008 excursion. I was reluctant but decided to surrender: 10 people or so wouldn't be so bad. The number turned out to be closer to 50 by the time we hit the road. I told myself that it would be a good way to make new friends. My intrepid mother, Jacqueline, had flown out from the UK to join us, too.

None of our party, which included elderly people and young children, were able to contribute money or services towards the trip, but Laura had the genius idea of renting a bus – known as the Diablo Rojo, or Red Devil – from one of her distant cousins. And it was a snip at $600. The soundtrack of thumping music and crying babies was provided at no extra charge.

We were to take the road to Puerto Quimba; from there, the boat to La Palma; and finally, another bumpy overland ride to Laura's home village of Nuevo Paritilla, a small settlement in the mountains where she had lived from the age of four in the care of her grandparents.

As our rag-tag group bumped over the potholes, we passed occasional stalls at the side of the road. Half a recently slaughtered cow, wearing a black fuzz of flies, was hanging outside one of the larger establishments and Laura demanded we stop the bus. She jumped out to negotiate with the stall-holder, unfurled a roll of dollars and bought the carcass as provisions for the journey. It looked like a lot of meat but, there again, there were a lot of people to eat it.

During our 45-minute boat ride, I managed to extract some information about Laura's aunt in Nuevo Paritilla. She was an honourable woman, I was told. That would make a pleasant change from the armed robbers I'd met so far.

As we approached the bustling, cluttered docking ramp at La Palma for the first time, I was entranced. The view of multi-coloured shacks and swaying foliage belonged on a picture postcard – even if the overpowering smell of raw sewage took away some of the charm. The soothing breeze blowing in from the bay at least wafted the stink back over the treetops. We were surrounded by a slew of Indian dugout canoes. Small cargoes of plantains and corn were piled onto boats by the shoreline, just waiting to be unloaded. Indian traders carrying woven baskets on their backs were busy chattering together as they traded or concluded deals.

So much for first impressions. We had barely walked up the slippery green ramp when I was coerced into hiring a bunch of rogue taxis to carry our travelling circus. Laura's cousin, Chai, was one of the drivers. He had a battered truck that had seen better days. We scrambled up onto the flat bed at the back, held on desperately to the roll bars and left the others, and the cow, to find their own way. Health and safety seemed alien concepts in this place. (I later learned that car insurance and road tax were for suckers, and that texting or phoning at the wheel was considered completely normal.)

After a while, we made a sharp right off the road and headed down a long makeshift jungle track. At our destination, a solitary campfire lit up the shacks. The place had the feeling of a gypsy encampment – indeed, the Gallardos considered themselves to be of gypsy blood – and I had the feeling that I was plunging headfirst into the unknown.

After I had unloaded our cases, I turned to see the rest of the convoy arriving from La Palma. To my amazement, the group had swelled to something approaching 100 people, having gathered more followers along the way. I wondered how everyone was going to be fed. My immediate course of action, however, was to find a toilet or outhouse. Considering the numbers of people in our group, I really didn't want to wait in line.

I was delighted to find said outhouse unoccupied. While I sat on the potty, I could see through the two-inch gap at the bottom of the plank door and noticed quite a few pairs of small, grimy feet. People seemed to be squatting in the bush just a few yards away, chatting to each other while they defecated and then using palm leaves to clean themselves. I made a mental note not to hold any of their hands.

Then, suddenly, there was a flash of movement on the ground and I let out an un-manly scream. A snake had just slithered between my feet on its way from one side of the rickety shed to the other. I have never before or since pulled up my trousers so quickly. Among the lessons I was learning in such short order, here was yet another: sometimes outhouses are empty for a reason.

The night settled in and more fires were lit by criss- crossing three huge logs for each one into the shape of a star and then setting an empty soda bottle alight in the middle. Once the flames were fierce enough, huge, witch- sized cauldrons appeared. I had never seen rice cooked on such an industrial scale. I was hoping that the cow – my cow, I felt – would also figure on the menu to provide some protein with all that starch.

Most of the people around me were very plump. Actually, the uncharitable description that came to mind was 'bloated whales'. Like Laura's family in Panamá City, they shovelled in gluttonous amounts of food. I suppose the fresh beef tasted better than the usual tinned corned beef they were used to. Thanks to the British gringo, they were all well- fed and in excellent spirits. We had taken the precaution of stocking up with an unholy number of Balboa beer cases in Panamá City before we left and had enough liquor to open a bar. By the time the morning came the ground was thick with empty tins, and it was time to make another run for supplies.

I knew our accommodation was not going to be of five- star quality, but I guess I was hoping for rustic but sanitary. No such luck. Mama Venni, Laura's grandmother, lead us into a rundown shack by untying some string that held the door to a nail in the frame. The level of security underlined the fact that these were people who felt they had nothing worth stealing. She flicked a switch that bristled with exposed wires. A single dim light bulb dangled from the ceiling and fat moths circled overhead. *Do the moths ever drop into people's mouths while they sleep?* I wondered.

The mattress of the bed was patched together with well-worn duct tape that had failed to prevent makeshift stuffing from escaping through long tears in the fabric. As mattresses go, it had the look of one on which entire generations had been conceived. I politely asked Mama Venni to remove two roosting chickens from under the bed before we retired for the night.

The 'bathroom' came complete with a bespattered bowl. I wished with all my heart that I was constipated. Darién, is known as the neck of a bottle because it blocks the flow of movement through the country, and has the delightful nickname of 'the tampon' or 'plug' of Panamá. Taking that as my inspiration, I tried to focus on thoughts of blocked movements in an attempt to make them apply to my own body.

Despite all this, I was on my best behaviour and made sure to keep my complaints silent.

The following morning, I could tell the family was up and awake by the blaring music. That bloody bed had done a number on my backside and I feared that I had contracted something nasty from the mattress. Things got worse as I managed – with apologies for the scatological tone things keep taking – to block the toilet as well. What a wonderful start to the day! They hadn't told me not to flush paper down it, and now the overflowing evidence of my mistake was just waiting to be discovered.

Who could blame me though? I had never been in a place where you needed to drop your soiled toilet paper into a wicker basket.

I told Laura about the mishap and she was furious, her eyes glinting like daggers at my stupidity. I feared that the whole family was going to turn on me and that all my attempts to ingratiate myself with the in-laws would end in bloodshed.

Word spread, disapproving looks continued but, thankfully, I was not the cause of the problem. The real culprit was the grandparents' septic tank, which was full of foam and had been leaking around the outside of the house. Anyway, as the rich supplier of so many unexpected goodies for the family, I think I would have been forgiven.

The trip, despite the hostile climate and the testing conditions, was actually exciting and good fun. We nearly drank the jungle dry by stripping young coconuts from the numerous palms belonging to Laura's clan and mixing the juice with a splash of the gin we'd thoughtfully brought along. The result was delicious and would have been even better if we'd had a lemon tree nearby for a final twist.

Our provisions for the journey included a multi-media projector we had brought from Miami. We wanted Laura's family to have a big screen experience, even if there were a few vital ingredients, such as popcorn and comfortable seats, missing. The jungle was our backdrop and we made a makeshift screen, using (less than clean) sheets gathered from various sources. Once stretched between trees and secured with homemade clothes pegs, these measured 12 feet across.

It was fantastic to watch the children's rapt faces as they drank in this brand-new form of entertainment. Willie had burned a load of pirate DVDs for us and we chose what seemed the most suitable of the bunch: some cheesy horror movies. The screams of the actors echoed through the midnight jungle and the screams of the audience answered. The kids were gripping their mothers, the mothers were gripping their kids. The atmosphere was one of total absorption.

I had bought a very fake-looking gorilla costume from eBay before we'd left, thinking it might be useful as an ice- breaker (and we Tuffneys have a weakness for pranks.) I squeezed into the suit halfway through the movie, then snuck into the jungle and emerged from behind the screen, running towards everyone and letting out my best impersonation of a King Kong roar.

Somewhat to my surprise, the jungle theatre emptied in seconds. I hadn't realised that I was so convincing.

With hindsight, it was a pretty stupid idea. Guns in that part of the world were as common as candy and I could easily have been shot by a well-refreshed and trigger-happy member of the audience who believed himself to be under attack.

The following day, we returned to La Palma to buy fresh supplies. We took the opportunity to introduce ourselves to the local police commissioner, González. I made the calculation that it was important to make a good impression on him, so that if we were caught later in one of the many pop-up police checkpoints in the area, I could mention his name.

It was a small town and word spread quickly. On our way back to base camp, Chai decided he needed more fuel if he was going to function as a taxi driver. We pulled up next to a shack, and Chai grabbed two five-gallon plastic drums before heading inside. He was met by an elderly grandmother who was sat in a darkened room pumping pink gasoline by hand from a big blue barrel twice her size. Gas stations as such didn't exist in La Palma. Fair enough: I just wanted to know why he was filling up the canisters without placing a drop in the tank.

There were no credit cards to use for fuel – or for anything else. Cash was king and the more of it you had, the more influence you wielded.

I got a clearer understanding of the local culture once I had the chance to talk to the locals with Laura as my translator. It turned out that families had been leaving La Palma for years because they were tired of swinging a machete for a few dollars a day. The population had dropped from nearly 12,000 in 1990 to just over 4,000 in 2010. Another reason for the decline was the trouble caused by the regular incursion of Colombian drug traffickers and the crime they brought with them. They were being captured on a daily basis, closer than ever before. I was also interested in the way the indigenous people, the Emberá, were treated as outsiders – almost disdained – by the majority, who had a mixture of Native American, European and African genes, thanks to Spanish colonisation and the slave trade.

The basic purpose of the trip was to research the potential of the region as the site for a sustainable teak and mahogany plantation, one that would improve the economy and provide employment. My in-laws certainly included a high number of men who spent most of the day swinging in hammocks. I was also interested longer-term in opening a tourist resort with an emphasis on adventure and the local fauna and flora, so all local information was useful. I could see that there was great opportunity for investment.

Everyone was exceptionally friendly, but I was nonetheless wary at first of their motives. It would have been foolish to discount the influence that money can have. Laura persuaded me that they were good people. Maybe not the most diligent workers in the world, but enthusiastic and honest. We communicated well enough despite my sub- pidgin Spanish, and I looked forward to co-operating with them.

Thanks to Laura, I was part of the family now, bound by the maxim that blood is thicker than water.

Ultimately, I bought land from Laura's grandfather, her uncle and her aunt in Darién. I also bought cows and 500 chickens from my in-laws, to be managed by them when I returned to the States. My house in Darién was built on the one-acre plot bought from her Aunt Nidia.

The rule was that if individuals had lived on a plot for a long time, they could apply to register ownership in their names. Laura's family supposedly applied for the title deeds (I was shown the completed forms) when they agreed to sell, so that ownership could then be transferred to me. The problem was that the deeds never actually arrived.

Initially, the issue seemed to be nothing more than bureaucratic delay, and therefore, on the basis of handshakes and hugs, we drew up homemade contracts and I paid the money up front. I was assured that as soon as the cheques were cashed, I would have full rights as the new owner. "Be patient," I was told. "Have faith. It will be fine." I proceeded with clearing the land and planting my first batch of 5,000 teak trees, which I did with their help.

As things stand today, I do not own any of the property or the plantation I paid for. There is no official record of the transactions and for that reason I have no status or protection in Panamanian law as the owner. It was only years later, after our marriage had broken down, that I discovered this fact. The breach of trust was crushing, especially after I had given employment to many members of Laura's extended

87

family. At the time, however, returning to Miami from Darién, this disillusionment was yet to come. I was convinced that my investments were sound, and that future investments would also be safe.

Laura, meanwhile, continued to live the high life of her dreams as an extra. She took great pains with her appearance, I noticed, and was unusually vivacious, telling me every day that she loved me. Hmm. Considering that she was spending more time off screen than on it at the station, I began to suspect that she was seeing someone else.

In around 2008 my fears were confirmed when I received an anonymous email from a girl going under the pseudonym 'Petal White'. In it, she baldly said, "I thought I'd let you know that Laura is having an affair with a guy down at Telemundo. It's not fair what she's doing." I am amazed, with hindsight, how calmly I took the news. I didn't even confront Laura to ask for the name of my rival. The reason may be that in my heart I had already known and detached myself from her to some extent. Maybe I was just a coward who hoped the affair would burn out. We had a son, after all, and he was my priority.

What the note did achieve was to concentrate my mind on protecting my own assets. For instance, I moved bank documents in case things went bad. I was most concerned about the titles of the properties I'd already bought, but satisfied myself that I should not worry too much.

A few months later Laura found fame. The soap opera's license was sold to Panamá and, mere extra or not, she became a superstar in the opinion of her family. Bolstered by their star-struck support, she became even more demanding, and my role began to feel increasingly more like that of bankroller and bag-carrier, as opposed to husband. Skippy and Jason kept me sane, but the marriage was in a mess.

This domestic semi-segregation drove me to find a new focus. Whatever my problems with Laura during those years, I fell in love with Panamá as surely as I once had with her –perhaps more deeply. We made several further trips to the jungles of Darién, sometimes accompanied by my mother. The level of abject poverty and neglect in the region was pitiful, especially among the Emberá Indians, and I wanted to help in a way that would improve their quality of life without disrupting their culture.

In early 2009, my mother and I established a charity, The British American Foundation (later the British American Foundation for Panamá), to send containers of donated goods that could be distributed across local institutions. My contacts in the supply business proved open-hearted and generous. Goods ranged from hospital beds, to bicycles, to children's toys and books. The energy I poured into the charity matched the energy I devoted to making sure that our new house in Darién – and the groundwork for my planned resort – would be a success.

I had supervised the construction from scratch. More than a place to live, it was a bricks-and-mortar expression of my hopes for the future. The fact that 90 per cent of the crew was made up of Laura's family, whose lack of expertise could be overlooked for rates of $7 a day, gave the enterprise symbolic significance as a joint effort. I learned on the job too, as this was my first attempt at playing site foreman in a jungle. Blood, sweat – a lot of sweat – and tears went into completing the job.

While the house was being built, we spent long periods in Darién, living in a tent next to Laura's grandparents' shack so that we could have an electricity supply via multiple extension cords. It was probably the only tent in Central America to have air conditioning and a plasma TV, and it used to attract quite a stream of admirers.

My plan was to rent out the Miami house and move down to Panamá while I established the plantation. The business In Florida was going well and we had seven highly competent employees by then. We didn't need a huge workforce because things functioned on the basis of what's called drop-shipping. Someone placed their order online, the order was passed to the wholesaler and then shipped to the customers, so we never had to handle or warehouse the goods ourselves – just seek out the business. I was at a level of seniority in which I could entrust the day-to-day schmoozing and selling to my staff.

I clearly remember the date – July 3, 2009 – when Jason, Laura and I returned to the jungle of Nuevo Paritilla to begin what I prayed would be a new and better chapter for us all, one in which we could distance ourselves from Telemundo. The house was up, the trees were growing strong and the first container shipment of British American Foundation donations was due.

I felt the day deserved some official recognition, but my invitation to the American embassy was rebuffed. Their staff did not travel to parts of Panamá considered to have inadequate roads. However, my good friend at the British embassy, Ambassador Richard Austin, replied to his invitation with an enthusiastic "Yes!" He was to become a stalwart and very much-appreciated supporter of the charity.

Richard's arrival coincided with that of the 40-foot container. Massed ranks of armed Special Forces police were gathered behind him and there must have been 600 Emberá Indians lining the track, clapping and cheering. He said that the reception made him feel like a member of the royal family.

It was a special moment for both of us. We drank fine wines and had a satisfying smoke while talking over my ambitious plans for the charity. To his surprise and delight I had managed to import some difficult-to-find British delicacies among the donations. Fray Bentos pies, Stilton and a jar of good old love-it-or-loathe-it Marmite were tokens of my genuine appreciation of his help.

Richard came with us to San José hospital in La Palma, the recipient of donated equipment, so that I could introduce him to the hard-working staff doctors there. They did a fantastic job in very challenging conditions. His observation was that they were working in the equivalent of a war zone, using great ingenuity to compensate for the essential supplies they simply did not have.

As a result of that trip, Richard became absolutely dedicated to the cause. He even donated an assortment of items from his own residence, including a washing machine and tumble dryer, to the hospital.

But July 3, 2009, was also a day that had severe unintended consequences. The opening of the container was something of an event and after it was done, we handed out celebratory beers. Laura's cousin, Dilsa, wanted to record the moment and she asked everyone to pose for a photograph. At that point, of course, everyone in the vicinity crowded into the frame. Kids who had been watching picked up empty beer cans and raised them in an exuberant 'cheers' gesture. It seemed totally innocent and harmless.

With hindsight, it was a misjudgement. That picture would be used against me years later, when the optimism around us had turned to dust, to support the absurd charge of corrupting minors with alcohol.

It was another misjudgement to have reported some Gallardo teenagers to the police after they stole goods from another charity shipment, destined for an Indian school in the town of Llano Bonito located deep in the jungle. The boys were demonstrably guilty and I was angry, but as far as their family was concerned, I should have turned a blind eye to the theft. It would have repercussions that I did not foresee.

The disparity between rich and poor in Nuevo Paritilla

93

My romantic dream that Laura and I would re-kindle our marriage in Darién proved to be exactly that: a romantic dream. To my wife, our new house was a status symbol to show her family. It was impressive but not necessarily somewhere she wanted to live. She preferred the excitement of Miami. Needless to say, the marriage continued to head downhill. We began to avoid each other. One day in 2010, when we were in Miami, we had the most almighty row that blew up over some petty domestic disagreement. She started to throw punches at me, I tried to restrain her, and it developed into a screaming fit, the likes of which I had never experienced before in my life. I am not a physically aggressive or violent person, and I was way out of my depth when confronted by such fury.

To distract her and, yes, to wind her up, I pretended to throw a folder containing her passport and other important documents into the water at the back of our house. Laura had put a lot of effort into getting those documents, most of all the prized green card that made her a legal immigrant after our marriage, and she went berserk.

About three days later I came home and was appalled to find that she had left for Panamá and taken Jason with her. To add insult to injury, she had also removed the plug from my boat and scuttled it in the dock.

On landing in Panamá, she hammered the American Express card to the tune of $10,000 in one day's shopping spree. She moved into her mother's house near the airport in Panamá City and bought building supplies, indicating that she planned to stay there for a while.

Jason was six when he was taken, and I have never seen or heard from him since. It still staggers me that his mother was able to remove him from the US without his father's permission. Her unilateral decision to cut me out of Jason's life, despite the fact that I was a good father, seemed to trump any effort I made to maintain contact with my own son.

I tried appealing to the American and British embassies for help. I hired attorneys in Panamá. I have the mountain of paperwork to prove how I trailed through the courts in a futile effort to gain access. Nothing worked. My Panamanian attorney was issued with a protection order that amounted to an injunction against me getting anywhere near Laura, and therefore Jason. Her family claimed that I had beaten her up. Breaching the order would have resulted in my being sent to prison. (Little did I know what was coming.)

When I did go to Panamá to find my son, I was immediately hit with a demand for $10,000 a month in child maintenance because of a warrant Laura had lodged with the police, though we were not at that stage divorced and the matter had not been discussed. Laura was fixated on bringing me down.

4

REVENGE WAS A BITCH

The campaign of harassment that ended in my imprisonment began almost as soon as Laura had taken Jason to Panamá.

I was in Darién on a regular basis, living in my house, despite the effective collapse of our marriage. I needed to fight obstacles put in the way of my seeing Jason, as well as distribute and manage donations for the charity, which continued to arrive from England.

The first arrest happened in 2010, when I was in Panamá with Angel, my translator employee and buddy.

We had set off early to load the truck with charity items from my depository near Panamá City, and then headed back to Darién. I wanted to give some of the donations to the police station in Meteti, a town about 20 miles from my house. The Senafront frontier patrol police in the area were responsible for keeping order in the jungle bordering Colombia, and I was keen to be on good terms with them.

Not only did they genuinely need stationery, I had a feeling that I might genuinely need their protection.

We duly unloaded our cargo from the flatbed of the truck and were introduced to the head of Senafront, Commissioner Frank Abrego. Angel noticed that one of Laura's innumerable cousins, who was a cop at the station, was talking intensely on her cell phone in the background. When we tried to say our goodbyes, we were told to hang around in the compound while some 'paperwork' was checked. Angel's hackles went up. He told me that something was wrong, but I couldn't understand why that would be the case, when we had just given them a donation.

After 10 increasingly tense minutes of waiting in the car, a cop walked over, pointed his AK47 in our direction and asked us to get out.

"I told you so," muttered Angel. They escorted me to a side room in the station, and that's where I was told that they had a warrant for my arrest, for non-payment of child maintenance. What child maintenance? I had no idea what they were talking about because I had never been served.

I was handcuffed and bundled into a police car, ready to be taken on a six-hour journey back towards Panamá City. Angel did not have a legal driving licence, but when I pleaded with the cops to allow him to follow us back to Panamá driving my truck, they agreed. I didn't want to leave it sitting unattended in Darién.

The police were doing a terrifying 80 or 90 miles an hour. Angel simply could not keep up. The truck was a beaten up Brazilian-made Chevrolet with inadequate wipers, and we were heading through a tropical storm. When I craned my head to see how he was doing, all I could make out behind us was a dim and distant pair of flickering headlights.

Somehow, we both made it to a place called Chepo, on the Inter-American Highway, where I was to be locked up for the night before proceeding under guard to Panamá City. Angel had to call through the bars of my cell window to ask how I was. "Tired. Confused. In need of a smoke," was my honest answer. I tossed my wallet out to him on the street so that he could find himself somewhere to stay for the night and buy me some cigs and a lighter.

It was pitch black by the time he returned, and he was trying to throw the packet to me through the window but he kept hitting the bars. My fags finally sailed through, followed by a lighter, and I was relieved to at least have some nicotine to comfort me. My issue was that I had to squeeze my face as close to the bars as possible to exhale the smoke outside, so as not to gain the attention of the cop on duty at the front desk.

When he finally caught me, he couldn't make up his mind whether I was allowed to smoke or not. The indecision went on for what felt like hours. In the end I took what in Panamá is always the pragmatic view and asked Angel to find my guard something from the boot of the truck. Sweeteners, bribes, inducements: call them what you like, they were the currency of officialdom in this country and they were necessary to oil the wheels. I got my smoke.

The next morning the police took me, with Angel at the rear, to Panamá City. We got there just as the electric gates of Ancón detention centre were opening. I had heard about that place and had no desire to go inside.

Just in time to save me, a message crackled over the police radio that I should be taken directly to the courthouse. There, I had to tell my attorney, José, what assets I had. Stupid idiot that I was, I listed the houses without saying that the one in Miami was mortgaged and told them about the land – not mine, as it later turned out – and the plantation. They assumed I owned everything outright and settled on a monthly figure of $10,000 in child support. The mentality was that if el gringo had so much, Panamá was entitled to it. I never actually found out what the initial sum, for which I was arrested, had been.

Laura was relentlessly on my case from that point onwards.

I paid the money regularly, but in Darién there were no banks. I had to go to Panamá City to make the transactions, and any kind of delay – sometimes of less than 24 hours – sent her scurrying to get an arrest warrant or national capture warrant issued. She used to sign them off herself at the police station.

ÓRGANO JUDICIAL

JUZGADO QUINTO MUNICIPAL DE FAMILIA
DEL DISTRITO DE PANAMÁ

Panamá, 20 de noviembre de 2012.

A cargo de la **POLICIA NACIONAL**, para que dejen sin efecto toda boleta de **CONDUCCION** emitida por este Tribunal a cargo del señor **NICHOLAS TUFFNEY** con número de pasaporte No.704249213, dentro del proceso de alimentos interpuesto por **LAURA GALLARDO.**

MAGÍSTRA. ELIZABETH HUERTA MORALES.
JUEZ QUINTO MUNICIPAL DE FAMILIA
DEL DISTRITO DE PANAMÁ.

Ubicación: Vía España, Edificio Dorchester, 3er piso, arriba del almacén Poppy, oficina 315. teléfono 212-7423. **EN HORARIO DE LUNES A VIERNES (8:00 a.m - 12:00 p.m y 2:00p.m - 5:00 p.m)**

/mg

Her whole purpose was to have me locked up – or dead, whichever came first. That was when I decided to invest in a bullet-proof jacket from eBay, purchased during my last trip back to Miami. She and her family were just as keen to have Angel arrested, because he was helping me through the maze of the Panamanian judicial system.

I became frightened of going out because there were so many pop-up police checkpoints on the roads. The police could feed my passport details into their system and, if there was a national alert in my name, had the power to send me straight to prison.

To illustrate how extreme the tactic became, I give the following example. On the day before the court hearing in which I sought access to Jason, I had paid money for child support directly into her bank at 5pm. However, it was in her interests for me not to turn up in court, and what better reason for that than my arrest? I drove to the courthouse with Angel and José, my attorney on the appointed day; pulling up in the car park, I was immediately surrounded by armed police. Laura had 'forgotten' to check whether the money was in her bank account the previous evening. I had to pull the transaction teller receipt from my wallet to prove that all was in order. This was while her armed robber brother Henry, who had by this time been released from prison and was running a taxi service, stood pointing at me just in case the cops ambushed the wrong man.

The court case had already been adjourned once, a year before, on the advice of my attorney. When we finally made it into court, the judge decided we couldn't go ahead because our official translator – a woman licenced and certified by the state – had not been personally approved by him. Case deferred for another six months. The whim of this asshole judge over-rode everything else in Panamá, which created endless opportunities for delay.

The catalyst for my second brush with the law was an incident in 2010, before Laura left me. Some teenage relatives of Laura and her cousin Dilsa were caught stealing computers and bicycles from the marquee behind our house that contained charity donations in Darién. They were guilty and I was angry, and I reported them to the La Palma police. The boys spent five days in the squalid La Palma prison.

Should I have dealt with the matter differently? Probably. The thefts were a cynical attempt to take advantage and I wanted them exposed, but I hadn't expected the boys to be locked up. The Gallardos considered my actions to be a rank betrayal. My status as 'family' had been conditional on spending plenty of money and playing the game nicely. When I broke the rules, they closed ranks against me. The isolation was brutal and fast.

Tensions were growing at the same time over the continued non-appearance of the deeds that were supposed to transfer ownership of the land and my newly built house, which I had already paid for. Dilsa in particular was nervous that she might actually have to hand over the titles in return for the money I had paid her for two plots, rather than keep stringing me along at her own convenience. Since buying the land, I had planted over 10,000 mahogany trees, so she was in the happy position of having money for the land and a plantation. What a plus for her if I went to jail, and was then then deported for life.

It didn't matter what I had done for the Gallardos to date, or whether promises had been made and contracts signed. I was suddenly the enemy, and all their weapons of war were now being deployed.

They ransacked my house while I was away and decorated it with dead and dismembered chickens that putrefied in the jungle heat. After that vandalism, they pulled all the air conditioning units out, leaving gaping holes to the outside. The Corregidor, chief magistrate of the zone in Chepigana, was called to document the scene and the destruction to my property. (I traced the air-conditioning units, eventually: two were at Laura's Panamá City property, and the other was at her mother's house.)

But the main thrust of their revenge came in early 2011. Together, the original Gallardo landowners and the parents of the plantation workers filed a Corruption of Minors case against Angel and me. Unbeknownst to me at the time, this was a popular way to remove enemies, known to the gypsies as the 'Death Blow'. They claimed, on the basis of Dilsa's photograph, that we had given their kids alcohol. They also said that we had shown them pornography. The truth was that Laura, not me, had included among the DVDs we'd brought to Darién from Miami a popular Spanish soap opera only broadcast in the States. My friend Willie, who had burned the copies for us, liked to watch porn and he had inadvertently left a blue movie in with the batch of soaps. We had just chucked them all in the usual drawer without checking what they were because they all looked identical. The kids, who had free run of the house, had apparently helped themselves as usual and chanced upon the unsuitable DVD while I wasn't even at home.

Willie willingly signed a notarised testimony in Miami to say that I wasn't responsible in any way for the DVD mix-up. When the case was brought before the courts a few months later, it lasted for less than 10 minutes before the judge dismissed all charges as unfounded.

My divorce from Laura came through in 2012, but it did not mark the end of the animosities. It was a living nightmare trying to cut through the wall she had erected to keep me from Jason. I appealed for help from the Child Abduction Agency in Washington; I employed an English- speaking solicitor to help me. My mission was to get my boy back home and it was exhausting, but what dad would not go the extra mile? I had no option except to be in Panamá full-time, which took me from my business in Miami and meant that I was vulnerable to intimidation from the Gallardos. They were still thirsty for every drop of my blood.

The attorney representing us on the original Corruption of Minors charge had mistakenly left that case, notes open, without sealing it. Therefore, it was possible to re-open the case at any time with an additional charge. The tactic chosen by Laura and co certainly deserved marks for ingenuity, considering their collective IQ.

In March, 2013, they watched a live late-breaking news cast on TV about witchcraft allegedly being practised 300 miles from Darién, in a place called Colon, on the Atlantic coast. Eureka! They decided that witchcraft was exactly the missing ingredient to spice up the corruption charge against Angel and me.

I had moved from the hostile atmosphere of Darién and was living mostly in Arraijan, near Panamá City, where I was also relatively safe from the monthly barrage of arrest warrants. In my absence, a shipping container belonging to the British American Foundation in Darién was prized open by the Gallardos, and some Halloween party favours donated by Amscan Ltd were removed. Next, they broke into my house and arranged the plastic snakes, toy dolls and various other trinkets in lurid, Voodoo-type tableaux. It added insult to criminal injury that they used my printer and A4 paper to copy the photographs they would later present as evidence of my depravity.

The Gallardos' final flourish was to invite the TVN-2 national news channel to come and film the Harry Potter scene props strategically placed in my house in Darién.

Viewers were treated to the sight of the reporter walking round my sitting room while various helpful Gallardos explained the significance of this knotted snake or that headless doll.

TVN entered my property to film a documentary called 'Terror en Darién', with the Gallardos by their side

I was painted as some kind of diabolical warlock living among the innocent folk of Nuevo Paritilla. My former in-laws, relishing their 15 minutes of fame, presented themselves as horrified by the discovery of such evil in their midst. If they sounded sincere, despite lying through their teeth about me, it was because they genuinely believed in some crazy bullshit. Laura had an uncle who lived a few doors down from us and claimed to be capable of curing cancer by summoning the right spirits. For a joke – things were at a low point in the marriage – I asked Laura's uncle how much he would charge to put a curse on Laura. He quoted me $800 and instructed me to gather specific plants that grew on the waterside about a 20-minute drive away, in a place called Sannon. On my return he scattered the plants around the perimeter of my property and performed a ritual. His mother-in-law applied a magic potion of tonic to my hair, but it did nothing at all and smelt like deodorant mixed with petrol.

Maybe I should have taken the family's weird suspicions more seriously. They certainly used them to set an effective trap. A revised charge of Corruption of Minors Using Witchcraft was filed against Angel and me in the La Palma prosecutor's office.

Three months later…

On the morning of May 16, 2013 – by coincidence, my dad's birthday – I watched the sun rise over Arraijan, where I was living. Dawn light was creeping through the windows when I stepped into the bathroom for a long, icy shower that I knew would invigorate me, even if it was a form of temporary torture. It certainly beat the Gallardos' torture, which had lasted a lot longer than three minutes.

Ordeal over, I threw on a bathrobe and poured myself a cup of tea: nectar of the Gods. The familiar flavour set my taste buds alight and brought back nostalgic memories of the UK. I could picture family holidays when I was a young boy, playing on the beach with my brothers, and the excitement of rushing across the sand to the picnic, complete with flask of hot tea, which my parents had prepared for us.

I felt a rare sense of optimism. So much at the time felt difficult and depressing, but today I had a plan.

I would be away for a few hours on a return trip to Costa Rica, taken for the sole reason of getting my American passport stamped. The 180 days of secure immigration status it would give was going to be worth more than gold to my mental health.

I had a legitimate, current Panamanian residence card on my British passport, and for that reason, I had to present it if I was stopped at a police checkpoint. But my British passport details were the ones programmed into the national police capture list, Pella, which flagged up any warrants against me. There had been two in the last month thanks to Laura's tireless attentions. Recently she had lodged a court order demanding that I increase my monthly maintenance payments to $15,000, supposedly for Jason's sake. In reality, it was for her and her greedy family.

The Pella crap was a constant cloud over my head and an impediment in my ongoing battle to gain some custody or visiting rights that allowed me to see Jason. Assuming my American passport details were not in the system, the

Costa Rican stamp would allow me to freely continue with my mission in Panamá for six months.

I took a good look from my wooden rocking chair at my sparse apartment: there wasn't much to secure before I left, and I would be home again within seven hours at the most. I closed the dusty shutters, reset the mouse trap and set out water and food for Skippy.

My adorable, ugly, black and white mutt was a constant source of joy to me. I loved her without reservation, and she returned the favour as a loyal and uncritical friend. My sentimental English attitude to pets was an oddity in Panamá, where most dogs were kept purely for guard duties and died of distemper. Skippy, on the other hand, was a true companion.

She made quite a scene of our goodbye by bounding over to me and nearly knocking the mug I was holding from my hand, her stumpy tail whirring. I wonder now if she had a kind of inkling, some canine sixth sense, of what was to come. I was travelling light when I set off to Tocumen International Airport: no bags, just my wallet, passport and sunglasses. My mood was light, too. I was looking forward to seeing Angel again. He was due into Tocumen after a month-long vacation in the UK with my family. The plan was for us to meet in the arrivals hall when I'd completed my lightning visit to Costa Rica, and then for him to head back to my place in Arraijan.

The 20-mile journey to the airport was the usual hellish dodgem ride on the Corredor Sur, with drivers swerving from left and right. At least the need to stay alive was a distraction from worrying about whether my Costa Rican jaunt would pay off. I parked at Tocumen and hid my key discreetly under one of the wheel arches, just in case. You never knew who else might need to use your car.

Airport halls, full of people greeting loved ones or saying goodbye to each other, always engage my imagination. I let my mind wander to longed-for scenes in my own future. I wanted to be one of the fathers embracing his young son but, beyond that, I wanted to be there at Jason's graduation ceremony, to be standing in church when he got married. Those were the ambitions that underpinned everything I did.

Pushing such thoughts aside, I breezed through the customs checks and settled into the first-class lounge without a hitch. By the time my call for gate 16 came up, I was daring to hope that my luck had changed for the better. The message that flight CM144 to Costa Rica was ready to board flashed up on the screens. My boarding pass, for seat 28A, was in my hand.

I stood and walked towards the sanctuary of the plane: just a quick check of my pass to complete. What could go wrong?

Mere yards from safety, I was stopped by a heavy hand on my left shoulder. "Senor Nicholas Tuffney..." I turned to see two Directorate of Judicial Investigation (DIJ) agents. They did not look friendly.

I had enough experience by then to read the signs, and I knew what was coming. They each placed a hand under one of my elbows and steered me to one side of the boarding gate.

"Passport, por favour." They made a big show of comparing my face to my mug shot and then told me with unnecessary pleasure that I was not going to be catching my flight. A third officer with 'Interpol' plastered across the front of his jacket showed up and began shoving me.

The metaphor 'I felt my heart sink' is one I'd used plenty of times without much thought, but at that moment I really did have the sensation of a lead weight in my chest. I tried to be cool and rational, but I was truly bricking it.

I didn't know what I'd done wrong because they hadn't told me, but, rather like the first time I was picked up for non-payment of maintenance, my ignorance was of zero interest to them. You reach a point of resignation, once you've had enough encounters with aggressive cops who don't give a f***, that would amaze a standard, upright British citizen. You don't scream about your rights; you just roll with the punches.

They marched me downstairs through the busy, over- heated arrivals hall and I had a brief fantasy that, after all the drama, they were going to place a fresh stamp in my passport and let me go. We headed towards a door marked 'Airport Director's Office' at the end of a narrow corridor and into a room filled with a bank of blue chairs. I sat and waited. There wasn't much else I could do.

A DIJ agent hovered over me, glaring as his gun holster gleamed under the lights. Those 10 minutes of waiting were the longest 10

minutes of my life. Suddenly the door opened and out walked my old associate, Commissioner González, in his new role of Airport Director. *Thank God*, I thought. *Someone's going to help me.*

By coincidence, Commissioner González had previously been chief of police in Darién, and the British American Foundation had refurbished his police unit in La Palma with a good $25,000 worth of donated equipment. The whole station was running thanks to my charity. I'd even picked out the interrogation chairs. Surely he could return the favour now?

He raised his eyebrows. "Why are you here?"

"Good question. Mistaken identity?" I offered. (After all, it had happened to me once in Miami, when I had spent two days in Dade County Penitentiary because a drugs smuggler was impersonating me and had jumped bail using my licence.)

Broward county prison mugshot of my double

"Listen," I said, "you can help me out here. Just stamp my passport quickly and I'll be on my way."

He paused for long enough to consider it, then turned away, muttering something about how he was sorry, but that I was in Interpol's hands now.

Mind you, he did wish me good luck.

There was to be no miraculous escape, no golden key, nothing. Whatever this was, it was unstoppable now. My mouth felt dry as sandpaper and I couldn't have made another plea for mercy even if I'd wanted to.

The DJI goons ran a chain around my waist and attached it to shackles on my hands and feet. The manacles were so new that they gleamed silvery white under the terminal strip lights.

"Venga," they said. I got up with difficulty and, waddling like a penguin, was escorted through the arrivals hall yet again, with Interpol agents on both sides of me. I felt humiliated, bewildered and scared shitless. The crowds of people I'd been watching an hour before backed away from me now that I was packaged up like the world's most dangerous psychopath. I kept my head lowered, but I saw the flashes of cell phone cameras reflected in the shiny tiles of the concourse floor as we headed for the exit.

There was a silver Ford Focus with non-tinted windows waiting for us. I was thrust roughly into the back seat and my new jewellery bit deep into my hands and ankles.

"That f***ing hurts," I shouted. The lack of response was deafening.

I was traveling back on the same route I had taken just two hours earlier, this time being chauffeured by Interpol. I guess my confusion was on a level with having been concussed. None of it seemed real. I

112

struggled to ask myself some sensible questions: What about Skippy? Who would feed her? Who would get word to Angel? How on earth would this effect my elderly mother? I dreaded her seeing my shameful arrest on BBC News.

I could see the driver's face in his rear-view mirror, hear him guffawing in Spanish about his fresh 'road-kill of the day'. I started to pant loudly. I needed a smoke. I needed something, a fix, to blur the horrific circumstance of being completely powerless and trapped in a tiny space with captors who regarded my misery as a joke.

The other gloating officer was chatting on his cell phone, "Hola TVN-2", he said. The lead weight in my chest got heavier. He was calling the TV station with a juicy piece of news: me. This was a nightmare from which I just couldn't wake.

Eventually the car stopped. We were now back at the Panamá City Central Detention Facility, Ancón. This place seemed to haunt me: only months previously, I had been at these same gates being brought back from Darién, thanks to one of Laura's tricks.

This place was known as the lion's den, where the guilty and innocent alike were sent to be devoured by time. You could wait and wait in Ancón , sometimes to rot, before your trial date was decided.

The hulking barbed wire-topped electric gate opened slowly opened for us, and suddenly we were surrounded by the glare of a hundred camera flash bulbs and TV lights. They were pressed right up against the car windows, blinding me. The police had tipped off the journalists that I was prize bait, and the journalists had paid bribes to the police so that they could film me from inside the perimeter fence rather than through it from the outside.

They got plenty of chances for pictures when I had to clank my way through the throng to get inside the facility. It was only then, when I was in their Interpol office, that I heard about the witchcraft allegations. Witchcraft? Angel and I were now practitioners of the black arts. The situation was dire, but I almost wanted to laugh at the absurdity of it.

We were both charged and wanted for questioning, but it was my American passport that had triggered the heavy- handed Interpol presence at the airport. When Angel flew into Tocumen from London a few hours later, he strolled through passport control in blissful ignorance and wasn't challenged by any officials.

I suspect at that stage I had been sold to the media as a rich gringo who'd done something really juicy, always the peg to hang a lurid story on. I didn't know if they had specific details of my alleged crime.

I was put into a special section of the police station, the 'grooming room', which stank of cheap deodorant and where Interpol officers spent hours primping themselves before they made TV appearances. There was a horrible carnival atmosphere because the live coverage was being played on a television in the cells next door to where I was being held. I could hear the inmates whistling and jeering. The majority of them came from the butt-end of Panamá City. They were tough as hell, shirtless, heavily tattooed — and they were watching me, in my smart clothes, being described as a 'millionaire businessman', or whatever else boosted the viewing figures. No wonder they were chanting for my balls on a plate. To say it was nerve-racking doesn't begin to cover it. It was bowel-loosening. It made me want to faint with fear.

The press and TV really got their money's worth when I was released from my chains and made to do a 'perp walk' for five minutes more, to ensure my notoriety was properly established and recorded. I was by no means a celebrity, but I had done enough in La Palma and Darién to have registered on journalists' radars. Persuading the British ambassador to visit a region considered too lawless for Panamanian statesmen was a coup that had gathered a fair bit of attention.

The guards were grinning from ear to ear at earning their kickback from the TV crews. I was a dead man. I was being broadcast on national television for everyone to see— and for all for the wrong reasons. Laura must have been ecstatic.

I was pushed through a side door and knew at once that the stakes had increased tenfold. Separated from me by iron bars was a massive holding-pen filled, as far as I could tell under the flickering light bulb, with semi-naked lunatics who were cat-calling and pointing from me to their TV screen. It was facing away from me so I could only guess what they were looking at.

I felt myself begin to slip away as the blood drained from my head, but somehow I managed to stay on my feet. I turned to see that the portable TV sitting on the guard's desk was showing the news. And at the bottom of the screen, on a repeating scroll were the words: 'Late Breaking Headline News: Captured Nicholas Tuffney.'

To my immeasurable relief, a friend arrived moments later. The British embassy, my cavalry, had sent their consul to release me from the horror. He told me carefully that he would do all he could, but that there were limitations to his influence. Limitations? Nothing that would keep me here another second, though, right?

José explained that he had arranged a meeting with the duty sergeant and that he had negotiated for me to be kept separately from the other inmates, for my own safety. Then he left.

I had acted as a warden for the British embassy in the Darién region before, a step down in seniority from a consul but with responsibility through a call system for rallying Brits if there was some kind of emergency. I thought of José as an ally and a colleague and believed that he would be able to help. How wrong I was to believe in our Foreign and Commonwealth Office.

My faith was short-lived. As soon as José had gone, the sergeant gave a nasty, twisted smile and beckoned me towards him. Other cops grabbed me and yelled at the baying men to retreat to the furthest end of their quarters. Then they pushed me inside the closest holding-pen, between the inmates and the officers.

This felt dangerous, and wrong. Behind the Plexiglas client-attorney window that overlooked the area were several lawyers, male and female, as well as my own attorney and another consular representative. None of them spoke up for me. I could also see through the slats of a mirrored window to the brightly lit offices where women were working. The combined audience was sizable, attentive and ready for a show. The police were in command of the entertainment. All I had to do was produce the goods.

I was asked to take my jacket off, to hoots and cheers from behind me. I reasoned that it was just for a pat-down. I was next asked to take off my shirt. Then, of course, I understood. He was going to make me strip.

The cop kept demanding and I had to keep obeying. Soon I was naked, reduced in this revolting place to a state of abject humiliation. It was a routine calculated to make the proudest man turn into a scared little boy.

At last, the officer allowed me to dress and ordered me to walk down the long, reeking corridor and through the cell doors. I had hoped that things could not get any worse. They were about to get a lot worse.

"Welcome to your new home!" he called. "Bienvenido a tu nuevo hogar, gringo."

5

THE NEW REALITY

The welcome beating I was given at Ancón could have lasted for 20 minutes or it could have lasted for 40:

I was not checking my watch. I can only say that it felt endless.

I was punched repeatedly in the head and lost two of my American-issue veneered teeth. I was jabbed in the kidneys, kicked, slapped, stamped on and told a hundred times by my leering, sweating attackers that I was going to be f***ed up the arse. (Thank God, I was at least spared that.) I think I may have screamed a few times. They were laughing like hyenas competing for a carcass.

Fresh meat was exactly what I was.

Even factoring in extra punishment for being a rich gringo whose face was on the TV, I expect that this was roughly in line with the initiation handed out to all new inmates. The prison officers simply stood by and let it happen. It was not them who rescued me, it was someone who broke through from the back of the crowd and spoke in English. "Stop. Enough!"

The light was too feeble for me to see him clearly, but he was a Rasta, built like a tank, and he had a lilting Islands accent. He introduced himself as Winston from Jamaica. I could have kissed his feet; I was so grateful. As far as I was concerned, he had saved me and we were friends for life.

Winston had been caught at Tocumen airport trying to smuggle in liquid cocaine disguised as perfume. That was the first I had ever heard of liquid cocaine, and thus began my prison education about the drugs, the crimes, the dodges and the survival techniques that might be alien to the law- abiding masses, but are common currency to people locked inside.

I curled up in a corner in submissive mode, pitifully shaken and cowed. The thin piece of cardboard under my backside did little to stop the damp from the concrete floor seeping into my bones. My priority was to make myself invisible until, a) I had recovered from my injuries and, b) I understood more about the rules, if there were any, of this place.

Ancón's central detention facility was infamous throughout Panamá City, probably throughout the country. Its latest captures were paraded on national TV, as I had been, to titillate viewers and to warn the miscreants out there of what awaited them if they were caught. It used to give me a vague feeling of dread when I drove past it, but

I always thought of it as a place for other people to fear.

The building was left over from the dictatorial reign of General Manuel Noriega and his personal army. The windowless cells had once been where he locked his enemies. Now they were crowded with about 200 inmates waiting to be processed through the Panamanian justice system. There were six cells in total, packed with bored, sprawling men, and a crowded corridor that lead in turn to a longer hallway and a dark room with two toilets and an open shower pan, connected with plastic tubing to a small concrete sink. A network of string, just above head height, held washing that never seemed to dry, and the permanent gloom was barely pierced by the naked, low-wattage bulbs.

It didn't take long to suss out the essential facts of Ancón. There were no beds for anyone, gang members excepted. Detainees had to sleep where and how they could. The few so-called surveillance cameras trained on the inmates were there purely for show: guards ignored them for 90 per cent of the time, and the inmates knew where the blind spots were anyway. They could always plan assaults so that they were out of range.

The veteran inmates and the gang kingpins with connections on the outside could live like royalty compared to the rest of us. They occupied little islands of privilege in the open cells on each side of the long corridor that lead to the bathroom. Not that it was wise to stare, but you could see they had queen-sized mattresses dressed with satin pillows and surrounded by toiletries, beer bottles, pizza cartons and phone-charging equipment.

In fact, it was an occupant of one of the Club Class mattresses who generally shut down arguments when they threatened to disturb his peace or his heavy programme of Kentucky fried chicken consumption. He was a skinhead in his 30s, his body scribbled with dense tattoos, and he was an important local gang member. He commanded total respect, even from the cops, who called him by his first name. He used to pull out a dagger when things got restless and flash the gleaming 12-inch blade it through the air until the combatants got the message and backed off.

Any misjudged gesture, movement or look put you on a potential knife edge of violence. In an environment where you were herded like cattle and personal space was near- impossible to protect, you had to be doubly careful not to offend.

That first night I found myself a place in the corridor. I was terrified that I might disturb someone lying right next to me and invite another beating, and the fear made me lie so rigidly motionless that my muscles cramped. Strangers snored inches away from my face on either side, releasing wafts of prison-issue halitosis.

The need to piss presented another problem. I had already wet myself several times since arriving, and I was beginning to smell of ammonia. I needed to get to the washroom, but it was at the far end of the corridor, at the back of the building. I would have to pick my way over sleeping bodies to reach it. In the near-dark I was bound to step on someone by mistake.

Fortunately for me, a huge fight broke out in the small hours between members of rival gangs. The guards calmed it down in their favourite way by spraying ammonia gas over the rioters. In the chaos, I was able to make my dash to a toilet at last.

The toilet cubicle doors had been ripped from their hinges, and I propped one of them up against the door frame for some privacy while I hunted for a sliver of soap. I settled for some moistened laundry powder leftovers and did my best to scrub away the urine that had soaked my trousers. I was acutely aware that my survival depended on being as bland as possible in every way. Having a personal scent of old urinal was not a good idea even in Ancón , where everything stank.

In the nine days I was there, I hardly ate, drank or went to the bathroom because I was so nervous of drawing attention to myself. I found my corner and stuck to it, except for trips to get subsistence-level rations. In any case, I decided that the prison slop was quite likely to give me food poisoning from the look and taste of it. You can imagine what my regime did for my kidneys. The combination of physical inertia and mental high-alert wasn't much good for the rest of me, either.

I was already stressed from the constant battle of wits with Laura, the hostile campaign from the Gallardos and the pressures of running a business and a charity. My adrenaline levels inside Ancón must have hit the roof. The speed of my debasement was apparent even to me. Since the day of my arrest, I was a changed man: watchful, silent, broken.

I kept having bleak flashbacks to some reading I had done about the Darién Scheme of the 1690s, a disastrous attempt to establish a Scottish colony in Darién, with the intention of plotting an overland route between the Atlantic and Pacific oceans. I have some Scottish ancestry myself, and I could imagine all too well the European settlers embarking for their new lives in a land supposedly rich with opportunities. They were supported by a huge investment drive from their home country and carried the expectations of their backers, who were hoping to establish a Scottish competitor to the East India Company.

But of those 2,500 settlers who landed in Panamá, only a few hundred survived. The dead were carried away by disease and starvation, made worse by incompetent leadership, military attack from the Spanish and English trade blockades. They had sailed on the base of dreams and promises, with no understanding of the land in which they were going to settle. In fact, the place where the Darién colony was founded, Guna Yala on the Caribbean coast, is still almost uninhabited 300 years later, and was a stone's throw from my house in Darién.

The similarities between my predicament and those of the Darién settlers made me uncomfortable. I wondered if I was going to be another victim of Panamá: someone who blundered optimistically into a new life and found out too late that he was unprepared for the reality.

The absence of natural light in the cells added to my depression. Without a chink of sunshine to distinguish night from day, you quickly became disorientated and unable to regulate your sleeping patterns. We were effectively locked in a dungeon like medieval criminals, but with the distraction of a cracked TV screen.

It might have been the second day, it might have been the third, when another incongruous new arrival pitched up. Smartly dressed and fidgety with nerves, he introduced himself as an air steward for Copa Airlines; it turned out that he had been captured on his arrival at Tocumen after flying in from Bogota. I got a clear mental image of him being frog-marched through the familiar arrivals hall while his colleagues watched aghast.

"I shouldn't be here," he confided. *None of us should be here*, I thought. A cheque he had written for his rental apartment in Panamá had bounced while he was out of the country, and his landlord had issued a warrant for his arrest.

Bouncing a cheque by mistake was something else to avoid in Panamá, then.

After three days inside Ancón, the air steward's attorney paid the cash that got him released without charge. I hoped for his sake that his employers would understand about his unscheduled stop-over in prison.

The dark monotony was broken by a surprise raid by the DIJ. We didn't know what or who they were after, but they came careening in with Mace canisters and caused mayhem.

There was a lot of furious shouting, but I couldn't see what was happening because I was caught by the gas and my vision dissolved. God, it hurt.

The nine days I spent in Ancón inflicted a series of traumas on my body. The Tuffneys have a family weakness to osteoarthritis – my twin brother suffers from it badly – and sleeping on the cold concrete floor did lasting damage to my knee and hip joints. When, at 3.30am on my last day there, a DJI agent appeared to tell me I was being transferred to La Palma and clamped me back in manacles, I had trouble supporting my own weight. I asked to see a medic, but was refused.

Panamanian law states that the well-being of an untried prisoner is the responsibility of the prosecution. However, since the national police are the ones charged with holding the alleged offender, they are supposed to share responsibility.

I was weak, dehydrated, emaciated and unwashed, and I assume that I looked like crap. There was a six-hour journey ahead of me. At the end of it I was expecting to face the prosecutor and give a cogent defence of my innocence. It was maybe just as well that I didn't make it to that stage.

On the turbulent boat trip across the Rio Tuira, which is the only way to reach the capital La Palma, I had a seizure.

The officers with me treated it as a mighty inconvenience. Having got me to land, they dragged me up the ramp, flagged down a passing pick-up truck and threw me into the cargo area at the back with the demand that I be taken to the San José hospital, three minutes away. When the driver demanded $5 for his trouble, they made sure to take it from my pocket.

At the hospital I was admitted and then immediately wired to two intravenous drips so that the doctors could push some fluids back into my system. Bloods were drawn for tests, and for the first time to date in this waking nightmare, I had the feeling that someone actually cared whether I lived or died.

I was lying, chained, in one of the very beds I had given the hospital from our charity donation drive in 2012. There was an Emberá guard appointed to stand over me with an AK47 just in case I made a break for the mountains, but even he seemed friendlier than the officers at Ancón .

It was bliss to be allowed to shower and change into crisp new scrubs, also provided courtesy of the British American Foundation. (It would have been less blissful to know that these were to be my only clothes for the next 18 months.)

It didn't take long for the director and sub-director, Doctors Garcia and Fausto, to hear about their newly admitted patient. I could see how dismayed they were at my condition. The obvious contrast between my health now and when I had last seen them eight months ago, during a sociable lunch to discuss future donations to the hospital, was almost embarrassing.

After weeks without contact from either the British or American embassy, José, a representative from the former, arrived, bearing a promotional Union Jack goody bag containing a Reader's Digest and a pack of pencils. Soap and toothpaste might have been more useful. The Reader's Digest, well-thumbed, included a true story from a reader at the back that went something like this: 'An elderly guy was on a BA flight and asked the flight attendant for one of the bacon sandwiches from the trolley. The flight attendant said, "We have none," but he could see them as clear as day. When he repeated his demand and pointed to the sandwich, she showed him that what he'd seen was the packaging on another item which read "BA.com".' That is the only thing I can remember from the FCO humanitarian survival bag

The consul, José, had previously met me in more pleasant context, at the embassy black tie Christmas ball held at the Inter-Continental hotel in downtown Panamá.

But no-one from the Embassy wanted to come out to Darién to see me. The round trip took a day out of their busy schedules and they were limited in what they could do to intervene, beyond filing a report, since they were 'prohibited from interfering with another country's internal matters.' This translated as complete impotence. José made no complaint to the authorities about my being chained to the bed except during visits to the bathroom. When I asked him to inspect the La Palma prison, in the light of my experience in Ancón, he disappeared and was back within minutes to tell me it was 'adequately safe.'

The American embassy stuck rigidly to its rule about not venturing off-road and refused to come anywhere near Darién at all. Bin Laden would have been safer here than in Pakistan.

Throughout my stay, however, I received visits from ordinary people in La Palma who had benefitted from various donation drives run by the British American Foundation. Indigenous people from Mogúe and Llano Bonito made the trek to the hospital with gifts of papaya. Their generosity touched me, and I will never forget it.

The doctors, too, did all they could. They got word back to the UK about what had happened to me and they risked antagonising the police to extend my treatment on the grounds of further evaluation. As was inevitable, their stance caused problems with the man in charge, Police Commissioner Luis, a super-sized fat bastard of a cop, known as the 'Jefe'. He forced them to sign me off after four days, on May 28, 2013. They did so with a verification that I had undergone a rapid and dangerous decline in health and was suffering from dehydration, acute gastritis, urinary infection, anaemia and extreme debility. In addition, I was diagnosed with acute depression and suicidal intent.

My weakened legs were near to useless when I was finally allowed by the cops to walk on them. I kept buckling at the knee because the joints had started to come out of their sockets. Necessity being the mother of invention, I was moved from the hospital to the police station on a dune buggy. The cops gave the impression they'd have dragged me behind it if necessary.

Whatever José from the embassy thought of the prison accommodation, I wouldn't say 'adequate' covered it, and the UK ombudsman report later in the book verifies their failings.

True, I was kept separate from the other prisoners, but that was because I was handcuffed and chained to the outside window bars of the station. The ground there often flooded after rain, when broad brown puddles would develop around my feet. I was on permanent display to anyone walking down the main street, including Laura's gawping, gloating relatives. (It seemed there were very few people in La Palma who weren't Laura's relatives. The Gallardos were everywhere, like flies. One of her cousins, Dilsa, had worked in the prosecutor's office, so she had contacts; others were distributed between government posts in the police, the national bank and the national lottery, Prodec, MOP.)

Prosecutor, La Palma

I remember the prosecutor himself strolling home from his work past the prison on the high street, gawking at me; he was the bible-bashing bastard who would not give me bail. He believed in the Lord's justice rather than the rule of law. One day the Archbishop of Panamá was also in town, but the man of the cloth was oddly deaf to my appeals for help.

The length of my chains varied, depending on the number of other inmates in the jail. If the police had captured a truckload of, for example, FARC guerrillas, I could be spared only a short single chain, which meant that I had to stand as best I could, all day and night. At quieter times when there was less pressure on resources, I was given a double chain with enough play in it to allow me to squat and to lower my arm.

The twice-daily bathroom breaks I was allocated ran on an erratic timetable, bound to the whim of whoever happened to be on guard duty, with the result that I had humiliating accidents. The only water available for washing myself and my clothes was in the cistern tank of the toilet, and that was if water was available at all. Due to the poor utilities in La Palma, many times the cistern was empty.

132

Given no chair or bed to rest on, fed like a dog from a bucket of semi-cooked swill, with no utensils, I remained at La Palma for 38 days.

I knew a few of my guards from the old days in Darién, when I used to entertain local officials at my house.

Those who remembered my generous supplies of beer and Cuban cigars were inclined to be more forgiving than the newcomers for whom I was just a skinny gringo who'd got himself into trouble. If the commando by the front desk was in a benign mood, he would tolerate it when those townsfolk who were not allied to the Gallardo clan stopped to say hello. Their kind words brought me more comfort than I can say. Mind you, I was also vulnerable to less welcome attention.

An elderly lady brought me some treats from her church in Mogocénega, complimented me on my previous charity work and then proceeded to lobby hard for a minibus. I had to tell her that I was quite keen to save my diminishing funds for my legal fees. She was good enough to wish me God's blessings in any case.

I did not receive another visit from anyone at the British embassy. As for the US embassy, despite their 500-strong staff, compared to the mere 25 in the UK embassy, no one came at all. After José's cursory inspection of La Palma's provision for prisoners, I was left to get on with it. The police station/prison was officially closed, having been condemned as unfit, but there was no local alternative to act as what was effectively a holding facility.

The police did not allow me to make any phone calls, but the doctors at San José hospital had managed to get word back to my mother. She and other members of my family in the UK were, of course, extremely distressed by my predicament and the difficulty of getting any information

from Panamá. (The BBC did pick up on my story from the wire, but then hounded my mother for more news.) I am thankful that they began to apply pressure on my behalf; thankful, indeed, for the way they did their utmost to support me throughout my preliminary prison ordeal.

My mum's attempts to involve the British embassy were usually met with unanswered calls or being pinged to the global response team in London, who knew nothing, or in bland assurances from a secretary that the matter was being dealt with. She did manage to engage a criminal defence lawyer named Fidel, who was willing to make the journey to Darién to represent me. (He was the one who snapped the covert photograph of me in chains in this book, to send as reassurance to my mum that I was still alive.)

Fidel called the embassy personally and told them that my human rights were being violated – the fact that a hardened Panamanian observer reached that conclusion is proof of the deplorable conditions. He requested a transfer for me to one of the national prisons. Notorious though they were, he felt they would offer more protection than I had in La Palma.

Case Note

12-PNP-719570	Panama	TUFFNEY	20-Jun-2013	17:01

		Status:	Filed
Post / HQ:	Panama City	**Originator:**	Keene
Note No.	44	**Topic:**	Conversation with Prosecutor's Office/attorney

Dear Abul/Celia,

We contacted the Prosecutor's office who explained that Nick would be transferred during this weekend, most likely on Saturday 22.

They confirmed that they did not have information about where he was going to be sent as it's Prison Service's responsibility.

We then contacted Mr. Euldarin, Nick's attorney, who explained that Nick needs to be transferred for his own welfare given that the facilities in Darien are not fit for purpose and keeping him there would be a violation of his human rights.

Mr. Euldarin said that he didn't know where Nick was going to be sent and he suggested that we asked the Minister of Justice to order Prison Service to send Nick to El Renacer.

We will talk to DHM in order to verify whether this is appropriate.

Thanks,

Karyel

Info:
Shaikh, Danial/Rio de Janeiro; FORSYTH, MARIE/Mexico City; Anthony, Celia/FCO Cons. Assist (CCT); Husen, Abul/FCO Cons. Assist (CCT); Keene, Karyel/Panama City; Mezquita, Jose/Panama City

The town was a claustrophobic little hot-bed of grudge- politics and petty posturing. The prosecutor, who liked to hand down aggressive prison sentences in the name of the Lord and quote long passages from the Bible, was so unpopular that he needed to go everywhere with a couple of armed police guards for his own protection. I was afraid that he would be biased against me by the oppressive influence of the Gallardo clan, who were true Bible bashers themselves. One of them, Dilsa, not only worked in his office but lived in the house next door to him. It was hardly in their interests to show leniency to the guy who was complaining that the family had swindled him over land rights.

Laura's cousin Dilsa's house – to the left of the prosecutor's office in La Palma

An appointment was made to declare my defence in front of the prosecutor. Before him were written testimonies, collected by Laura, from several minors who claimed to have been plied with alcohol and shown pornographic films by Angel and me. One by one, over the next 18 months, these testimonies were to be withdrawn while I was in jail, though I did not know that at the time, as the children admitted they had been bribed by the Gallardos to make false allegations. Result? Laura and some of her family was scolded by the prosecutor but never charged with manipulating evidence or corrupting witnesses, all while I was sweltering in the 10th worst jail in the world.

Fidel refused to letmebe rushed through the interrogation process. He stood his ground over those two days and diligently defended me against the crazy allegations. In the infuriating way of Panamanian justice, no conclusion was reached and there was no immediate change to the grim monotony of my days.

The prosecutor paid little attention to the charges levied against my friend Angel, who had heard how I was being treated and had taken the sensible precaution of staying away. In order to avoid arrest he decided to leave Panamá City to be with his family and children in Sona, and then move to the mountains in Veraguas, from where he kept in contact via Fidel. I fully respected and understood his need to take responsibility for his family, and his reluctance to face prison because of a malicious false allegation: Angel knew this family's game-playing as he was married to Laura's cousin, Adnelys. Five years previously, his brother, Bascilo, had had a similar altercation with the Gallardos and was accused of the same crime, then later released without charge. Angel also had experience of another toxic feud with the Gallardos that dated from when he had made a loan to a member of the clan, an employee on the plantation, and also a relative of his wife, who was now refusing to repay the money. Angel's expectation of a fair trial in La Palma was therefore every bit as low as my own. It so happened I found out that I was the seventh victim over the years to be charged by the Gallardos using this method.

Sr. Abdiel Gallardo
Testigo

Though neither Fidel nor I knew it at the time, the decision had been taken somewhere in the rusty cogs of officialdom to move me to La Joya. I was simply being kept in La Palma until the indeterminate date when a bus, then a boat, and then another functioning vehicle with sufficient petrol could be found to take a busload of prisoners to

Panamá City. It was a surprise to me when I was told that I was going to be transferred with about 20 others.

I was still in a very frail physical and mental state, having deteriorated again after my all-too-short stay in the hospital. A relief though it was to be leaving La Palma, I was no closer to being free. I felt hollowed out and utterly powerless, and I feared the degradations ahead.

On the police boat across the fast-flowing Rio Tuira, on our way to meet the battered ex-US prison bus in Puerto Quimba, I watched the khaki-coloured water rush by and thought how inviting it looked. I was weighted with manacles and chains, I was wearing no life jacket: if I tipped myself overboard, as I was desperately tempted to, I would drown in seconds or be hit with the force of a train by one of the huge logs being carried towards the sea from the jungle. It would have been a quick resolution of what threatened to be an endless losing battle in a foreign country far from my family. Thank God that the thought of my children being left without a father pushed its way through the darkness of my depression and pulled me back from my suicidal thoughts. During that 45-minute river crossing, death offered a potential escape, but I chose to fight on. I am profoundly happy to have done so, even if the damage I experienced in Panamá still haunts me.

6

THE LA JOYA RESORT AND SPA

Before I left La Palma, I was given a welcome pack by the consul from the Foreign Office telling me what to expect when I arrived in La Joya, which translates as 'the jewel'. The description of a barbeque area and freely available treats such as crisps made my next destination sound positively wholesome, possibly even five- star, compared to my existing shit-hole. I hadn't realised that I was being transferred to a sort of outward-bound hotel for naughty boys, where regular family visits to the cells came provided.

It was a complete fantasy. The brochure had not been updated since 2000 and I doubt it was any more accurate back then. I used to joke that the La Joya resort and spa, with its long laundry list of goodies and benefits, failed to live up to expectations.

I arrived there weak and exhausted from the journey, clutching a meagre carrier bag of possessions. The first thing the guard at the main arrival gate did was to pull out my clothes and scissor my red Manchester United shirt to ribbons. Red clothes, he growled at me, were banned because they made it too difficult for the cops too see if you were leaking blood after being shot or knifed.

There is a provision of food within the prison. Prison food is free but may not be sufficient to fulfil your dietary needs. You would need funds to pay for supplements to your diet, which can be bought at from the prison shop (run by other inmates as a source of income), or from the cafeteria and restaurant (open on visiting days).

Approximate prices (US$) of basic products are as follows:

Bread	(loaf 1.50 / 0.15-0.30cents per piece)
Coke (fizzy drinks)	(0.50 cents per piece / 1.50 litre)
Tea	(0.10-0.20 per bag 8 bags for 0.75 / 0.25 prepared cup)
Coffee	(0.25 per cup / with milk 0.30 / pack 85 grams 2.00 – 170 grams 4.00)
Water	(0.50-0.60 bottle / 1.50-2.00 litre)
Rice	(0.45-0.50 per pound)
Sugar	(0.50-0.75 per pound)
Tuna	(1.50-1.80 per tin)
Meat	(2.00-2.50 per pound)
Milk	(0.80 ½ litre bag / 1.60 litre) powdered sachet 3.20
Crisps	(0.50-0.60)
Chocolate bar	(0.85-1.30)
Potatoes	(0.50 per pound)
Fruit (bananas)	(0.15 per piece) (1.00 for 5 apples / 1.00 for 10 bananas)
Vegetables	(0.15-0.50 per piece)
Cooking gas	(4.50-5.00 for refill / 35-40 for new bottle)
Blanket	(5.00)
Mattress	(10-100)
Clothes washing	(1.00-1.50 for 10 items)

Welcome to one of the worst prisons in the world, where your chance of dying by suicide, murder, a drugs overdose, disease or alcohol poisoning only added an extra layer of jeopardy to the disgustingly over-crowded and insanitary conditions, the miserable rations and the police brutality.

I watched the heavy yellow barrier rise to admit our bus into the compound and thought, *Now we're really in hell.* Around us loomed old warehouses and helicopter hangers from General Noriega's era, each surrounded by a double fence and bristling razor wire, and overlooked by gun turrets. The bars on the windows of the buildings were thick with discarded food waste that, in the sauna- like temperatures, had spawned thousands of maggots and flies.

We trundled on, into the belly of the beast. Although we were supposed to be checked for communicable diseases and any other health issues at the Merced medical clinic, the guard on the bus took one look at the prisoner queues snaking through the door and waved us directly on to the prison itself. This was despite the fact that we could have been incubating any kind of tropical disease from the Darién jungle.

We passed La Joyita prison facility first, which is La Joya's even more overcrowded sister-prison exclusively for Panamanians, then headed towards La Joya itself. It housed a mixture of Panamanians and internationals in different blocks. As a British/American passport-holder, I was destined for La Joya's notorious Building Six, where foreign nationals were sent.

Another checkpoint, more barbed wire and a new order to disembark. That was the point at which it became obvious that I just couldn't walk any further. My punishment in Ancón, followed by the prolonged crouching while chained at La Palma, had crippled me. Someone found a wheelbarrow – cost: a dollar tip of my own money to the barrow boy – and I was manhandled into the scooped tray with my carrier bag on my lap. I was still wearing my by-now stained hospital scrubs from San José, along with the black business shoes and socks I had managed to salvage from the time of my arrest. The heat and humidity were intense. I remember the sun beating hard on the back of my neck as I took my first good look around me. Every barred window seemed to have either people's arms or drying washing hanging through it. There were random, stinking piles of garbage in the yards and, spaced more regularly, hundreds of yellow five-gallon buckets lined up like soldiers. (They were there to utilise the single standpipe that was turned on for one bare hour a day to provide water for the needs of everyone inside. That number totalled 640 by the time I left, with still only one stand pipe controlled for one hour a day.)

145

The scene reminded me of the slums of Panamá City around Calle Sta Cruz. I had driven into this 'no-go' area by mistake once and immediately felt a panic-inducing need to get out. Even the air had tasted dangerous.

We were processed and registered in the administration building before being allocated to either Building Six or Eight, both of them equally dingy slums set aside for international prisoners. While we waited there, we looked around and saw that sweating men had been chained like dogs to every immovable part of the interior. There were prisoners attached to the banisters all the way up the staircase and prisoners whose chains had been looped round railings or pipes. The officials seemed to enjoy the chaos and, above all, to relish the depressing effect it had on our morale. They barked questions I could barely understand or answer in my halting Spanish.

I was given the prisoner number 445. This indicated serious over-crowding, considering that when the building had been made into a

Once the easy part of the admission process was done, it was time to enter what I feared would be hell itself: the cells. The desk commando left it to custodians – trusted prisoners who were working off their sentences (or running smuggling rackets) – to escort new prisoners inside. These custodians were in theory supervised by guards, but in reality they were treated as proxies for boring jobs such as unlocking gates, accepting new inmates or transferring them to other buildings.

147

One by one, the new boys were sent through. The other prisoners made it as intimidating as possible while we waited for the padlocks to be opened. Threatening us and screeching in our faces was a rare spot of entertainment for them, a ritual to be enjoyed three times a week on Mondays, Wednesdays and Fridays. We could hear them howling through the bars and making the time-honoured promise to new inmates that they would first f*** us and then kill us.

I could remember too well the terrors of Ancón. The surroundings at La Joya were still unfamiliar, but the shouts of "Venga, el gringo!" and "Carne!" were just the same. Never in my life have my survival skills been tested so harshly.

The guards colluded in setting up the bear pit. They took sadistic pleasure in the cacophony of abuse, and they relied on the initiation rite to keep new inmates subdued for a few days.

Tipped from my wheelbarrow, I presented a sorry sight. I had trouble supporting even my diminished weight, I was scraggy and haggard and I was dressed in a ridiculous combination of what looked like pyjamas and office wear.

I decided to exploit my only possible advantage: I was going to play the cripple to the hilt. Given my current state, the performance wouldn't be much of a stretch and my survival might depend on it.

As soon as the gates slid back, I hit the floor like a sack of spuds. I kept one eye slightly open to see if the dozy bastards around me would take the bait. They did. The guard ordered some inmates to dump me in a corner of the converted so-called gymnasium hall that was now the sleeping area for new prisoners, where I looked too feeble for anyone to bother assaulting. I made a mental note to thank Mrs Curd, my primary school drama teacher, for all she had taught me.

I knew I had to use brain rather than brawn to keep myself safe among these thugs and gangsters. I was determined to soak up every bit of useful information I could while I had the chance, so I sat quietly, evaluating my options and doing my best to observe how the power structure worked. I told myself that I was trapped in a lion's den with animals that had just been fed and weren't yet hungry again... the only certainty was that they soon would be. I had no intention of offering myself as the next meal.

The place was absolutely rammed with people. At the back of the building, behind the gym, was the accommodation for the more affluent prisoners who could afford to pay from $300 to $2,000 for a cell. These were arranged as two facing rows of 18 cells separated from each other by a rat- infested service corridor. Each cell contained six concrete platforms, in bunk bed style, fixed to the walls, along with a concrete wash tub, a slimy green shower pan, minus taps, and a toilet bowl, minus seat, cistern-lid or flush handle. Water – when it was available – had to be poured in manually. When it wasn't, another inmate's urine would have to be used.

The cells held an average of 15 people each, with another nine sleeping on platforms that had been suspended in the attic space above the cells using hammocks tied to the roof girders of the building. The penthouse-dwellers had fashioned a guttering system from plastic soda bottles cut together to carry urine directly into the cell toilet below. If they needed to shit, they'd do it into a plastic bag and then throw it outside through the window bars.

In an attempt to personalise their sleeping areas and claw back an iota of privacy, prisoners used scraps of material to make curtains for themselves where there was space to hang them. The flapping floral material gave a strangely homely look to some corners of the prison, at odds with the filthy surroundings. The doors to the cells were left open, allowing anyone who passed to stare inside and facilitating the constant milling circulation of inmates. Within the prison buildings themselves, no guards patrolled.

The majority of inmates were Colombian and Mexican nationals, bolstered by Venezuelans, Guatemalans and a few Europeans. I was one of only three Brits and there were also three Canadians. Most were incarcerated for drug offences or homicides.

There was incessant activity and haggling among people doing drug deals, and the Chinese had cornered the market in selling moonshine, portioned out in plastic bottles. The rules of the prison were posted on the walls in plain sight and every minute of every day, the rules were broken. The place was a free-for-all, governed by its own internal hierarchy. As crazy as it was, Building Six did have a kind of government.

The unofficial president of the La Joya prisoner republic was Nikki, a Venezuelan drug lord who lived in Cell A16.

He kept the key to the door between the cells and the gym. The nightly lock-up prevented the police from making any surprise raids while inmates were sleeping.

He had what you might call a vice-president Nixon, an English-speaking guy with an unlikely side-line as a barber. I used to pick up juicy pieces of general prison gossip and privileged information about Building Six while he cut my hair. I paid for the intelligence he offered by giving him $3 per haircut instead of the usual going rate of $1. The extra

$2 was well worth it. My informant was released in 2014 after a lengthy sentence and deported back to Holland, where he was murdered upon arrival. It happened a lot to ex-inmates involved with drugs. Prison was often the safest environment for them. One of

Laura's criminal cousins who had been in La Joya was also killed – shot in the back of the head – hours after his release.

The drug lords, usually Colombian and Mexican, were the serious big-hitters, right up at the top of the tree. They were pulling in Western Union payments via the prison money laundering system of $5,000 and $10,000 at a time from their criminal activities on the outside. They employed their own chefs, ate scampi and steak with the finest of home- brews, and lived in VIP rooms, complete with double beds, created in the attic space well above the cells, where there was a superior grade of accommodation. They were served by a network of fixers and hangers-on, who had hangers-on of their own.

Attic space located above the cells, where a community of more than 150 people had hammocks tied to the roof joists

In the middle of the pile were the men just trying to get by, some of them by running micro-businesses. At the bottom were the unfortunate sods – nearly always drugs mules – too poor or vulnerable to benefit from connections inside or family money outside. They were the ones whose only hope of representation in court was from 19-year-old law students on work experience. They were also the ones who tended to be serving 10- or 20-year stretches.

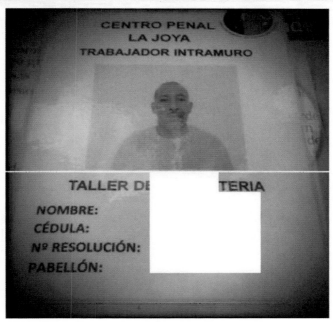

CENTRO PENAL
LA JOYA
TRABAJADOR INTRAMURO

TALLER DE   TERIA

NOMBRE:
CÉDULA:
Nº RESOLUCIÓN:
PABELLÓN:

155

Grande on the left

The first person I spoke to was Grande, a huge but friendly Colombian guy. Believe me, I was desperate for help from any ally I could find, and here was just the sort of person you would want on your side in a fight. Grande realised that I was from England and went to find Ben, a hard-nut east Londoner who had already been in La Joya for five years on a drug running charge. Ben's best mate was Leo, a Brummie drugs baron and boxer. He used to work out regularly and was solid muscle: another reassuring sight. Together, my compatriots gave me an excellent insight into how the prison ecosystem functioned. (Sadly for Leo, his own downfall had been at the hands of his daughter, who had blown his cover by taking his passport from his ranch house in Panamá to help with her own application for a UK passport. Leo was flagged by intelligence services and captured as a result, along with more than $500,000 of cocaine, on his ranch. At the time of writing, he has served over 10 years in La Joya and is wanted upon his release in Russia for drug crimes.)

Unsteady though I was, I was taken on an introductory tour. We stopped at B-18, the Jamaican cells, to say hello to a few more English speakers. They were talking in their local patois but switched immediately to a more standard pronunciation for our benefit. They were good guys and could be relied on in a crisis to support anyone from the other Commonwealth countries, and they were resourceful. Somehow, in the limited natural light, they managed to grow a spinach-like green called callalu for a reminder of home. They kindly gave me a sample to try, and I am sorry to report that it tasted like crap.

In fact, I was amazed by how closely the place resembled a busy Arab street market. There were pop-up micro-stores at every turn. If you had the cash – which was smuggled in by a well-tried route via a prison officer's wife and the prison director, Ronaldo Lopez – you could buy coffee, cakes, haircuts and even medicines from various entrepreneurs. It was best not to worry too much about hygiene standards as applied to any of the above. The fact they were available at all was a miracle, considering most of the items on sale were banned.

I learned where to find the guy who brought the black- market cigarettes in, how to get hold of a phone, and that the Chinese were in charge of the liquor that flowed through the prison. Much of it was made from Welch's grape juice. (Among the Chinese were the crew of a ship called the Chung Chon Gang, captured in the Panamá Canal on its way to North Korea with undeclared weapons of war hidden under sacks of sugar. In February 2014, after paying a hefty

$700,000 fine, the crew and their ship were free to leave Panamá without their cargo.)

My instincts as a salesman and businessman made me respect the shows of enterprise, and I understood at once that survival here depended on the ability to negotiate. The ancient skills of ducking, diving and making a deal would be vital in the months ahead. They helped me not only to stay afloat, but to keep my sanity.

I was initially very nervous of the aggression that swirled alongside all this commerce. Armed fights, usually between rival gang members, were common, and I tried my best to side-step potentially violent situations or people. Not that I always succeeded. One of the stupider things I did soon after arriving was to get into an argument with a well-known nutter over a 25¢ banana.

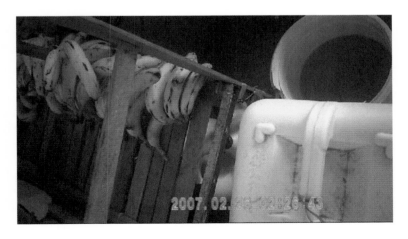

2007. 01. 15 01:10:42

Fresh fruit was supposed to be banned in case prisoners fermented it into alcohol or used it to conceal drugs, but somehow an illicit consignment of bananas had found its way inside and I was at the head of the queue to buy one. I handed over 25¢ for my single banana to Mr Angry, but as I pulled it off the bunch it slightly ripped the skin of the banana next to it. I was told that I had to buy both for 50¢. I told the guy to f*** off and a slanging match started to develop. Once male pride was involved, of course, neither of us wanted to back down.

I had the sense to stop myself from going head-to-head against the guy over 25 cents, but the incident was a warning of how petty grievances could escalate in the pressure-cooker environment of La Joya. Many of the inmates were mentally ill, and the system pretty much guaranteed that they were either off their meds or on something more potent.

Ben made finding me some more space his priority, because that was a major preoccupation of just about everyone in the prison. He explained that the going rate for a bunk in a cell was very expensive. It wasn't exactly an irresistible deal, and I quickly realised that if there was a fire in the building, and there was every chance of one caused by a rogue spark from a cigarette or all the home-made electrical connections, those in the cells would be roasted alive before they could get out. There was the additional danger that most of the people were high as kites on drugs or alcohol. Even though the cells were situated at the back of the facility next to a fire door, it had been welded shut. In any case, the gate separating the cells from the gym was locked at night by Nikki, and in an inferno the fumes caused by the plastic hammocks suspended from the rafters would have overcome you before you fumbled your way out of bed. With no fire alarm, water or emergency lights available, a conflagration in Building Six would have been tantamount to a death sentence. All in all, I preferred the relative safety of being right by the front door in the gym.

I had been told already about a fire in the juvenile prison a few months earlier, when the police had decided to teach unruly kids a lesson by locking down the building and lobbing in tear gas. One of the canisters had ignited a sheet and six people had died in the blaze that followed.

I had naively hoped from what I had read in the FCO prisoners' welcome pack that La Joya would provide me with a basic foam mattress as part of the service. Instead, Grande kindly found me an old cardboard box and a discarded rice sack for my bedding. Even the postage-stamp sized space I found for myself in the gym was disputed by another prisoner. In the end we reached a compromise and agreed to share for the night.

I stayed in the gym – known as the 'gancha' – because the location gave me a prayer of escape if the place burst into flames, but that was the only positive thing to say about it. I was nose-to-nose with farting strangers of dubious sanity again, just like the madhouse of Ancón.

I had owned a big house in Miami and estates in Panamá, and now here I was fretting that if I fell asleep someone would steal the shoes from my feet during the night. Losing any of the few possessions I had left would have been a blow to my fragile mental state. I didn't want to be one of the sad creatures shuffling round the building with pieces of stained rags tied to their feet for shoes.

The shift in my circumstances was such a shock that I still struggled to believe it could have happened. At times, I didn't know whether I was imagining my past life or my current one. I remembered driving past the entrance to La Joya many times, on the Inter-American highway on my way to Darién when I was a free man, and thinking that the tall arch gave it an unsettling resemblance to the Auschwitz-Birkenau concentration camp. The idea that I myself would one day be an inmate was absurd.

Yet here I was, aware of the strange irony that five months earlier I had made some charity donations to the prison for the specific use of male and female British prisoners. The contributions included instant Cadbury's hot chocolate, tea bags, toothbrushes, toothpaste and loo rolls delivered via the British embassy. It was a shame I was too late to benefit myself, but Leo remembered the stuff being handed out like unexpected party gifts and thanked me for the kind gesture. I was woken before dawn on my second day by the musky smell of pot in the air. The guy next to me was having his early fix. Another neighbour was preparing his dose of crack with the aid of the base of a Coke can and a lighter. I had never in my life taken drugs or been involved with people who did, but here they seemed as commonplace as a morning cup of coffee.

163

I got up, careful to step over the mass of prone bodies, and headed to the toilet.

I was confronted by a stained five-gallon paint bucket, full to the brim with foaming urine. (What the hell were they *drinking* in here?) The stench was worse than that of a dead body, and the mere sight nearly made me heave. Even roaches were dying in here. There was no proper flushing system. Taps and free-flowing water were non-existent and there were no sinks. The only method was to pick up the bucket, protecting yourself from direct contact with the handle by wrapping it in tissue, and pour the contents over whatever you wanted to get rid of. Because of my weak legs,

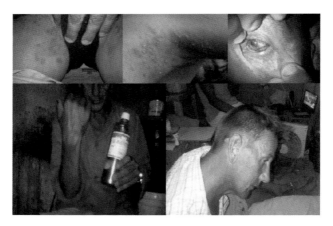

I was unable to squat over the pan in the way everyone else did and had to wipe the rim with tissue before sitting on it. No wonder I would later find myself plagued by infections.

I could not believe it when I was told that for 50¢ a day an inmate was expected to scrub this area, without protective gloves or clothing. He had no alternative source of income to buy essentials such as water

– always limited and impossible to guarantee unless you paid for it – that were necessary to life.

Still recovering from the hideous toilet, I took advantage of the relative quiet to try and gather my thoughts. Rising early became part of my daily routine because it gave me a few moments of peace and privacy, impossible once the rest of the inmates were awake. Through the barred doors I could just about see the dawn mist clearing as the morning gathered heat, and I felt a stab of sadness to be disconnected from the natural world. The greater sorrow was being parted from my family and stuck in this festering pit for God knew how much longer.

The mornings were also when our duty commando arrived to take charge: a joke in itself. I could see him slam the outer perimeter gate behind him and slip the padlock back in place as he jangled his fat bunch of keys. He would circle the building to make sure all was calm, run his baton over the iron bars to listen for the tell-tale changes in tone that indicated hacked metal, and nod to the guard in the tower as a way of checking in. (The guards did not use their radios except in emergency situations because they didn't want Central Command eavesdropping on their conversations.) The commandos were then based outside in the yard from 8am until 5pm, at an old metal desk complete with wire-mesh chair and scuffed logbook.

Building Six, or pavilion six, as the Panamanians called it, was considered a good gig by the cops. Compared to the blocks for home-grown criminals, it was calm and self- regulating. And it was bursting at the seams with money.

Colombian and Mexican drug lords and their lieutenants were regularly admitted, and provided a lucrative income stream in the form of back-handers and bribes, until such time as they bought themselves out again, or paid for someone else to take the fall on their behalf. North Americans and Europeans inside for financial or drugs crimes poured more dollars into the greedy hands of the guards and the many hovering lawyers. There wasn't a single layer in the administration of the prison, from top to bottom, free of corruption. The commando's radio silence was a calculated way to avoid detection if he wanted to set up a little business of his own, while protecting his cut from rivals.

Sergeant Fat Boy 'Santa Rivera' finally opened the main door and walked towards me, bringing a tantalising breath of what counted for fresh air around here. We exchanged glances and I nodded, eager to make a good impression. He was the sole supervisor and my welfare depended partly on his good opinion. It was like being back at school, if the teacher's weapon of choice had been an AK47 instead of a cane.

No more than five people were allowed out in the yard for exercise at once. That was the official rule. The unofficial rule was that a dollar bought you 15 minutes outside and $20 paid for a few hours, unless the chief, the commisionardo, strolled by and closed down the scheme.

It was a small risk, as the chief rarely ventured beyond his air-conditioned office, from where he issued orders by phone or radio.

I reckoned that unless I took decisive action, I was doomed to be penned inside with 500 or so inmates for days, if not weeks, on end.

Grande joined me and we stood together. The cop's interest in us was on a strictly pay-to-play basis. He paused to establish where I was from and his tiny eyes sparked with interest when I mentioned London and Miami. Big cities in rich countries were an indicator of possible wealth. Had I said Nicaragua or Cuba, no doubt he would have placed me a lot further down the food chain.

I realised that a kind of interview was taking place and that if we both played our hands well, we could come to a mutually satisfying arrangement.

Exercise time finally came. "Five minutes," the commando said as a goodwill gesture, before nodding and strolling away. Today's outing was a freebie, but the next one's would not be. That man was to be the first out of over a hundred cops I paid off while I was in La Joya.

I feel no guilt for my contribution to the endemic corruption. The kickbacks bought me a few slivers of comfort and privilege in an otherwise grim existence. They were vital in helping me to survive.

Many were not lucky enough to have money or family behind them. They lived in La Joya for years on a meagre rice-based diet, often destined to die there wearing the same clothes in which they had arrived. All they owned was scavenged from the dead or from the discarded property of those who had left the prison. These poor souls scraped a few dollars a time by doing chores for others, such as washing their clothes or cleaning the cells. Grande, for instance, supported himself by selling black market sodas and phone cards.

Everyone needed to be helped out occasionally by people who could afford to pay, but such acts of generosity were rare. You had to grasp quickly that everything had value, nothing was free: you had best be prepared to pay in one way or another for what you needed, including sex.

A strange community spirit, with its own codes and customs, prevailed within the prison. Not exactly 'honour among thieves', but an acknowledgment that the inmates were all doing their best to manipulate an unjust system.

The most driven prisoners set up little kiosks. A baker from Guatemala managed to power up two old frying pans by adding a hob and inverting one over the other to make an oven, in which he miraculously cooked the most delicious cakes and croissants, made in a basic kitchen rigged up in the corner of a cell. He sent the profits home to support his family and generated a thriving trade in smuggled flour and eggs.

The electricity supply system was designed for 150 people and, in reality, served four times that many, so it was always overloaded. The strain was only increased by such cunning inventions as an oven made from a metal filing cabinet, with all but one of its drawers welded shut and coiled heating elements installed top and bottom.

Some inmates managed to bake fairy cakes with sprinkles on top and sold them for $5 a time. You really couldn't have made up these weird, mad inconsistencies.

Others, who hailed from coastal communities and had been caught while piloting drugs boats, made hammocks out of plastic ice bags that had been patiently stretched into long cords and woven as if they were fishing nets. I bought one of these extraordinary creations for $30 and I thought it a bargain, considering the month's work that went into it. I still have it, and use it at home in memory of those times.

While it was easy to admire the ingenuity of men like these, the drug dealers were harder to love. They spread misery, or relief, according to your perspective, and they were ruthless in exploiting their captive market of addicts. As for prostitution between inmates, the other dark aspect of prison life, it happened. 'Gay for the stay' was such a common phenomenon that no one paid much attention, except for a bit of a stir when the transsexuals were on the prowl or in a cat fight over a man.

The matter of universal urgency, the one that united every man in the prison, was the quest to find enough drinking water. You would have thought water was an essential that even the heartless regime of La Joya would make available as a matter of course. Not so. Prisoners had to find their own makeshift ways to hoard this precious commodity.

A strict limit of 15 people at a time was applied to using the standpipe, and it operated for just an hour a day. As a consequence, there were many inmates who went for long periods without being able to collect supplies and who became seriously dehydrated when whatever they had managed to save ran out.

The yellow plastic buckets I had noticed on my way into the prison were available for $5 each, and then it might cost more money to fill them if you missed your turn at the standpipe for long enough. Prisoners wrote their names on their buckets and guarded them with a jealous passion. (Grande slept with his solitary pail at the head of his bed.)

Rich inmates like the Mexican drug lords were lucky enough to have more than half a dozen filled pails each, or huge, 80-gallon blue barrels that allowed them the luxury of washing. Some of them even managed to tap the supply to the standpipe and use a pump to divert it to their cells through a hose. They sold this contraband at $5 a bucketful, complete with free sediment.

Prisoners collected rain whenever possible by making wobbly guttering out of halved one-litre soda bottles and positioning it to catch the run-off from the prison roof. The result was often orange from rust, but it was an essential supplement to our inadequate and erratic rations. The police were quite capable of reducing the daily operating time of the standpipe if they were in the mood to torture us. For all the things that did make it past the guards into La Joya – drugs, weapons, delicacies such as hamburgers – bottled water never seemed to be in circulation. However, insulated cooler boxes were bought by some inmates from the guards, at extortionate prices, and sporadic deliveries of ready-made ice used to arrive to be sold at $2.75 a bag, double the street value.

The strict prohibition on fresh fruit or vegetables, which rarely made it past the checks, meant there was a chronic shortage of vitamins in our diet. Considering what was used to make moonshine, this was a typically dim-witted restriction. But once a fortnight, deliveries of canned goods, rice and meat were waved through for those who could afford them.

It was safe to say that the individual welfare of prisoners was right down at the very bottom of the La Joya administrators' list of priorities. The concept of health and safety was non-existent.

My earlier fears about electrical hazards were well-founded. The proliferation of ropey, two-ring cookers, all of them missing their thermostats, hot-wired directly into the mains, resulted in frequent explosions of sparks that fused the lights in the entire building. Too often, I found myself trapped in a press of bodies in the pitch-blackness, afraid that thieves would use the confusion to steal what they could from whoever was closest.

I heard that in Building Nine of La Joya the police had once decided to punish unruly inmates by, for a change, giving them too much water. The cops had sprayed it in through the bars with a hose pipe. An inmate died of electrocution when he grabbed hold of the light switch while he was standing on the saturated floor. No one was ever charged with his manslaughter, and his parents were not informed of what had truly happened until two days later.

2007. 01. 16 23:11:08

The unlocked cells were a pragmatic way to ease severe over-crowding; they dated from a protest in 2010, well before my time. The prisoners had finally rebelled after a sick man was left to die, as many had been before him, because it had taken so long to open the doors and summon emergency help. The following day they had torn off all the padlocks of the cells and used the barbells in the gym to smash them to smithereens.

Unless an inmate was close to death, the police were reluctant to remove him for medical treatment – and even if they did, it was still 50/50 odds on his survival. If it became a necessity because his fellow inmates kicked up a riot, the patient would be put in a wheelbarrow and taken up to the admin building, where he might have to wait for attention until staff clocked in the following morning. Only then, assuming he was still alive, would he be taken to a clinic two kilometres away, or moved to the main gates of the prison.

Ambulances were not allowed within the compound boundaries, although it can't have been as a security measure because transport trucks and private lawyers' cars drove in on a daily basis. The logic was typically flawed, heartless and disrespectful to human life.

All these things and more I was told by my guides, Grande, Ben and Leo. Their crash-course in prison etiquette included some useful history and offered practical tips I didn't always want to hear. Among these was the advice to get myself a plastic shipping crate to store my personal items and a satchel to hang from the ceiling for anything I considered valuable. Why? Well, the crate and your bed – if you had one – would need to be thoroughly cleaned every few days to evict the dozens of cockroaches, bugs and huge spiders that would make their homes there.

No doubt about it, the La Joya experience was one that would have been hard to sell in a holiday brochure. I was just pleased after the isolation of my previous prison stay that I had at least found some apparent allies to talk to. For all its evident menace and squalor, for all the physical deprivation and discomfort, La Joya was still better than La Palma. I had an inkling that it would be possible for me to adapt here while I continued to work towards proving my innocence. That thought alone represented an improvement on my bleak state of mind in Darién. I had regained the tiniest flicker of hope.

7

MY NEW HOME

I spent what might sarcastically be called my honeymoon period in La Joya resting, establishing myself in my new surroundings and in pursuit of a permanent pitch. As luck would have it, I managed to obtain a couple of mattresses, one from a guy who had died and another from someone who was released. Regardless of its origin, my new bed represented pure luxury to me. Anything was better than sleeping on that cold, hard floor.

After three days of being moved around the gym like a pawn every night, I finally put my name on a coffin-sized rectangle of concrete near the exit. It cost me $100 without title or taxes, which I paid to a Colombian crack addict, and it gave me a fighting chance of getting out alive if there was a fire. Not much to boast about when two months earlier I had owned a total of five properties and 160 hectares, but it was a turnaround in my status. I was no longer a refugee. A disadvantage of living in the so-called gancha, which translated as 'hook', was that it was a dead zone for electronics. There wasn't a single socket or light fitting. Nights were a total black-out and it was a nightmare trying to navigate your way across the space by just the lamination off your cell phone.

During the day, the gancha would be used as a kind of church by some of the prisoners, who cleared away half the bedding then spent what felt like hours praying and singing in multi-faith groups. The noise reminded me of Nora's house. The difference was that here I had no way of getting away from these nutters.

Another problem was that because I was located near the sole entry point, all the animals who wandered into the prison to get out of the rain then back again used to pass by me, usually after leaving a package on the floor for me to tread in. Prison security did not, sadly, extend to excluding stray cats or reptiles, including scorpions. Coral snakes, which are generally venomous, used to slither past, and one in particular held me as a motionless hostage while it circled my pillow. On another occasion I was attacked by a thankfully not very poisonous scorpion.

It was common practice to sleep with a tea-towel or cloth over your face in an attempt to stop the cockroaches from climbing up into your nostrils or ears, but the little bastards still managed to penetrate every orifice. It was disgusting. Then there were mites called chinchas that made homes in the mattresses and would emerge at night to feed on you and leave you covered in itchy bites. Rats and mice were such a common sight that they were hardly worth mentioning.

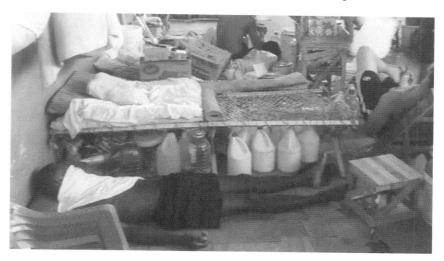

The physical discomfort of prison was constant and cumulative. It built on itself: you slept on hard or damp or lumpy surfaces that made your bones ache; you were either too hot or too cold; you were sweaty, or thirsty, or you had stomach cramps; your teeth hurt; your eyes smarted; you were never clean; you smelled bad – and if you didn't, the person next to you definitely did. The insects were just another component in the mix, and you had to endure them. At least complaining about your latest crop of bites was a way of bonding with everyone else who was suffering. I always worked on the principle that it was better to make friends than to keep myself aloof. My interest in my fellow inmates was genuine and I wanted to know their stories.

Introducing myself to my new next-door neighbours in the gancha was the natural thing to do.

On my left, a man called Sandy shook my hand and asked me to refer to him by the pronoun 'they'. He (they) was (were) a well-educated American who looked like a transvestite or a mariposa – the Spanish for 'butterfly' – with his long hair tied back in a sleek ponytail. We started a conversation and my curiosity made me desperate to pose that tricky prison ice-breaker of, "What are you in for?" When I did ask the question, I wished I hadn't.

He calmly told me in his soft, cultured voice that he had been a resident of La Joya for 18 years now. Go on. It transpired that he and his brother had killed a young girl, and then eaten her as part of a horrific ritual murder in Los Santos, Panamá.

Sandy went on to say that all the inmates had seen me on TV. Me? "Yes, you're the British guy who was arrested for witchcraft in

Darién… We thought when we saw it that the report must be a joke! You are famous in our cult circle!"

Jesus, I thought, *I now have a fan club of cult killers and weirdos.* If I was going to be famous in any circle, I would rather it was a different one – and for a different reason.

To the other side of my bed was William, a Colombian drug mule and pothead who was also addicted to porn. The fumes from his ever-present spliff were so over-powering that just being in his vicinity was enough to make you feel high.

I could not have asked for better bed fellows (it made me nostalgic for the days when Skippy curled up to sleep at the bottom of my duvet). William spoke little English but seemed friendly enough. I just hated lying next to him while he stared at his fully charged portable DVD player and jerked off. The guy had no inhibitions whatsoever. I wouldn't have shaken his hand when we first said hello had I known what it was usually doing.

Thinking about those nights even now gives me goose- bumps; those sad individuals were the only people I had to call my friends. Yet six months earlier I had been chatting to Prince Andrew – he may since have had troubles of his own but, come on, he's a Royal, not a cannibal – and the chief of police at the British ambassador's residence in Panamá.

I had obtained some funds from my family in England through our unique La Joya money laundering system, Western Union. It was more efficient than Amazon Prime. Large amounts of cash were not normally allowed into prison because it caused trouble by encouraging inmates to lend, gamble and trade black market goods. The maximum donation from the outside world was supposed to be $20, but La Joya was hardly a model regime and the guards had no incentive to obey the rules when disobeying could bring them a profit.

2007. 03. 23 00:08:17

There was a guy called José Londono in the prison whose wife was having an affair with the prison director, Ronaldo Lopez. Londono was very forgiving of this infidelity because the arrangement was very profitable for him. I would contact my mother on WhatsApp, initially on Benny Boy's mobile phone, to ask for money. Mum would go to Western Union's little franchise office in Strood, Kent, and arrange the transfer of whatever amount – we started small with $100 – I had requested. She was such a regular visitor that the girls behind the counter got to know my story and used to ask how I was doing on a weekly basis. Senora Londono would collect the transferred money and send her husband a message to say she had it in her hand. That was his cue to pay me – minus commission – from the cash he carried in his bum bag. It took about 45 minutes from my calling the UK with the request to my having the payment delivered inside Building Six.

Finally, Senora Londono gave the money she had collected to her lover, the director, who'd pass it on to Londono to cover what he had paid out, minus a 10 per cent kickback. Londono took a further five per cent. Any custodio or guard attempting to muscle in on this magical retirement fund generator from outside the circle of trust found that he did not last long at La Joya. There was roughly $200,000 a month going into Building Six alone, and our fine, public- spirited captor-in-chief was keen to protect the revenue for himself.

To illustrate the flourishing health of the trade, in 2014 a guard at La Joya was apprehended while carrying more than $15,000 in cash to be distributed among his prisoner- clients.

Inside prison, as outside, cash made you king. When every item from the lowliest piece of cardboard had a value to someone, it also had a price. Those locked up without access to money could find their lives utterly restricted and miserable because they were trapped right at the bottom of the dung heap. Some of the suicides – and there were many in La Joya – were committed by men who were so desperately lacking in the most basic rations that death seemed preferable to their comfortless lives.

After my release in 2014, I wanted to support the less fortunate prisoners who remained in the prison, and some others, such as Grande, who had left but were still in poverty. For a while I sent the odd $50 back to Panamá. It wasn't a vast amount but Western Union decided that my pattern of money transfers constituted 'unusual activity' and it closed down my account (if only they'd been aware of quite how unusual the activity in La Joya had been). I was then visited at home by two British police officers who arrived with their squad car lights flashing. They wanted to know why I was sending money to Panamá, Colombia, Peru and Mexico. Was I involved in an international money laundering scheme, by any chance?

I switched to Money Gram after that ordeal. Within a week, that account was also closed down. Now, I use a third party to handle the cash that I still send to this day.

As my endlessly supportive mum had already been blacklisted by Western Union and Money Gram because of the payments she was making to me, we're now both criminals in the opinion of the international money transfer companies.

Money allowed me to purchase some decent food and vitamins to supplement the appalling prison slop, to help others who were less fortunate and, most importantly, to pay off guards for privileges such as being allowed out in the exercise yard.

The kiosks sold hamburgers and sub sandwiches that certainly tasted OK, despite their origins and the fact that there was a distinct shortage of quality control involved in their preparation. Not the best of diets, but it gave me some type of basic protein and the energy I needed to function.

And thank God that I was able to buy some painkillers to control the grinding and throbbing in my knees, and the discomfort from multiple infections. The pills made it possible for me to walk around rather than be marooned on my mattress from one end of the day to the other, and to be integrated into prison life in a way that gave me some semblance of normal human contact.

One of the Belgian inmates, Mikey, set up a pop-up pharmacy five beds down from me by using tablets stolen from the prison clinic. He had a Panamanian contact in there who would razor open the corner of the paper prescription packets, slip out a few pills, and then turn the fold back over so that no-one noticed the theft had happened. He also had a highly lucrative side-line in used clothing, from sports coats to running shorts, mostly from dead men, which he displayed on hangers strung around the gym walls. He made the place look like an outreach branch of Oxfam.

I'd been told to be wary of Mikey as the guy was a ruthless profiteer, in business to make the money needed to keep his obese body packed with food at all times. Whatever arrangement he'd cooked up with the guards, they allowed him to ply his trade in full view of the authorities, although they were well aware that his prescribing skills amounted to zero.

The gap in the market he chose to exploit was created by the gross inadequacy of the prison medical clinic. It was held just once a fortnight and admitted only 10 patients to each list. The only way you could guarantee an appointment at the clinic was by paying for it. The schedule did not come close to catering for the rich array of diseases and conditions that afflicted the 600 or so men in our building. Those with cancer did not have a chance. Prisoners did their own tooth extractions with the help of utility pliers and cocaine. If you had a bacterial infection you bought whatever antibiotics you could on the black market and then you prayed. If that option was not available people turned to the next best thing: mouthwash.

Mikey sold condoms that would have been available for free in the prison clinic if it was possible to get an appointment there. He also supplied injections that were popular with body-builders like Grande. What was in them – vitamin C, steroids or plain old bullshit – we could not be sure, but they seemed to work. One of the things it was possible to do in La Joya was work out, and some of the men had dedicated themselves to becoming as solid and ripped as prize fighters, but I always wondered what the point was. By the time some had completed their 47-year stretches, their muscles would have wasted away.

His dubious qualifications aside, Mikey was the only – and therefore a valuable – source of painkillers and anti- diarrhoea tablets. As far as I was concerned, that made him an upstanding member of the community. And if his generous portions of opioids helped to numb the reality of jail for some inmates, then maybe he deserved congratulations.

The double-standards, hypocrisies, sleights of hand and unequivocal crookedness that bubbled through the regime at La Joya was nowhere better illustrated than in the cops' attitudes to mobile phones.

Phones were illegal and classified as contraband. If you were caught with one you could guarantee a hard time from the authorities. Yet, as all the cops were keenly aware, you needed a phone to contact your family, your embassy and, of course, your lawyer. Or, if you were a drugs baron, to set up deals from your cell

The cops understood, too, the psychological importance to inmates of having a connection to their families. Phones were a lifeline to normality. Whether the treasured photographs they stored were of the kids cuddling up to the family dog back home, or of your girlfriend without her clothes on, they were a sweet reminder of freedom. Texting was something you could do privately, without being overheard, and it provided the emotional intimacy lacking in the macho prison. It was instant, too. No queuing involved. For some of the most anxious, unstable inmates, the loss of their phones was enough to tip them into a meltdown.

I desperately needed to secure myself a way to call home. It had to be a small, discreet model that could be easily concealed, especially as my bed was within two metres of the entry door, and I managed to buy a Blackberry phone and SIM card for $150. Where to hide it though? Sandy came to my rescue. He had constructed a bed out of discarded tote boxes for himself, and I asked if he could build a hollow extra leg onto the side that lined up with my mattress, as a kind of safe for my valuables. The DIY work cost me $20, but it offered the perfect solution.

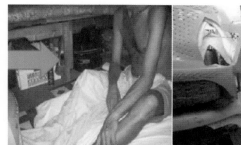

Surprise police searches were on the increase – although we questioned the motives for all that official diligence. Cell phones were a good commodity to trade, especially if you were a cop. Every police raid or 'requisa' would yield about 30 to 40 phones, with a resale value ranging from $100 to $500 each – the equivalent to a cop's monthly salary. Some raids would bring in a jackpot haul of Samsung tablets and HP laptops as well. These raids really shook me up, as did the thought that so many cops were hungry for my phone, my cash and my meagre personal processions. According to the rules, $20 was the maximum we were allowed, but I had been lucky enough to win prizes from three pop-up lottery dealers who sold lines of numbers based on the national lottery results. They would get a sheet of paper, draw a grid from one to 50, then wait for the results to come up on the TV. The winner was the one who matched the numbers. I had placed the same bet with three independent touts so all three had to pay up, but that didn't solve the problem of what you did when a requisa descended and your pockets were bulging.

A requisa on Building Seven. Good luck, guys

You never could predict in those circumstances which additional items the cops would decide was fair game. On the last raid I witnessed, I saw a guard walk past with a box containing the usual phones, liquor and routers but also three giant purple dildos. No one knew when they had become prohibited.

There was no doubt that the cops were playing the system. A morning raid, for instance, would lead to the redistribution of phones by early afternoon; those frantically calling their own numbers would be answered by a person in Building Five, opposite, who had just bought himself a lovely new phone from one of the guards.

It was a running joke among inmates that the alternative offered by La Joya – four payphones mounted onto the gymnasium wall, near where I slept – was hopeless. No more than two of them were ever working, and even if they had all been in perfect order, the ratio of inmates to receiver would have been 150 to one. Who had the patience to take his turn on those odds?

Nevertheless, I bought some black-market Mas Móvil phone cards and phone chips from Carlos, just in case my phone was stolen or confiscated in a raid. The cards had a scratch-off panel at the back over a unique 16-digit number that gave you chat time: a better option than popping in quarters, because small change was hard to come by. I was told to keep my code hidden. Many of the inmates were opportunist thieves, of course, but some of them also had a MENSA-level ability to memorise number sequences

There were literally hundreds of used mobile phones circulating throughout the prison population. They came in a range of brands, models and colours that would have delighted any retail outlet. Getting hold of one, if you had the cash, was not an issue. Getting one to work was more of an effort.

The nearest phone mast was too far from the prison to provide a reliable signal and police phone blockers were causing issues. One of the drug lords who had not been getting a signal managed to destroy one of the outside blockers by using gasoline supplied by his crew. This drug lord needed to get a good, clean, uninterrupted reception from a router in order to have the limitless internet access that allowed him to run a profitable empire from Building Six.

I soon learned that it was best to wait until night to make serious calls or to download WhatsApp videos – and I was told that the best place to do so was up in the attic space, where I had not been thus far. The first time I climbed up into this alien territory, using bars and makeshift ladders welded to the cells, I was astounded by what I saw.

There were at least 150 to 200 people living on platforms constructed out of anything, as far as I could tell – from corrugated plastic, to old pallets, to strips of plywood, lashed in place with the same home-made ice-bag twine that was used to make hammocks, as well as strips of fabric and bungee cords.

There was a whole hidden community above our heads, like a band of high-tech, aerial hobbits.

The router lights were so dense that they made the area look like Heathrow airport at night. There was something cheering and almost Christmassy about the glowing colours. The combined output from the units provided enough signal to cater not only for all the occupants of Building Six, but also for the guard in the watchtower.

Many of us had noted that the guards used their phones to alleviate the boredom of their long shifts, despite phone use being forbidden while they were on duty. So, to expedite prisoner-guard relations, I had supplied them with a password to our system. Anything to oil the wheels. They were very grateful for the improved signal quality.

Every now and again, some of the more enterprising prisoners would try and get better reception for their phones by placing their routers slightly outside the overhang of the metal roof. That might have improved their signal, but it also raised their chances of losing the router entirely. The cops would send out occasional patrols armed with long sticks with a sharp blade on the end in order to cut free the offending routers and watch them plummet to the ground. To prevent that from happening, an elaborate lookout system was in place whenever the stick patrol was spotted approaching the building. The warning whistle would sound, and a flurry of activity would take place as the guards approached and – most times at least – the router would be snatched back inside to safety with only seconds to spare. To smuggle a router in would cost $500, but it would not take long to get a return on the money by charging users $7 a week in line rental. There were always more than enough clients.

The system was generally working quite nicely when we were hit with some bad news. After months of sporadic work repairing the blockers, the high-ups who weren't benefitting from the thriving trade in used phones succeeded in setting up a new batch of signal blockers. They were worried by the amount of crime being directed from prison cells by the drug lords, who could order multi-million dollar deals and even hits from inside La Joya. The star player for the government in the clean-up campaign was an Israeli mobile military truck loaded with antennae.

The effect on morale was immediate and depressing. Tensions rose as inmates began to panic that they would lose contact with their loved ones — or, in the case of new-ish girlfriends they had just found on Facebook, that the loved ones would lose interest in them. Because we originated from outside Panamá, most of us knew no one who lived close enough to visit in person. Without the consoling substitute of contact by phone, we were entirely isolated from family, friends and our attorneys.

The guards who had been happily piggy-backing on our system were annoyed at not being able to call home during their shifts. Those who had been making big bucks from the profitable router Wi-Fi rental market were also distraught for less sentimental reasons. The drug lords were mightily hacked off, too. Being disrupted half-way through deals was a major inconvenience for them.

The blockers worked a little too well, which was not something you could often say of the Panamanian justice system. A few unfortunate civilians who lived near the prison found that they also lost their signal. There was a scandal when the house of a woman a few streets away burned to ashes after she was unable to call the emergency services in time.

The local outcry was vociferous and TV stations and newspapers lapped it up. Soon, the government and police came under pressure to reverse their blocking tactics before any more tragedies occurred in the neighbourhood – possibly with loss of life for the unlucky householder. Bad news for the police was surely going to mean good news for us. In short time, sure enough, the blocking truck was removed and normal service was resumed.

8

THE GAME CHANGER

Once in a while, a little good news pierced the prison gloom. Mine was that William, the porn addict and habitual masturbator next door, was to be released and repatriated back to Colombia. As a result, his bed space was up for grabs.

Now that my funding from the UK was secure and regular, I was able to put my money to a good cause. A frail old man given the nickname of Abuelo – 'Grandad' – had been recently sent to La Joya on a mammoth sentence for acting as a drugs mule. He was struggling with the conditions in the gancha and had been having a very rough ride. There seemed to be no one from his family who could support him. I bought him William's bed, plus some toilet paper and a pair of flip flops from Mikey: such minor luxuries were disproportionately important in jail. He offered whatever services he could by way of thanks but that was not the point. He was alone and I wanted to help. I often lent him my mobile so that he could call home.

Our relationship certainly grew stronger over time and I remain in touch with him via WhatsApp. He is due for release in 2028.

Abuelo - Grandad

Abuelo's plight was the catalyst for my new sense of mission inside La Joya. I suddenly saw that I might be able to achieve something beyond my own survival. I could be useful as a campaigner against the appalling conditions and also as someone who could offer a layer of protection to the more vulnerable inmates in Building Six.

My complaints about the ineffectual efforts of the British and American Embassies to challenge the abuses in La Joya were a constant background theme. My main contact was still the consul, who I counted as a friend. Once every three months they would come to see Ben, Mark, Leo and me and bring Prisoners Abroad funding, which was $90 a quarter and supposed to cover extras such as toiletries.

Now, you might imagine that an embassy is there to protect you and your rights as a citizen if you run into trouble abroad. The truth, as but I learned in Panamá, is that they exercise their very limited powers purely on personal discretion.

I drafted a letter, with help from a highly articulate Canadian inmate called Mark, to detail the horrors of La Joya and to say that I was holding the British embassy and Her Majesty's Government responsible for my welfare and well-being while inside the prison. I felt I was putting them on notice.

I had expected to hand the letter to the consul, José, at our meeting the following day, but to my surprise and by total coincidence, the new acting ambassador, Matthew Phillips, was present too. He had replaced the previous ambassador, my old mucker Richard Austin, after he had retired from the post at around the time I was sent to prison. I asked him, as a representative of the Crown, to sign the letter, and he agreed. This potentially incriminating document was photocopied in October 2013 by the administration office staff, and the embassy acknowledged its receipt. Still, it had no effect.

If you wanted anything, such as a fan, brought in through the official route, your family had to send money to the embassy, which then requested permission from the director for it to be brought in on your behalf. The director, being contrary, crooked as hell and unable to get a cut via this method, would more than likely refuse.

I quickly realised that I had to be persistent and clever in my approach, because corruption was endemic and thrived at all levels of Panamanian society. The fight to expose injustice would be certain to embarrass some influential people.

To be recklessly verbal about injustices would get you nowhere except a transfer to La Joya's vile 'Chutra', a stinking, communal dungeon that ranked as one of the most God-awful pits ever created for the punishment of men. The Chutra was hidden from the view of visitors and NGO goodwill organisations, but every prisoner knew it was there.

For that reason and for many others, my cause was not one I took up lightly. However, I remain utterly committed to seeing it through, whatever the sacrifices. As long as there are prisoners in Panamá whose basic human rights are being abused, I will keep gnawing away at the problem. I owe that much to the people who are still trapped in La Joya and to those inmates, such as my fellow campaigner Dr Arthur Porter, who have since died.

I mentioned Arthur in the prologue, and he truly was an inspiration to me during my detention in La Joya. He was a burly, gregarious man with a cosmopolitan background and the air of someone who was used to moving in somewhat higher society. Mixed Danish and Kenyan by descent, he was a citizen of Canada and the US, and a former US ambassador to Sierra Leone. He was licenced to practice medicine in Canada, the UK and the US, and had been offered the position of surgeon general of the United States by President Bush. His resume was as long as your arm and he had connections that spanned many African countries, including Libya.

Professor, The Honorable Dr Arthur T Porter PC MD MBA FRCPC FACR FACRO FAAMA

Charges officially abandoned against **Arthur Porter**, two years ...
CBC.ca - 4 Aug 2017
Crown prosecutor Nathalie Kleber said she filed **Arthur Porter's death** ... Porter
died in Panamanian custody in 2015 after being detained in that ...
Arthur Porter officially declared **dead** by Quebec Court judge
International - Montreal Gazette - 4 Aug 2017

I met Arthur on my first day in La Joya, when I introduced myself, but we did not establish a friendship until later. I just knew that he, like me, had been recently picked up at Tocumen, and that he was in prison awaiting extradition back to Canada.

This brilliant former student of Harvard and Oxford was doing his best to fit in with the throng of inmates crowding him with offers of cigarettes and homemade liquor. Being an outgoing person by nature, he managed to adapt. I clocked him as an English-speaker and someone with whom I could have a conversation without having to wave my hands around like a mad man.

As a trained oncologist as well as a hospital administrator, Arthur had diagnosed his own lung cancer before entering La Joya and knew that his chances of recovery were not great, despite the connections that allowed him to bring suitable chemotherapy drugs into the prison. Yet he was able to think beyond his predicament to the importance of revealing La Joya's dirty secrets.

I was to gather 600 hours of rock-solid, filmed evidence of the abuses suffered in that place, thanks to his help in obtaining spy-ware, but I began with a letter-writing campaign. This developed in time into a concerted assault on the human rights violations of the Panamanian government.

It is required under Panamanian law for inmates to be examined by a medical officer, at 'Merced' clinic, on admittance. This did not happen for me at La Joya, although I was clearly weak and ill, with badly damaged knees. Months after my arrival, what we did get was cursory and inadequate. We were handcuffed in pairs, lined up and asked by a doctor whether we had any diseases: yes or no? Each individual was given a few seconds' attention before being signed off.

It would become obvious that Tuberculosis and Hepatitis C were rampant in my building and that a number of inmates were slowly dying of AIDS. Bacterial problems of the type that plagued me were everywhere because infection spread so quickly in the insanitary, over-crowded conditions. It is now the case that Covid-19 has also entered La Joya.

I had all kinds of horrible rashes and boils on my head, groin, legs and armpits the whole time I was there. It didn't matter what precautions I took, there were just too many germs and too few antibiotics in circulation.

Controlling the infections was next to impossible when washing facilities were basic, at best, and most prisoners could not afford the luxury of keeping clean. The kitchens where inmates were deputised to prepare food for the rest of the prisoners were often fly-blown, and so were the surfaces used by individuals for making the treats they would then sell for profit.

The population of rats, cockroaches and bed bugs compounded the problem. In all my months of incarceration, only once did I see the building washed down and fumigated, to control a plague of mosquitos that threatened to spread dengue fever. The block was pumped with a choking fog of insecticide that was almost as dangerous to the humans as to the resident bugs.

The dismal standard of care became understandable, if not excusable, when you considered that the prison medical clinic serving both La Joya and its neighbouring prison, La Joyita, had only two doctors on duty at any point, with a combined patient load of between 11 and 13,000 prisoners. Urgent injuries from knife fights and gunshots ate into most of their time, and there was little left over for tending the remaining inmates.

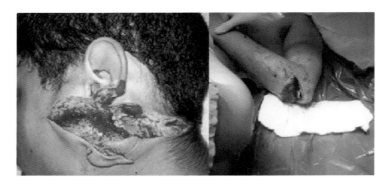

Those who were seriously ill and in need of regular care dominated. New cases could wait months on end, and the selection process was skewed by favouritism and the payment of back-handers.

My own request to see a clinic doctor was for various reasons repeatedly cancelled. It wasn't until two weeks before my release in 2014 that I was finally taken to the clinic – which was some 13 months after my original application. I had managed to enlist the British and American embassies to pressure the director to grant me a letter of 'extraordinary permission' for the appointment. This was a privilege no one else received without paying a fee to the supervising guard, or commando, parked at his desk outside.

It was a development highly unpopular with the guards, who worried that it marked a threat to their position as gatekeepers to the medical clinic – and to their bribes. But one glance at the queue of ragged inmates still eager to secure some kind of privilege should have reassured them that those were not at risk.

Whenever the British embassy staff visited the prison, I told them that I could not get proper medical care. The filthy conditions were plain for them to see, but I described them repeatedly anyway. They didn't pursue it at all. I wrote a letter personally to the ambassador and my attorney hand-delivered it to his office, yet they still didn't respond.

Eventually I joined forces with Ben to write a letter to the prison director requesting a medical assessment for Arthur, who had stage four cancer, and myself. This letter was stamped as received by the director's secretary, then promptly returned as unacceptable because it wasn't written in Spanish. The prison guidelines regarding the rights and obligations of inmates gave an assurance that internationals who communicated with the authorities should be able to do so in their own language, and that their words should be accepted. Apparently, that was not the case in Panamá. Ben, a Spanish speaker, re-submitted the request in Spanish. Once again it was stamped as received but no action was taken.

This second letter requested permission to bring in several essential pieces of equipment to improve safety and comfort. As a teaser we asked for a smoke detector and a fire extinguisher: at the time there was not a single example of either in the whole of Building Six. We also wanted a first aid kit that would at least allow minor injuries to be treated with clean bandages. Last on the list was a fan, to alleviate some of the stifling heat in the tin-roofed structure and to deter mosquitoes.

As was becoming a habit, the director turned us down, even when we put the request to him via the British embassy. Lopez already had a beef with me because he knew I had complained to the public ombudsman in Panamá about my treatment in the prison. All the same, I filed copies of the letters and cited them later in a complaint to the international authorities. I also filed a human rights case against the Panamanian government for the treatment I suffered while I was in Ancón and La Palma.

We would discover that the only way to import items, whether deemed essential or recreational, was by making arrangements through the unofficial channels that ran parallel to the official ones. You had to pay the director a tip, or 'propina', ranging from $20 to $100. This was common practice, accepted as the only way to improve conditions for inmates. If you attempted to act on principle and obtain items in the approved manner, you were screwed. The incomprehensible part of the system – if it could be described as such – was that it was highly selective: televisions were available via propina; first aid kits and 'exit' signs were not. Entertainment ranked higher than things that most state-run public buildings would consider mandatory.

The commando who first approached me in La Joya had alerted me to the advantages of buttering up those who could make life a little easier. Once I realised how things worked, I made a point of befriending each guard for favours. It was easily done, although my Spanish was piecemeal and mispronounced.

The commando on duty would often have four or five inmates hanging around his desk, some seeking a deal, others inviting him to enjoy a can of soda or a cup of coffee. The atmosphere was almost festive on some days. I think he liked the flattery almost as much as he liked the tokens of appreciation. Many guards loved to boast about themselves, their families or their conquests once prompted by a few questions

The older commandos assigned to La Joya to wait out their retirements had generally been members of General Noriega's army, and were still devotees of his dictatorial style. In the prison it was their turn to play commander-in- chief, even if it was only over a battalion of inmates.

I endeared myself with attention and with cash. It was a deliberate strategy to find my niche in the hierarchy.

When I told Leo and Ben that I intended to pay off the cops for privileges, they both said I was stupid. Their attitude was that the police should be treated like shit on principle. But I could see how to make it work for myself and for other people around me who I wanted to benefit. Without the sanction of my fellow Brits, I decided to give

$100 a week to whichever cop was looking after Building Six. Word got around the various cops in the compound that a mad Englishman with deep pockets was in town, and they all wanted to work in our building after that. It even reached the stage where they were pulling straws for the privilege. After all, $100 per week was exactly what they were being paid to work in La Joya.

I would also pay the custodial prisoners, the ones who acted as the guards' doormen by unlocking the gates or escorting prisoners, for occasional favours such as getting a letter posted.

The cops were happy for their proxies to get a cut because these guys saved the guard from the tiresome business of rising from his desk to actually perform any physical tasks. He was then able to concentrate on surfing the internet, eating and consuming drinks that were often spiked with cell-made liquor.

The money I handed over bought me a transactional type of loyalty and freedom of movement. Sometimes a guard would just give me the keys that allowed me to cross to another building. It meant I could let people such as Arthur out into the yard when I had the opportunity. Without that flexibility, you might easily be locked inside the building for a week or more.

I was able to talk to the inmates from Building Five through the fence when they had their allocated one-hour exercise period. The conversation turned one morning, as conversations did in La Joya, to how much it cost to take out a contract on someone in the outside world. I had stumbled on what seemed to be an established side-line run from the prison, and it shocked me to the core. The price list was extraordinarily precise and rattled off like a McDonald's menu: $500 to kill a single person and $1,500 for a whole family. If you only wanted someone maimed that would be $2,000 because that kind of precision job was more demanding and would give the victim lifelong pain.

Another inmate I met on my rounds was a Panamanian from Building Seven who was loaded down with gold bling and used to parade around the prison with his pet Rottweiler. Anyone else sporting that amount of gold would have been a marked man, but this guy had immunity because he was a kingpin who had bought the guards' blessing to have the run of the place. No-one dared say 'boo' to him.

He had so many connections on the outside that he boasted he could get hold of anything you wanted. I thought I'd test his distribution network in the days leading up to Christmas. I told him I wanted a case of Heineken, a ham and a bottle of Scotch, along with assorted festive goodies. He promised to get the stuff to me within a couple of days. (For reference, his mark-up on a bottle of so-so Scotch that might be $12 in the shops was about 1,000 per cent.) While I stood talking to this commander of commerce, I noticed a sweet kitten playing on my side of the fence. The animal made the worst decision of its short life by slipping through a drain hole to emerge in the Building Seven yard. Within seconds, the Rottweiler had snapped its jaws, crunched through a few bones and swallowed kitty whole, head first. I could hardly believe what I'd seen but the guy didn't even flinch.

I had entered La Joya as the lowest in the pecking order: friendless and unable even to walk properly. However, being able to bribe the guards and spend money to obtain goods helped to boost my credibility, and that in turn gave me some influence.

I also figured that spreading payments around to people unfortunate enough to have fewer resources not only helped them, but also helped me by providing a form of insurance. I had an arrangement, for instance, with the inmate who had the job of laundering other prisoners' clothes at a rate of 15¢ a garment. He was allowed out to the standpipe when it was turned on so that he could collect enough water to run his pop-up laundromat. I would pay him to put my bucket of water outside in the sunshine each morning so that it could warm up. The arrangement allowed me the luxury of washing outside just before the sunset, using water that had heated throughout the day to a bath-like temperature. The guy used what I gave him to help buy creams that alleviated the damage caused to his hands and feet by the constant contact with detergent powder.

My access to different parts of the compound was to be invaluable when I needed to collect footage of the conditions. This was done stealthily and steadily over the course of many months to give the widest possible overview.

9

AMBASSADOR IN THE PEN

The collaboration between Arthur and me began one afternoon when we both happened to pass $20 bills to the guard at the door of the exercise yard so that we could squeeze outside for a walk. As we chatted and discovered that we had nationalities in common, he opened up slightly. He explained that he was a medical doctor and the former head of the review committee, keeping tabs on Canada's spy agency. In other words, he had been one of the country's top spies.

He had fallen out with then-Prime Minister Stephen Harper and decided to leave Canada, but had been arrested with his wife while in transit to St. Kitts and the Bahamas, where he had a house. He was ticked off with the feds because, prior to leaving, he claimed to have made a deal with Harper to keep quiet about the government's indiscretions in return for being left to get on with his life.

I didn't know whether to believe this tall tale and grabbed Leo, Arthur's cellmate, by the arm for confirmation. Leo told me it was all true. As for the allegation that Arthur had defrauded some $22.5 million from the construction of the new McGill Medical Centre in Montreal, where he had been a director, Arthur dismissed it as a put-up job. He said the real problem had been a clash between his outside interests as a board member of Air Canada and a member of Canada's privy council with his government position.

A few weeks later, Arthur and I teamed up again and decided that we would work on a plan to improve prison conditions and get him some medical help. It seemed that his case was being frustrated by unknown forces in a way that tallied with my own experience. Our small talk became very interesting. The more we discussed the atrocious conditions and the struggles of the poorer inmates, the stronger our conviction became that something had to be done. Seeing people struggling to retain their dignity as they tried to get by without shoes or toilet paper or even a few cents to their names had deeply upset us both. We were both Christians and the flagrant human rights violations offended us on a moral level, as did the routine injustices of the prison system. If we, with our financial resources, found it tough, how much worse was it for the people who could not buy a modicum of comfort?

We had a brainstorming session and our crazy idea was born: we were going to attempt an undercover operation like no other – and I was to become a spy. The terrible reality of La Joya – and, by extension, all Panamá's rotten jails – was going to be revealed to the world, something that, as far as we were aware, had never been done before in the country's history.

Arthur planned to arrange for his attorney to smuggle in an HD video spy watch. With this, I would be able to covertly record the incidents of squalor and brutality that we prisoners had almost come to regard as mundane. We made a pact that whomever of the two of us was released first would expose it all. Panamá deserved to be shamed on the international stage and censured by the United Nations. In other words, we thought it was about time that Panamá received a public spanking.

Arthur's arrest was bigger news than mine. A Canadian reporter from CBC, Dave Seglins, even flew down to interview him. The entire prison population was agog as the story unfolded on mobile phones. He became an object of particular fascination to inmates with Canadian passports and to the Jamaicans, many of whom felt a connection to him because they were mixed race, as he was. Arthur strenuously denied that he had bilked the Quebec government and laundered the profits, but word was out that he had a lot of money. His Jamaican mates were anxious both to befriend and protect him from the constant approaches for 'business' funding, and they made room for him in their cell, B16. They even built him a sleeping platform and a privacy screen. He stayed there for a few weeks, until the mayhem and constant reggae music became too much for him.

The odd thing was that he didn't at first glance look ill, and his apparent good health sparked more rumours: that he had faked his diagnosis with the benefit of his medical expertise, or that he was bluffing for sympathy in the hope of a more lenient hearing. The fact that he was able to tend to ill or injured inmates – he had a basic medical bag with him in La Joya – or to give them advice, added to the impression that he was more robust than he actually was. Arthur helped many prisoners on an informal basis, within the limitations of the facilities and the available equipment. One of the most bizarre cases involved a Romanian guy whose balls had swollen to the size of an elephant's and who came to Arthur desperate for a cure. It transpired that the Romanian had somehow inserted seven ball bearings into his scrotum. Then began a minor, but toe-curlingly delicate, surgical procedure. Arthur eventually moved to one of the attic living areas, with a couple of other Canadians and Leo. It was situated just above the commando's desk and it was the closest thing the prison could support to a five- star hotel: they had a plasma TV, a sink and a penthouse view of the surrounding country through the window bars.

Once, when we were sharing some food up there, he let me in on a secret.

I had started a conversation about one of my constant worries: what would happen if a fire started. It was my opinion that the advantages of his quarters were seriously undermined by the difficulty of escaping in an emergency. He agreed, adding his own concerns about the toxic fumes from burning mattresses. We both knew that the cops would ignore prisoners and get the hell out if the place started to burn, and that those at the back of the building or high in the ceiling would have the worst chance of all. Arthur started to chuckle, and he pointed to the window. He had been patiently working at sawing through the bars closest to his bed. When he cut through the metal, he did an excellent job of sticking the severed ends back together with gum so that there was no sign of his vandalism. The only way anyone could have detected the breaks would have been by running a stick across the bars and listening for the tell-tale change in tone; as Arthur's window was located in the attic area, it was well beyond the reach of the guards below.

Arthur had devised his own fire escape. One push and the bars would give way, allowing him to climb down the outside of the building on knotted bed sheets. It was reassuring – and useful – to know there was a way out from up there.

He had the same type of power within the prison as the drug lords, considering his wealth and global contacts, but with far greater credibility. For hours every day he was busy talking on his phone, writing his book or texting, in consultation with his Panamanian attorney to arrange some kind of house arrest. He stood his ground and when Panamá failed to provide him with a hearing within 60 days, he sued the government for $150 million for illegal detention. If only the rest of us had the power to sue governments! We would have plugged up the courts for years to come.

My own legal trials were not so newsworthy, but they patently caused me enormous stress and ate up huge quantities of money. From La Joya I was able to communicate on a regular basis, via WhatsApp and Gmail. José, a young energetic attorney in his mid-20s, was representing me on my domestic, civil battles, while Fidel was dealing with my penal case.

José tried to regain control over my assets in Darién and Panamá City, but it was a process that proved unexpectedly difficult and traumatic when it emerged that I was no longer the owner the properties I had bought. My supposedly secure investments were collapsing one after the other, as surely as a line of falling dominoes. And there was not a thing

I could do about it from La Joya. Laura had me positioned exactly where she wanted me. Confining me to jail was her dream outcome

213

because it meant under Panamanian law that I had no voice or authority – especially when it came to gaining access to Jason.

When I had divorced her in 2010, Laura's attorney had wanted to delay the division of property, which I had found strange. I didn't really understand why at the time, but I went along with the request, with the novice attorney I was using at the time as my guide.

José discovered that just before my arrest, Laura had generated a special power, making her sole title holder of the assets, including the Darién plantation of 36,000 teak and 10,000 mahogany trees. José went to the national registry archives looking for the vital document – 2910 –supposedly signed by me and showing the transfer of ownership. Strangely enough, the original had somehow disappeared from the notary's records, as well as from the national archives. José knew immediately that we were dealing with a forged and fraudulent grab for my property. My beautiful Miami house had gone into foreclosure in late 2013, and half of the equity of $50,000 had been paid to Laura without any notice whatsoever having been served to me in La Joya.

I should have paid more attention to the gut-feeling of unease I'd had ever since the divorce. As circumstances stood, I was effectively powerless. Not only that, I was having to divide my attention between two fronts: my divorce and the corruption of minors charge.

I had to make a decision about which was my priority. My criminal defence lawyers were expensive, and the related costs were placing a strain on my family back in England. On top of that were the outstanding credit card balances that I could not pay while I was stuck in prison. I just could not afford to fight Laura's commercial crime at the same time. My immediate focus needed to be proving my innocence from the horrible and absurd criminal charge.

My statement of denial in the case had been made back in June 2013 by my defence lawyer, Fidel, to the bible-bashing prosecutor in La Palma. By the Autumn I had still not been notified of any hearing at which I could put my case. At last, Fidel managed to secure a date: November 13, 2013. That was when the logistical jiggery-pokery began.

The court would need the judge and the prosecutor to be present, of course, along with all my witnesses and a certified translator because my Spanish was shaky. I, as the accused, would have to be accompanied by the national police, and we would all have to travel separately on the six-hour journey into Darién – assuming that the police had an available truck with enough fuel to make the journey (court and hospital appointments had been cancelled before because they had run out of fuel or working vehicles).

Crucial to the case was my co-accused, Angel. Without him, nothing could move forward, and I faced being held indefinitely. It was up to my lawyer to locate Angel and convince him to appear, but it was doubtful that an actual arrest warrant had been issued against him. It wasn't the Panamanian they were after: it was the gringo who had outraged national decency, despite the fact that Angel was accused of the same crime. Gullible as I was, I was convinced that my release was imminent. The day before my court appearance I did my best to spruce myself up with whatever Mikey had to offer, and Abuelo offered to polish my shoes so that I would make a good impression. Freedom felt within touching distance!

The fateful morning dawned, and the guards appeared to take me to the admin building so that I could be searched and chained, then loaded into the vehicle. I had managed to hide $100 under my shirt collar in order to pay for any necessary extras on the journey. I was as prepared as it was possible to be.

We crossed the half mile between Building Six and the entrance to the prison compound, where it faced the highway. I could see the yellow barrier ahead of us and my heart was beating faster with the excitement of imminent escape. That was when the message came over my guard's radio: "El Gringo, we're cancelling your day in court."

It was barely light when we set off and too early for any government employees to be at work, which meant that the police must have known the day before that the hearing had been cancelled. Yet we had gone through the charade of preparing. Angry and bitterly disappointed, I wondered whether incompetence or cruelty was to blame for the false start. It was going to be a long wait, after all, to defend myself.

On speaking to Fidel, I learned the reason for cancellation: my accusers, the Gallardos, could not be located even though they lived just minutes away from the court house. It would seem that their only objective was to keep me in prison for as long as possible.

I had often heard people complain about the unreliability of Panamanians, especially in relation to court cases. It was a nightmare trying to get three or four in the same place at the same time. If it was inconvenient, they simply got sick or didn't show up. However, it seemed that this pattern of behaviour was so common that judges simply shrugged their shoulders and enforced no disciplinary penalties on the police for failing to round up the relevant witnesses. It meant that those being held before trial could languish in prison for months or years before their fates were decided.

A second hearing was ordered in January of 2014 – and then cancelled. Each time, I had paid the chief custodial officer $100 in advance for transporting me to court in Darién. He did not offer refunds.

Aware by now that my case was locked in ping-pong mode, I wanted to lobby the highest levels of government for fair treatment. But I was informed by the British embassy that this would be meddling in 'internal affairs' and advised not to rock the boat.

I ignored their typically timid and mealy-mouthed advice and decided, with the help of my attorney José, that the president of the Republic of Panamá should be petitioned to correct this travesty of justice. We reasoned that even if President Martinelli personally failed to act on the petition, the problem would have been brought to light and that someone in the government would take notice.

On December 19, 2013, the letter was written, transcribed into Spanish and hand-delivered to the Presidential Palace, where it was signed for. We did not expect an immediate response: it was Christmas, and after that there was a prolonged period of partying in the New Year, but by February of 2014, we had still heard nothing.

In an effort to expedite the case and to put some pressure on Panamá to conform to the norms of justice and human rights, letters were then written to the ambassadors of the US and UK governments asking them to intervene on my behalf. Although the 'no meddling in internal affairs' line was a standard response in cases such as mine, both the US and the UK had bigger obligations under law to protect their citizens, especially when it came to human rights.

The US, the UK and Panamá are all signatories to the Geneva Convention's International Right to a Fair Trial agreement. And my rights in this regard were clearly being violated.

Although the letters to the embassies were, again, hand-delivered (to the consul or Charge d'Affaires), neither ambassador bothered to acknowledge receipt or to respond. I found their attitude profoundly upsetting and disappointing. It reinforced my impression that existing trade deals and the promise of future ones would always supersede human rights.

In the eight months since my first hearing was cancelled, four other hearings were scheduled and then snatched back on the very morning that they were supposed to take place. The same cynical pattern was played out on each occasion. The prosecutor or the judge then cancelled because one person or another for the prosecution could not, or would not, be in attendance.

My attorney believed that my case was being deliberately delayed because it was not politically expedient for it to proceed. It was simply too high-profile and embarrassing to the incumbent government.

But as of July 2014, Panamá had a new president-elect: Juan Carlos Varela. Before that date, he had been vice- president in the previous government under his one- time rival Martinelli, and the two had bad blood between them. Varela had a point to prove against the previous administration: namely, that he could do a better job of running the country. I hoped that this change of president was an opportunity for me to find justice.

I wrote yet another letter, this time to Varela, appealing to his integrity (and his vanity) as a politician:

> *In accordance with your election campaign platform to bring in a new era of fairness and justice to the Republic of Panamá and its ordinary citizens, as well as an earnest campaign for transparency in government in the absence of corruption, I am writing to you in that belief.*

I went on to explain my situation and included a copy of the letter sent to President Martinelli, believing that it just might make a difference. It did not. Varela seemed equally immune to my pleas and arguments invoking my human rights. His government installed a new cast of favoured bureaucrats and judges to replace the previous incumbents and they gave every sign of carrying on exactly as their predecessors had done. I had yet another appointment for a hearing on July 9, but that too was cancelled, because the judges were in transition.

Why the hearing had been scheduled in the first place was anyone's guess. I almost began to wonder if the individual guards being paid to get me to La Palma were in league with the Varela government, just to spite me and extract a bit more cash in back-handers.

My attorney had a smooth tongue, and he was always hungry for more money. Every delay was an opportunity to ask for more, with him offering further investigations at $1,000 a pop.

I can understand in many ways why guards in La Joya were forced into corruption, especially when they had large families that depended on them. The cops were not even supplied with a uniform by the state. They had to pay for everything, from their boots to their essential travel expenses - and they had to do so without complaint, because their employment contracts forbade them from protesting. In a failed effort to halt corruption, the government sent cops who were serving their last post before retirement to work far from their homes, where they were less likely to have local connections. All our cops in La Joya, for this reason, came from David, an eight-hour bus ride away.

In reality, the government practically encouraged them to supplement their wages with what they could from the prisoners. It was a culture of deniable collusion that created not so much a few bad apples in the barrel, as a brimming vat of putrid fruit.

Many of us had experienced first-hand the casual way that our belongings were confiscated and never returned. What happened to all the personal possessions of those captured at Tocumen International Airport? Laptops, money, cameras, electric razors… vanished into the bottomless pit of police greed. And we heard plenty of stories about hauls of smuggled cocaine disappearing in the same manner. To this day the practice continues.

My possessions from Darién have never been returned to me, despite numerous requests.

Arthur quickly acquired a reputation as a man with money. He was an easy mark for inmates in search of funds because he would rather pay people off than be confronted. He was especially popular with the guards. He knew that on Wednesdays, the last day of the week before the new duty commando took over for the next seven-day shift, he would have to fill his pockets with cash.

Every commando regarded Wednesdays as a pay-out bonanza. The more favours the officer had granted inmates over the preceding days, the higher his 'tips' as he collected his rewards. And the service charge in La Joya was never optional. It was a ceremonial hand-over that no one dared to ignore.

This one cop was charged with supervising up to 500-plus people: that amounted to a basic starting point of $500-plus. Many of the grasping bastards took full advantage of their authority. Nixon and Nikki would be delegated to act on the commando's behalf, and would pace the building with him to collect the loot. Arthur's penthouse was the last call on the visiting list and would usually net a bonus of $200.

Before entering our building, the cop would have given a nod to his buddies at the checkpoint, who would radio to warn him if the big boss was around. (Blatant though the system was, you didn't collect tips when the police commissioner was watching.)

Leaving the building, however, was more difficult if you were bulging with cash like a piñata stuffed with dollar bills. The cop had to find a friendly drug lord who could process the money discreetly into $100 bills. His net gain once he factored in side-deals could easily top $1,000.

One week in La Joya's Building Six was equivalent to two months' wages. Go figure why we were so popular.

10

You Have Been Framed

It was glaringly apparent that nothing would improve for the average prisoner as long as corruption was allowed to persist.

The wealthy were buying their way out of prison and enjoying a diet of steak and cheesecake while they waited for their paperwork to be fiddled by a compliant official. The poor could be detained without trial for years and then given long sentences for relatively minor offences. It always seemed to be the drugs mules, not the drugs lords, who suffered. Some who had spent five years or so awaiting their hearing would eventually find out that their sentence was less than the detention period they'd already served. Others would be found not guilty when they finally got to court.

Five years without a hearing

Signing off your sentence

In La Joya there were several different economies at work, but the same vulnerable people formed the bottom layer of every system.

How could I prove that corruption? How could I try to institute change?

Arthur's attorney was a colourful character called Ricardo Bilonick, whose past clients included the 'narco king' Pablo Escobar. Ricardo had been the Panamanian ambassador to Washington in the '80s, as well as serving time in a US jail for smuggling drugs. He was the man who managed to track down some HD video spyware disguised as a watch. He passed it to Arthur during one of their meetings in the administration building by slipping it off his own wrist. The charger was delivered at the next meeting.

Suddenly, our imagined campaign became real, with real risks and penalties attached to it. I kept my James Bond-style fantasies firmly in check. This was not a game, but would be a game changer: I would be punished with a minimum 10- year sentence on a national security violation charge and a spell in the chutra if the cops caught me filming.

Arthur was in no physical condition to carry out the task as he was attached to a respirator to help him breathe; therefore it fell to me. He was elated that I was able to take action, though. Our friendship had deepened and for all the differences between us, we also discovered many things in common, such as our American citizenship and our bruising experience with the judicial system.

As my bed was located right by the front entrance, I had the perfect base from which to track the activities of inmates and guards. The privileged access I had already established to the outside space, and to inmates from different buildings within the compound, meant that I could gather a wide variety of material without arousing suspicion.

I will give credit where it's due to the British embassy for backing me in the argument that I needed regular exercise in the Building Six yard in order to strengthen my damaged legs. Although my emoluments to the guards were probably a more decisive factor. By handing out small, tactical donations and continuing my policy of befriending cops, I could infiltrate an even wider area. The police gave me total permission to go into restricted areas, including the infamous chutra, as long as I could satisfy them with some vague explanation about doing business there. My prison status as a wheeler-dealer certainly gave me additional credibility.

The first issue I had with the watch was that it looked like a cross between the world's most blingtastic Rolex and a controller for the Space Shuttle. My show-off, rich man's timepiece attracted a lot of attention and, under the circumstances, attention was not what I wanted. I had to parry admiring questions about where I'd bought it, while whoever was asking was talking straight into the camera. There were several occasions when I nearly soiled my pants with the stress. I wished a thousand times that Ricardo had found something less exuberantly 'drug-lord' in appearance and a little more nondescript.

The other problem was that I had no way to be sure the watch was recording once I had pressed the multiple buttons. I put a lot of effort into learning the configurations by touch so as not to draw attention to what I was doing, but it was complicated and one wrong step in the sequence could give me a faulty voice recording, or a still shot instead of moving footage. I never did manage to change the factory-set time and date, which was stuck permanently in 2007.

2007. 01. 15 19:00:35

I had a running commentary of instructions in my head. *Keep it properly aimed on the subject matter,* I told myself. *Too high, and you'll be filming the sky; too low and you'll be framing the guy's nuts.* In an effort to ensure steady footage, I began walking more stiffly than usual when I was filming and I'm pretty sure I looked as if I was recovering from a stroke. No one seemed to notice. The only thing I knew for sure was that when the watch's lithium battery came close to dying, it would start to burn my wrist. At least it was a reminder I couldn't ignore.

There was so much at stake, so much hanging on whether I collected the right evidence, that I became utterly absorbed in the task. I was damned if all the hard work was going to be wasted.

It was vitally important, for now, that Arthur and I kept the project secret. I had to resort to hiding in the gancha toilet in the dead of night when the watch's memory chip needed to be extracted and replaced. I remember having to perch on the edge of the bowl, breathing in the foul smell of ammonia and praying that I didn't lose three days' worth of filming in my amateur efforts to grapple with covert surveillance technology.

226

There was a particularly nerve-racking moment during the first week, when I honestly thought it was all over. I had managed to capture what I hoped would be excellent footage of commando Santa-Maria in the act of taking cocaine when he turned to me and pointed straight at my wrist. He wanted to know why there was a light frantically blinking blue and red on my watch. I could have told him that it was because the watch was recording via its pin-hole camera – and had, indeed, just recorded him snorting a lavish line – but I decided against it.

I quickly spun some ridiculous tale about an alarm function that had not been disabled and he swallowed the explanation. Thank God I was as high as a kite on moonshine because the spirit, in every sense, of creativity took over. Had I been sober, I doubt I'd have mustered up such a convincing cover story.

It was hardly an auspicious start for a novice spy, and after that I became still more careful. I went away to re- read the instructions, which is when I discovered that a 'red and blue light continuously flashing means chip is full' and vowed that I would never again leave a chip in place for long enough to risk that particular klaxon going off.

My next issue was where to hide all those microchips. One police raid would be all it took to screw me and the entire operation. I came up with an ingenious idea of hiding the chips in plain sight, deciding to slide them gently in between the corrugated section of the folded flap of a cardboard carton next to my bed. I used the other side of the carton to write down phone numbers and other oddments, as if it were my notebook. I could make the manoeuvre quite easily without looking furtive or as if I were trying to conceal something valuable. Only a fire could destroy the evidence, or so I believed.

Every time a cop palmed a bill from an inmate or took time out for a cosy gambling session, I was there with my camera. I felt the thrill of the chase, the satisfaction of capturing footage and a growing sense of responsibility. Not only was I gathering a damning archive of La Joya's regime, the activity made the dragging hours pass more quickly. Working out how to get the sharpest image, without any stray sunlight to make the picture flare, and staying out of the wind so that I could clearly hear the conversations, was also a welcome distraction from the tedium of prison life.

I filmed when whole sacks of chickens that had been stolen from the prison kitchen were waved past by the police so that they could sold off to the personal chefs of wealthy inmates. I filmed cops smoking and drinking on duty. I recorded Mike, a hit man from New York who'd been thrown into the chutra for fighting, then passing me a note asking if I could supply him with some plastic bags for him to shit in.

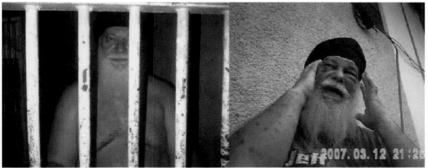

Mike's handiwork, which landed him in the chutra

People used to die in the chutra on an even more regular basis than they did in the main prison. Their afflictions ranged from knife wounds to snake bites to the terminal stages of AIDS or hepatitis. You'd see their bodies being removed in wheelbarrows. Once in the chutra, there was not the faintest whiff of a chance you would qualify for medical attention.

An inmate from Holland working in the administration building managed to smuggle a note to me via one of the guards on Mike's behalf after three days, begging me to get him out of there. No wonder he was desperate. People could be stuck in there for up to seven months on end for fairly petty offences. In Mike's case, it was because he had fought with another inmate by the nickname of Santa Claus after Santa had criticised his parental choices. Whatever.

After I left in September 2014, la chutra was closed because someone from an NGO saw it, was horrified and made a public stink. In its place the compound opened a similar facility called la chutrita, which holds half the number of people but is still hidden from view. I've seen videos smuggled out in 2019 from inmates being held there, and it is every bit as terrible as its predecessor.

Arthur and I kept knowledge of our covert operation on a 'need-to-know' basis, but I did have to semi-involve Grande out of necessity. Charging the watch to its full recording capacity of 90 minutes was difficult for me because there were no electrical points in the gancha. I asked him if he could plug it in near his cell – and he referred me to his cousin, also housed in Building Six. The guy showed zero interest in my flashy jewellery and guarded it like a hero.

That watch had a charmed life. It was never stolen or detected as a fake, though it did at one point suffer a minor breakdown. The constant opening and closing of the memory chip compartment eventually caused a fly lead from the battery to detach itself from the circuit board. Once again it was Grande to the rescue. He knew the electrician in cell A-1, who charged $5 to solder the wire back into place. The guy wisely asked no questions and I was relieved when I was spared from spinning any more lies.

Maybe the intensity of the surveillance skewed my judgement. When I met both the US and UK embassy staff in our administration building on their three-monthly visits, I told them blatantly that I had been filming since soon after my arrival and could expose hundreds of human rights abuses. The very human rights abuses they were so reluctant to acknowledge.

With hindsight, this was a poor choice on my part. By giving them the information, I made myself toxic. Their fear of being embarrassed by the evidence caused them to back away, instead of rush in behind me as I'd hoped. At the time of my unfair deportation, none of the embassy staff weighed in to help – they just wanted me gone quickly, and without the possibility of return.

Once I got back to the UK, I put in an FOI (Freedom of Information) request for the contemporaneous notes made by the consuls at the meeting and discovered that our conversation hadn't even been mentioned. Luckily for me, I had recorded it.

Something else I recorded was the scam that allowed rich inmates to buy off chunks of their sentences by cheating their work records to gain unearned credits.

All prison work – in the kitchens, for instance, or clearing rubbish from the yard – counted towards time off your sentence, and for that reason plenty of inmates volunteered, or paid to volunteer, for duties.

My fear of losing my precious collection of recordings never abated and, thanks to the over-eager housekeeping of Abuelo, three months' worth of material did, indeed, vanish. He took it upon himself to spruce up my sleeping area by throwing away that piece of old cardboard carton I always kept near my bed. When I found out, I hurled such awful insults at him that the poor old guy was completely bemused. He told me that if it mattered so much to me, my cardboard was now in the dumpster area.

Even with my access, that was out of bounds. It required me to pass three armed checkpoints and two barbed wire perimeter fences. It was torture because I could actually see the dumpster through the wire. Abuelo was so contrite that he offered to go there himself, but the idea was crazy. If he was caught with the microchips it would just mean that we both faced longer sentences. I had to write off all that hard work. It was heartbreaking.

My usual method of smuggling the chips out of jail was by using my attorneys as unwitting mules. José had no idea why I was giving him random pieces of cardboard scribbled with names and numbers and asking him to post them to Kent. He probably thought I was a lunatic.

When I was eventually released on August 24, 2014, I had the problem of getting the watch safely out of prison, along with any as-yet unposted memory chips. I asked Fidel, my other attorney, to visit, ripped the battery from my watch, inserted eight chips in its place and handed the re-sealed watch to him with instructions that he wear it to leave the prison. He, in turn, passed the thing to José, who finally delivered it to me in the UK while he was on holiday there.

In 2014, all my videos were eventually handed over to John Jones QC, the renowned London human rights barrister. He stated in a letter to President Varela:

> *I would mention that an inmate recently released from La Joya Prison, Mr Nick Tuffney, has hundreds of hours of footage, which he secretly filmed in La Joya Prison with a small camera. This shows a catalogue of human rights abuses, corruption by guards, drug-taking by prisoners and guards alike and a host of other incidents, which further put Panamá to shame. I have seen footage with my own eyes, and will ever be haunted by many of the images, including a prisoner who was chopped into pieces by another prisoner, due to the fact that the prison negligently allows prisoners access to machetes.*

For all the activity of my evidence-gathering tours round the building, prison weighed heavily on me.

A particular low point was in March 2014. I had witnessed the deeply upsetting suicide of a friend and some particularly brutal bullying, and my own mental and physical health was poor. All the energy I had poured into letter-writing had yielded no hearing and no prospect of release. The prosecutor in La Palma had been informed that I was frail, but his attitude remained one of stony indifference.

The feeling that you have been abandoned is one of the most destructive for a prisoner. It saps your motivation and replaces it with the dangerous questions of, "What's the point?" and "Who cares?"

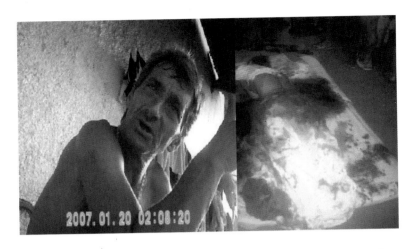

An inmate who slept three beds down from me and acted as my occasional gopher had recently taken what must have seemed the easiest way out. 'Portugal' had said that he was missing home, as we all were, but evidently his torment ran deeper. He slit the arteries in his groin with a razor blade, which he then swallowed.

I had risen early, when it was still dark, to use the toilet, and then I stood by the window to have my morning smoke and watch the sun rise. As the light crept over the gancha it illuminated the inmates one by one, and that's when I noticed Portugal lying face down in a pool of blood.

I raised the alarm and ran to find towels to staunch the flow, but it was too late (this being an out-of-hours suicide, the authorities would have failed to respond immediately in any case). Arthur was the only person with medical training to attend the scene, and although he hurried to help, there was nothing he could do except confirm death.

The reaction from other inmates to Portugal's suicide ranged from sorrow to derision. In the hardened, dog-eat- dog atmosphere of La Joya, the most vulnerable were not necessarily given much sympathy.

Sometimes their treatment amounted to mental torture and the guards colluded in the bullying culture.

I could see directly into the opposite yard of Building Fifteen, which housed Panamanian prisoners. Every morning that I was there, in weather that spanned rain and blistering heat, I noticed a young inmate standing naked at the right-hand corner of the yard by the fence – always in exactly the same place. Someone would fill a bucket, grab a bass broom and use it to wash the boy down as if he were a mangy dog. After that ordeal was over, prisoners would taunt him and chase him round the yard with sticks. He was degraded and humiliated in this fashion every day, right under the noses of the authorities.

The spectacle of his misery made me cry with pity and with anger. I imagined the pain of his parents if they could see the way their son was suffering. It made me despair of how barbarically people could behave if they were allowed to. I caught the poor, persecuted inmate on film – I'll call him Senór J. Doe – as further proof of La Joya's cruelty. As I stood there, recording, our guard passed by and I asked him what was going on in Fifteen. Sergeant Solis just laughed and told me, "That's the crazy man!" The prisoner was a joke, there for the entertainment of others, and in Solis's book deserved no further consideration.

I doubt whether the young Panamanian had any concept of rehabilitation or the protection offered by a lawyer or the state. He was defenceless. I would like to think that he eventually found a release, but I am pessimistic that that is the case. His plight touched me, and I dedicate this section of the book to him.

These vulnerable individuals desperately need our help and a voice. They need a platform that will shine a spotlight on Panamá and seek change on their behalf, by pushing the country to enforce the code of international human rights it only pretends to follow.

Mental health problems were everywhere. A Jamaican in Six became an obsessive Christian evangelist, cornering anyone with the patience to listen to him and quoting long passages from the Bible about salvation. As his sanity deteriorated, he went on loud rampages throughout the building. As usual, our requests for intervention fell on deaf ears. Then one night the Jamaican upturned several 45-gallon drums of water stored in the roof and soaked many people sleeping in the bunks below. The authorities did rouse themselves to action at that point and removed him from the main building, not for the psychiatric assessment he needed but to slam him in the chutra. He returned a month later, having lost all contact with reality, in a more unstable condition than before.

La Joya worked on the basis of containment, punishment, institutionalised corruption and severely rationed human decency. Rehabilitation was not on the agenda. Everyone knew that the director was crooked as hell. He was even screwing one of the inmates' wives. And on the subject of dishonour, I came to find out that while Angel was in hibernation, his wife was having an affair with my attorney, Fidel. He even sent me a photo of both of them in a cosy, romantic pose. To this day, I am not sure if Angel knew what was going on.

I needed to document as many offences as possible to build my library of evidence, so I asked around to see if any of my contacts would, for a fee, film in other buildings on their cell phones. The response was initially wary but within a week, my WhatsApp was alive with damning footage from Buildings Seven, Eight, Nine, Eleven and Thirteen.

I immediately forwarded the clips to London, and they now form a significant part of my library. The footage would turn out to be vitally helpful for my campaign.

Word spread beyond La Joya, to other prisons in Panamá, of a swelling underground protest movement. Just when I was beginning to feel nervous about what I had started, I was contacted by someone who made my anxiety levels rocket. William Dathan Holbert, aka Wild Bill, an American-born serial killer of five people, contacted me from his Chiriquí cell more than 150 miles north of La Joya. He said that he wanted to join the cause. Hell, he could even rally a movement for us!

American serial killer **William 'Wild Bill' Holbert** and ex-wife....
Sky News-15 Aug 2017
... ex-wife have been jailed for the murders of five other US citizens in a Caribbean holiday resort. **William Dathan Holbert** nicknamed **Wild Bill**....

Wild Bill was a big-mouthed exhibitionist originally from North Carolina who already had his own campaign going. He had established Panamáhumanrights.com using WordPress on his phone. I suggested that we should mount a co-ordinated exposé, but Bill was only interested in slamming the Panamanian government on his Facebook page. He apparently took many beatings from the guards for his misjudged tactics.

Afterwards, Wild Bill generated renewed interest from newspapers, including the *Daily Mirror*, and from various TV channels, but instead of telling the media about the poor conditions for inmates, he made it sound as if he was living the life of Riley by boasting that his cell was better than most Panamanians' houses and showing off his plasma TV. It was a massive ego trip splattered across the press for all the wrong reasons. The tone of the coverage was catastrophic as far as I was concerned, because it trivialised serious issues and undermined the case I was still planning to build.

Bill had his own agenda. He could not carry out his campaign without funding, so he decided to change his persona from that of tubby, unrepentant murderer to muscle-bound prison pastor and redeemed man, so that he could gather in donations. I'm amazed that he was allowed to use YouTube, and that he is still using it, from inside jail, to gain an audience and raise money.

His opening pitch for Panamá Prison Ministries went like this:

> *"Panamá Prison Ministries seeks help to cure tuberculosis patients/inmates. $168 buys a cure for the disease that is killing seven inmates in the Chiriquí Public Prison. These are reformed, born-again Christians who deserve a second chance and not to die. Please visit williamdathanholbert. com to see what Panamá Prison Ministries does to bring Jesus Christ to the 1,200+ inmates of the notorious Chiriquí Public Prison."*

Amen, Wild Bill. Do you take PayPal?

I'll give him his due: he was resourceful. However, he never mentioned to his flock that he had divorced his third wife and was in a new relationship with a 20-year-old prostitute who regularly visited him in his Colon prison. At the time of writing, the couple have married and now enjoy sanctioned conjugal rights when she comes to see him. He also posts frequent footage of himself barbecuing sausages on an outdoor grill and downing beers with his acolytes. Maybe Bill, of all the people who have suffered in Panamá's unspeakable judicial system, has discovered that elusive resort and spa experience while serving his 47-year sentence.

He was good enough to provide me with a rare treat after we finished our telephone conversation, though. He used his contacts to provide me – for a mere $10 – with the first McAngus and fries I had tasted in well over a year. It wasn't exactly piping hot by the time it reached me and it had probably been smuggled into jail inside some cop's trousers but, man, it tasted delicious after removing the gherkin.

There was clearly huge potential support out there for my campaign. It caught an existing flood of resentment towards the Panamanian authorities and it represented an opportunity for me to accelerate my evidence-gathering.

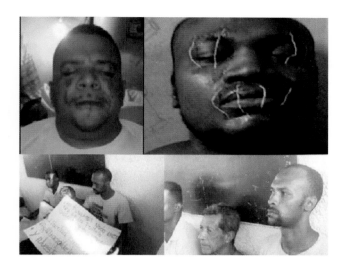

Many in our building went to extreme measures to show exactly how they felt, especially a cadre of nine angry Venezuelan prisoners. These guys were used to dictatorship, and any punishment La Joya could mete out was probably a comparative breeze. Early one December morning in 2013, there was a commotion outside in the yard. The Venezuelans wanted to make a dramatic point about how they were silenced and ignored in prison to a visiting Christian group. As the guests approached our building, the Venezuelans unfurled a 'Libertad!' banner of protest – but there was something more shocking. The inmates had sewn together their own lips and eyelids. Blood was streaming down their faces like tears.

Their courage definitely made an impact on me, but on the Christian group, there to save us? To my amazement, the people in it walked straight past without comment.

The majority simply wanted to avert their gaze from the scandalous conditions of Panamá's prisons. It wasn't even as if all the inmates could be dismissed as guilty, given the high number who were trapped there awaiting trial.

Some who didn't avert their gaze were Prisoners Abroad, a dedicated UK charity supporting the essential needs of UK citizens imprisoned overseas. Their $90 every three months was greatly appreciated, as was their assistance in locating essential documents and mustering support. On my trip back to London, one of my missions was to visit them personally to give them a big thank you, which I finally did in 2014.

I appreciate now the gratitude I should feel for living in a country with freedom of speech. In Panamá, saying the wrong thing or 'insulting the flag' in any manner deemed expedient by the government could lead you to several years in jail.

Okke Ornstein is an investigative journalist from the Netherlands who used to live in Panamá and who ran the Banana Republic website. In 2012 he ran a number of pieces exposing fraud and corruption. One of the individuals named, Monte Freisner, filed a complaint that resulted in Ornstein being issued with a criminal defamation charge. In 2016, Ornstein was picked up at the cops' favourite spot of Tocumen International Airport and slapped in prison. It was only the international outcry against Ornstein's heavy- handed treatment that got him released, by presidential decree from Juan Carlos Varela. He was granted a pardon, but chose to leave Panamá in any case. As he put it himself:

> *"I have kind of had it with the Panamanian hostility towards journalism and transparency. There is still yet another case pending in the courts — despite a presidential pardon, mind you — that Monte Friesner filed as well, for example. Of course, that'll be dealt with, but it's impossible to publish on a blog like this in a country where everybody and his brother can file a bogus criminal defamation complaint and where the public ministry will in 99 per cent of the cases then run with it."*

Okke now lives in the Netherlands with his family, as far away as possible from Panamá, the country that hands out Interpol red tickets like confetti.

Dutch journalist Okke Ornstein jailed in Panama for ... - Refworld
www.refworld.org › docid

29 Nov 2016 - **Ornstein**, a **Panama**-based journalist who runs the news website Bananama Republic, was arrested in relation to a 2012 criminal defamation....

In my research, I came across a case from the last century that made me wonder if the Panamanian habit of imprisoning impudent foreigners has deep historical roots. In 1911, a 32-year-old American, James Perry, spent five months of hard labour in a Colon prison for alleged false imprisonment. He eventually returned to his Brooklyn home for the sole purpose of suing Panamá for $10,000 – or around $500,000 in modern money.

In memory of those who did not make it out alive from Building Six, in this their lives will live on. I have built a special website especially designed for you the readers. It isn't open to the general public, and you will have unlimited private access. I assure you that you will see everything live as if it was yesterday; all the people mentioned will now come to life before your very eyes. Enjoy my friends!

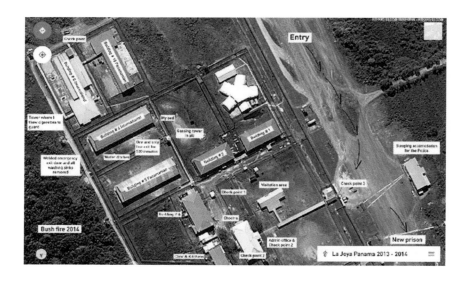

247

11

YOU HAVE GAS

The whistle, sharp and urgent, from the look-outs perched in the attic spaces, was our first warning. The sound rang from building to building, amplified by the thin walls, and it told us that something bad was brewing.

That August morning in 2014, cops began massing at the administration block soon after daybreak. There were at least 200 of them, armed with guns, batons and gas masks, and they were obviously preparing to mount a major raid. What we couldn't tell was which building or buildings they planned to target.

The sight of our normally indolent captors rigged out in full combat gear was quite a draw. Each building they passed erupted in cheering and catcalls from the inmates who were pressed against the windows and the entrance door. This was the most entertaining spectacle we had been treated to for months. We just needed some popcorn to get the full cinematic experience.

But as the cops marched past Building Five, then Building Seven, the truth hit us. They were bloody well heading straight towards Building Six. Now, all the laughter and jeers were going to be at our expense.

The smirking faces of the cops acquired a sinister meaning. They knew, whatever the pretext for the raid, that our building held La Joya's mother lode of cash. We were the source of the fattest dollar bills, the choicest liquor, the best phones and laptops in the compound, and if we could be panicked into abandoning all of the above, the cops would have easy pickings. They were practically salivating at the prospect.

Many of the inmates had lost their precious possessions in past sweeps and they had no intention of losing them again. There was an immediate rush to hide cash and prohibited items and devices.

As the cops breached the front door, all hell broke loose. They moved en-masse into the gancha area, but it took them valuable time to make their way across it to the inmates who had retreated and were still busy stashing goods, while pushing and shouting in the chaos. I should have been one of the first to get out, considering my prime position by the door, but I, too, needed to hide my phone. My Blackberry was my lifeline and I fumbled it into the false leg of the next bed in the sincere hope of seeing it again when the raid was over.

The cops wanted to get access to the cells, where the richest drug barons slept, behind the gancha, but there was a problem. They did not have the key to the door separating the two areas. Nikki, the designated inmate key-holder, was still high on cocaine from the night before and he was at the furthest end of the building in cell A-18, too out of it to hear the guards' orders.

It was hilarious to see these tooled-up cops pumped with adrenaline and clanking with weaponry being forced to stand and wait for a stoned convict to let them in. Predictably enough, they began to get seriously pissed off. Their rage mounted with every passing minute and, finally, they threw CS gas canisters through the attic roof space to get a response. But canisters crashed red-hot onto the inmates below, in both the gancha and the cells.

Suddenly, everyone was screaming. It was impossible to see more than a few inches in front of you because of the thick fumes billowing in the air. In the rolling fog, as the gancha erupted in panic, the cops unleashed a barrage of pellets from their guns. One shot ricocheted and hit me in the eye. At first, I barely felt it over the combination of ammonia and chlorine released by the CS gas, but it soon began to hurt like hell.

When coke-addled Nikki finally emerged after his wake- up call and opened the door to the cells, there was a solid mass of more than 500 desperate men shoving their way towards the single exit, a few feet from my bed. The outgoing tide of inmates was strong enough to sweep along anyone in its way. As I was pushed through the door to the yard, I was able – being taller than most – to see over the heads of the other prisoners that two cops were firing pellets from their guns directly into the dispersing crowd.

This was no accidental reaction. The guards were crouched down on one knee in firing position and they were aiming at people's backs. I could hardly believe it. Police are not supposed to carry live weapons inside the prison compounds, never mind discharge them at the fleeing inmates.

You could hear the pellets bouncing off walls and the savage yells of those who were hit. Prisoners were still streaming out of the building. Once outside, they collapsed choking and flailing on the ground like wounded animals.

I was glad when I tripped and sent one of the guards sprawling. I certainly didn't stop to apologise. All I wanted to do was run to the far end of the yard, next to the perimeter fence and, I hoped, out of harm's way.

Every breath I took was agony, my vision was swimming and the back of my throat was scoured raw. The injured eye was a solid blood red and I had to squeeze it shut against the light, hoping to God that my sight was not permanently damaged. My best buddy, Arthur, had been badly trampled in the stampede and was now slumped against the fence, gasping for air, as he tried to clear the gas from his damaged lungs. Someone had run back into the building to collect his oxygen respirator, but no other emergency equipment was available to help him.

Plenty of us counted ourselves lucky that day to have made it out alive. We could have easily been poisoned by the fumes. Or one rogue spark could have caught a mattress and incinerated the lot of us.

The building looked as if it was exhaling fog from every window: there was a toxic mushroom cloud hanging above it – and that was the point when the previously still day began to whip up a wind. The front cover of the book depicts this event and was taken by an inmate opposite us, in Building Five.

The acrid gas started to drift uncontrollably over the rest of the compound and then to disperse into the surrounding blocks. You bet the cops were scared of what they had started! They had created a perfect storm out of their own incompetence, brutality and greed.

I'd grabbed a scrap of dirty cloth that I pressed over my mouth to try and stop the gas from penetrating my lungs. I don't think it worked.

A few inmates had ripped the gas masks from the cops inside, and were now wearing them. Others had pulled their T-shirts up over their faces.

Semi-disguised as they were, some prisoners talked about staging a breakout while the guards were distracted by the havoc around us. Many of us were simmering with all the pent-up aggression and anger that had built during incarceration in La Joya. The mistreatment, the humiliations, the shitty conditions, the revolting food, the boredom, the fear, the overcrowding: the daily lot of the average inmate, endured because he had no choice, was now the fuel that powered a riot.

Simply put, this was a chance for serious revenge.

It was the first time I had ever seen inmates rally together for a cause. Many of the men had been convicted of violent offences, others had been members of Colombia's rebel force: they were the natural candidates to lead a fight-back. But we had all been hardened by prison and even the quieter guys were filled with a warrior spirit. An increasing number hid their faces by rolling up their yellow T-shirts like bandanas so that all you could see was their eyes and they began to look like soldiers readying themselves for battle.

The jumpy, fully armed cops on one side faced the mutinous inmates on the other. The atmosphere reminded me of a Formula One starting line: revving engines everywhere, just waiting for the flag to drop. You could feel the tension and excitement crackling in the air. No one was about to back down, but who had the balls to turn the confrontation into an out-and-out fight?

The experience was vivid and unreal at the same time, like being caught in some manic scene from a movie. If not for the pungent smell of the CS gas and the pain in my eyes, I could have persuaded myself that I was on the set of a live-action prison drama. I'd seen enough of them; I just wasn't sure I could predict the ending this time.

The mob of inmates was certainly angrier than the cops. They had ripped the goalposts from the earth in the yard to set up a blockade around the gate to the perimeter fence, and then piled it with rocks and chunks of broken concrete until it was at least six foot high. There were further pyramids of debris, to be used as possible missiles or to be climbed as look-out points, scattered round the yard.

The chants of the inmates rose and fell rhythmically as the day gathered heat. Some strutted back and forth, their chests puffed out, issuing a stream of contempt for the prison regime. We loudly agreed with them that the director was a cheating bastard. The Venezuelans, being from a country where civil protest was common, were especially eager to escalate the situation, but the rest of us were wary of coming under fire again or being sprayed with more gas.

By 9.30am the administration staff had begun turning up for work. The warden and the police commissioner did their best to calm things down and it went a long way to achieving some kind of peace. We negotiated to have the sickest of the injured prisoners seen by doctors. Arthur was loaded onto a food cart and then taken to the barricaded fence, where cops agreed that he could pass through to the clinic. Other men who had been peppered in the back with shot lay in the dirt with blood seeping through their T-shirts. Their cries for help were overwhelming.

Meanwhile, a phalanx of police guards had lined up behind the fence with grenade launchers and shotguns at the ready and a SWAT team had assembled in ninja gear, their shields and batons held high, as they awaited the order to strike.

The police commander, a big man, strolled up to the fencing. The prison director, who wasn't as confident, remained behind him, preferring to let someone else come within range of a possible hail of rocks. The commander held up his hands in a T shape, indicating that it was time to talk. He reinforced his superior fire power by stating that his men could be ordered to shoot, but that that would result in needless casualties.

"You should all just peacefully return to your cells," he said. (We'd been pretty peaceful in there before the police had arrived, but he seemed to have forgotten that.) The request did not go down well with the hard core of three dozen or so inmates who were aching for a fight. They had gone beyond the point of complaining about conditions and just wanted to draw first blood.

Breakfast was delivered, but not allowed through the gate. As Six was temporarily uninhabitable because of the gas canisters, the inmates had nowhere to retreat to and had to follow the shade of the building to avoid the by-now blazing sun. A few did re-enter the cells to retrieve their phones because they wanted to take photographs of the devastation or roam the yard filming all the cops. This was probably the only time that the police got an inkling of how many mobiles were truly in circulation.

Just to add to the noise and confusion, the sensationalist local TV station, TVN-2, scrambled a helicopter to circle the prison in hopes of filming a blood bath. The camera crew got shots of inmates holding up banners that proclaimed 'Libertad' and 'Abuso Varela' in huge letters and the story broke as live news all over Panamá. You can't say that we failed to take advantage of the media attention.

The standoff lasted into the late afternoon. By then most inmates were thirsty, hungry and exhausted, and still nursing injuries from the earlier pandemonium. A rudimentary clear-up operation got rid of the exploded gas canisters and inmates trickled back inside the building to their cells and beds. However, it was not until the following day that those hit with pellets were taken for medical attention.

Next, representatives from various embassies reluctantly began to appear – the visits were outside their normal duties and disrupted their calendars – to take statements from their citizens about what had happened at La Joya.

The whole sorry episode gradually faded. For all the drama, it achieved nothing of any value; conditions did not improve, they got worse, and the cops did not even get their hands on our phones, as they had planned to that fateful morning. The animosity towards them simmered for weeks. There were other protests about the conditions, other shouts of "Libertad!" and on several occasions the cops had to barge their way inside the barricaded buildings.

The near-riot had an odd fall-out for me, though. The following day I received an unexpected visitor.

In through the gates of Building Six walked the police commissioner for the whole of Panamá, Samuel Zambrano. Even our usually tough old guard was stuttering and quaking with nerves. Zambrano was top dog: no one screwed with him. He reported directly to the president of Panamá and the orders he passed down the chain also issued straight from Varela.

The cops around us were astounded. They did not know that Zambrano was dating a very good friend of mine from the British embassy, who I knew via my charity work and from the years when I was a regular guest at ambassadorial black-tie events.

We stood in the yard, beyond the earshot of the duty guard and the many onlookers peering through the bars. Zambrano asked about my dark red eye and I casually said that his guys had shot me as we were escaping from the gas in Building Six, and that my vision was now impaired.

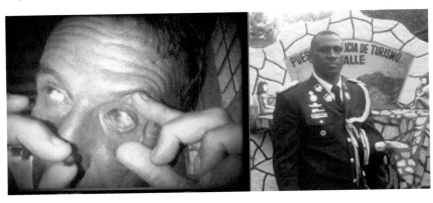

He decided to take a selfie of the two of us standing there and pulled out his mobile – at which point Leo could bear it no more and ran over to offer his services as cameraman. He was also quite eager to include himself in a shot or two. Who can blame him? This was probably the closest he would ever get to Varela, and when you have already served 10 years, any lifeline is better than none. It was a one in a million opportunity for him and we were all running on the fumes of a dream. He hoped that he could get a presidential pardon, but the sad reality is that he is stagnating in La Joya to this day.

If it did nothing else, Zambrano's impromptu visit vastly improved my credibility within the prison community and made both guards and inmates more respectful towards me: I was now someone with possible influence. The practical benefits of my supposedly hot government contacts were, however, non-existent. The directors rewarded our rebellion by seeing that standards plummeted lower than ever and I suffered alongside everyone else from the muddy water and meagre scraps of food.

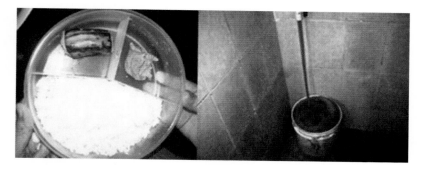

During the administration of Martinelli, our meals had been contracted out. The food delivered was barely edible, generally poorly cooked rice with such things as putrid chicken scraps mixed into it, feathers, smashed bones and skin included. All at a daily cost of $1.49 for each prisoner.

With the new Varela presidency in 2014, the food provision was moved in-house and inmates were given the task of cooking. This helped to improve matters short-term... until those working in the kitchen figured out how to feed themselves lavishly, make a profit by selling off supplies on the black market, and get away with off-loading rubbish on the rest of us. We were lucky to get a can of mixed vegetables mushed into a vat of stodgy, tasteless rice. The kitchens boys got away with it because they made sure the police were well fed.

Even for one of the worst prisons in the world, La Joya excelled itself with the supper of two stale biscuits and a small can of sardines – minus ring pull – we were served one evening. We wondered if we were being set up in some cunning scheme to discover illicit weapons. The only way to open the can was with a knife. A look-out scanned the scene for guards, we got an all-clear and suddenly out of pockets, shoes and God knew where else, hundreds of knives appeared. I had thought only a few existed inside the prison, as they were normally kept carefully hidden. It turned out that I was one of the few not to have a homemade weapon, fashioned from the very same metal as the sardine cans. Prisoners had discovered that the thin, flexible tin was the perfect grade for making blades and copying keys – soda cans being too flimsy. They used to open and flatten the sardine cans so that they could score the exact shape and outline of whatever key they were counterfeiting. It was a method that had worked on several previous escapes. There was some poetic justice in the fact that our terrible supper would come back to bite the cops in the ass later.

Edmund, an Israeli kidnapper, was someone who almost made it to freedom with the help of sardines. He managed to hide himself in the administration block after a meeting with his attorney – behind the ceiling of the toilets, in fact. When night fell, he used his new set of keys and a stolen cop's uniform to make a run for it. The daring bid would have worked, had he not fumbled at what was literally the final gate.

August 3 2014 was my 51st birthday. It was a milestone date for me, in a month that was to be scarred by death and unrest. I was desperately missing my kids, my twin brother and the rest of my family. The reality of prison meant that there was nothing to celebrate, but I decided to do it nonetheless.

I put on a brave smile for my children and sent them a picture of me posing in the gancha, with the message that I was 'in a good place'. I hope they missed the joke. I wanted them to think that I was coping and happy but that was far from the truth.

I gathered together a group of close friends that included Grande, Ben and Arthur and we celebrated by sitting together on the cold floor and drinking moonshine by the light of our phones. A talented Colombian guitarist serenaded us while we toasted the future, and for two hours it was just possible to enjoy the beautiful music and forget ourselves.

It was the first time in months that I had mustered a smile. The next morning, I was greeted with many back-to-back 'bings' from well-wishers on my phone. The sound was always a good one. It was a reminder that out there, in the world beyond prison, someone loved me. Reading the messages from my family and friends was bittersweet. Though it was great to be remembered and missed, I wondered how many more birthdays I faced in this dump. I had no calendar to mark off each day that I'd already spent there, but I had devised my own equivalent by chalking marks on the wall using the gaps in the wire fence. Every morning I drank a cup of tea while I stood outside, and every morning I swung the used teabag at the fence when I'd finished. The attached string lassoed itself to the wire and the bags hung there like forgotten Christmas decorations, hundreds of them.

I had spent 15 months in La Joya to date and been through the disappointment of seven cancelled hearings. There was never a satisfactory answer when I asked what was causing the delays, and the numbers were stacking up against me. It was a constant effort to avoid tipping into depression, but I gave myself a pep-talk to ward off the doldrums. Keep going. Work harder. Think positive, Nick.

I heard an inmate shout from the yard. "We caught a sloth!" A *sloth?* I ran to the scene, and could see what looked like a cute, cuddly bear with long claws being prized off the perimeter fence by two inmates. They were almost hysterical with excitement. For a mad moment I wondered if a prisoner had some scheme to turn this wild animal into a pet, and then it became obvious that more basic plans were afoot: sloth stew.

A crowd gathered and began to stoke a fire. The sloth's throat was slashed while the guard took his $5 to turn the other way and ignore the knives openly on display. Then the gutting process began. You could tell that some prisoners got a fix from using their bare hands to rip out the stomach and intestines, all of which went into a cooking pot.

I'd been a fisherman used to reeling in big catches, so I wasn't squeamish, but it still upset me to see another creature being treated so callously. The bloodlust of the kill was unsettling to watch, and it revealed the true nature of some prisoners.

Never mind my reservations, those from rural Colombia regarded sloth as a rare delicacy. The stew was auctioned off at $2 a bowl and it was a wildly popular with other prisoners. Chunks of meat, even if they came garnished with bits of fur and gristle, were a big improvement on our usual greasy chicken skin and feather soup. All the same, I decide to give the bush meat experience a swerve.

The unfortunate sloth was not the only animal to be handed a Building Six death sentence. Our yard backed on to an area of dense, swampy jungle that was home to all sorts of wildlife. A month earlier, the pop-up prison barbeque had featured a lovely crocodile stew. Before that, roasted boa constrictor had been on the menu.

I often thought it was a toss-up which of the many species you met in the yard was more primitive: the innocent strays from the jungle or the two-legged predators from inside La Joya.

12

DAY OF THE DEAD

The endemic abuses and violence of La Joya were of course appalling, but worst of all was the thing you could never escape: the utter, grinding boredom.

The monotony of day after pointless day, packed in with the same people, staring at the same filthy walls, induced a sense of claustrophobia that was too much for some to bear.

Suicides were common, but people are inventive souls, even in the most desperate circumstances, and the prisoners found ways to occupy their time that, in many cases, bore a distinct similarity to their pastimes on the outside – namely, gambling and booze.

The presence of all this liquor relieved the tension for some, while causing problems for others. Nights would be filled with parties, which would start after the guard had closed the door at 5pm. These parties would be fuelled by the enthusiasm of both Colombians and Mexicans, who'd be shouting and screaming over the blaring music.

This was no different to typical city life. By the time night kicked in, the place would be full of drug selling, pop-up hairdressers, cantinas and casinos. Everyone was trying to make a buck out of the day's trade, and it was amazing seeing this village come to life, bursting with energy.

If you wanted to be involved in the genuine national lottery, even that was possible. Yet how would you be able to cash in, especially within the confines of this hideous jail? As for the booze, everyone indulged, including me.

God knows what effect it was having on our livers, but it made the days pass more quickly, and the fact that it was generously dispensed to most of the guards made our time more bearable too. One of our building commandos, Solis, was unable to resist the free drinks on offer and we were happy to provide them. As soon as he was shitfaced, we'd be free to do whatever we pleased. Perfect.

Solis regularly downed a six pack of Miller Lite and would stumble around like most Panamanians, who drank like fish. On one occasion Solis wasn't even able to stand or walk – totally pie-eyed. Unfortunately, his commanding officer then arrived for a brief patrol around the building. Solis had to be steadied by me and Portugal, and neither one of us was exactly sober ourselves, but we did our best. We slapped a pair of sunglasses on him quickly to cover the glaze of his eyes. We could have left him to deal with his own shit, but if discovered, he would most certainly have been replaced with a stricter officer – one that could perhaps ruin my plan completely.

One such was Sergeant Santa Maria, a money-grabbing bastard who was on my WhatsApp. This little punk took advantage of his authority and milked every ounce of strength I had. When he rolled up to Building Six, he was only focused on me. "Tuffney!" he'd shout.

The second I saw his fat ass, I would head straight to the back of the building. He'd then have to waste his precious time trying to find me, which was not easy. After all, there were around 477 other inmates to go through.

The first thing you must understand is that La Joya is the last grazing ground before police retirement. They all had to do their stint there before hanging up their badges. You would never see young cops in Pampers at La Joya; those officers were seasoned veterans from Noriega's era, and needed to extract as much money as possible in six months. The unofficial motto was, "What happens in La Joya stays in La Joya."

Drinking that local La Joya moonshine was actually a form of gambling in itself, but as some were to find, the stakes were so much higher than a few dollars.

A pair of young men from cell A-14 sadly got into the hooch early on, and they would drink on a daily basis starting at around 6am. The stuff was as close to pure alcohol as you could get. It was rough on the old stomach: the liquid would catch fire from a lighter, which was how you'd know it was the good stuff. You could have probably run a car on it.

I remember warning both of them, but especially Mark Bodden, a Caymanian serving a sentence as a drugs mule. That stuff packed a punch, and could severely damage his liver since he was really going all in. I never saw him without his chipped ceramic tin mug in his hand, mixed with a splash of orange juice, having seen many like him before on the streets of Panamá during their seriously shortened lives. Some drunks had fallen from the attic space above the cells before, their bodies bouncing off the wet concrete floor. I saw many sustain serious head injuries, and most ended up in Santo Tomás Hospital for weeks chained to their hospital beds. Most such accidents occurred when inmates were scaling the side of the cells to enter the attic space.

This was exactly how young Mark, inevitably nicknamed 'Cayman' after his island homeland, tragically died on August 18, 2014. He was due for release less than a year later.

He suffered a massive head injury after falling out of his bunk – eight feet above the concrete floor. So, a drunken accident plain and simple? Well no, not exactly – this young man's tragic death was not only predictable, as you'll see, but was also entirely preventable, and culpability extended not only to the prison service, but also to the British embassy.

I just can't forgive them. The British consul came out to La Joya two weeks before Mark's death, accompanied by an envoy for Central America. Because the Caymans Islands is a British Overseas Territory, their citizens are able to use the consular services of the UK Foreign Office. On my covertly filmed video, you can clearly hear Cayman demanding that the consul come and inspect his living quarters, and find him a safe place to sleep.

Leo and Ben both said that he needed to sort out his sleeping accommodation because it was so horrendous. Leo and Ben told the consul in a heated meeting, "You need to get this guy a proper bed because where he is sleeping is too dangerous!" They said his sleeping accommodation was not acceptable because he was a very tall guy sleeping on a rickety bed.

These British government officials were a total joke, their visits just fan service. The embassy did their best to walk away from even partial accountability for any part of Mark's death. Before going on your next holiday, it is worth Googling the term 'Beyond Discretion'. It tells you what the embassy will not do; it'll open your eyes to the legal implications, to the fact that you are their servant. Remember this before you venture abroad.

The embassy's most common catchphrase was and probably still is, "If we do that for you, we will have to do it for everyone." I've had a lot of time to wonder why our diplomats abroad are so useless and a few conclusions have come to mind.

The British embassy was always scared to raise things with the Panamanian authorities because they didn't want to rock the boat – it was all about trade. But the fact that they used Panamanian staff rather than British to save money was also part of the problem. Those guys had different standards when it came to prisons, and when they heard of a case like Mark's, they just shrugged their shoulders and said that it happened all the time. London puts these people in place to save a buck and they don't consider the long-term effects. I would say that more than half of the staff in the British embassy were Panamanian, yet the Americans don't operate that way: all their staff are Americans. The British embassy runs on a shoestring when you consider that the UK does $5 billion in trade with Panamá each year, with a total staff of just 40 (half of them locals). The Americans do $15 billion in trade and have a staff of 500 people, all US natives.

Naturally, the consul didn't take up Mark's invitation to come into Building Six to inspect the bed for himself, but if he had, he'd have seen that Mark had built it way up above the door-line by suspending a thin piece of wood between the rafters. Two weeks later, Mark was hitting the liquor again from early in the morning. It was his usual combination of moonshine and Ron Abuelo, literally 'grandfather rum', a brand made by the president of Panamá's own company, ironically enough. At around 8.30pm, he went up to his top deck bed and lost his balance, falling eight feet headfirst onto the concrete. Everyone could see at once that he was seriously hurt. He was unconscious and blood was oozing from his ears in ominous sign of brain injury. I gasped at the sight of his left arm, which was bent at an unnatural angle, but broken bones were the least of Mark's problems.

We had a medical emergency on our hands. Arthur was called and came as quickly as he could, armed with his stethoscope and a flashlight and trailing his vital personal supply of oxygen. There was little he could do but stay close by and monitor Mark's condition. A sheet was slipped underneath him as a makeshift stretcher so that he could be carried to the front door of the gancha, as close as possible to help when – or if – it arrived. He was laid gently on the floor at the foot of my bed, where he suffered seizures and seemed to drift in and out of consciousness.

It tore me apart to see him in such a pitiful state when a few minutes earlier he had been laughing during a call home to his parents and happily celebrating. It was a brutal lesson in the sheer, random cruelty of prison life.

Arthur told us that Mark was probably bleeding internally, and that the blood had now built up in his brain. There was absolutely nothing he could do. Everyone could sense how desperate the situation was, but we were just as powerless as Arthur. Our cop had signed off four hours ago, and after he'd finished his shift there was no one in authority to intervene. Whatever happened in that building after hours whether the crisis was murder, fire, epileptic fit or fatal injury – we were on our own.

Night had fallen and it was totally black outside, except for a beam from the one security flood light that swept over the silhouettes of the feral cats in the yard. The nearest point of contact was the guard tower way off in the distance, adjacent to Building Five. We all frantically tried to get its attention. Inmates took to shrieking from the attic space and through the window bars. But although the guard in the tower must have been able to see and hear us, he wasn't about to come down or to radio for help.

Desperate to raise the alarm, the guys in the gym snatched all the weights out of the cupboard and four of them lifted a 500-pound dumbbell and started to ram it against the door of Building Six as hard as they could. I wondered how much punishment this door had soaked up over the years. Like the stubborn guards high up in their towers, it didn't yield an inch. What else could we do? Some of us even tried to summon assistance by using the payphones to call 911. Yet I knew that neither the Panamanian police nor the ambulance service were going to arrive. All that was left to us was to attempt to make Mark comfortable while his body shook in spasms and blood trickled from his ears.

I kept asking myself, *What if this were my son?* It was such a terrible waste of a young life, such a needless, traumatic end far away from home and the family that doted on him, especially his beloved grandma. His death was a direct result of the lazy, uncaring Panamanian police attitude to prisoners. It was preventable, and that is what makes it so barbaric.

All night, he lay on the floor at the foot of my bed – 12 long hours during which he received not a shred of the medical attention that might have saved him.

The guard came at 8am, by which time Mark had badly deteriorated and was more out of this world than in it. Even then, the cop was in no hurry, despite the fact that we were all screaming at him to call an ambulance. He placed his coffee carefully on his desk, opened his backpack, withdrew the day's ledger, then walked round the building before finally getting around to opening the door.

In place of an available gurney or wheelchair, we lifted Cayman on his sheet onto a soiled food cart and made our way up to the administration building, where he waited another three hours for a vehicle to arrive. The last I saw of this young man was when the police dumped him like a carcass into the load-bay of a pick-up truck. God bless you, Mark. Panamá, you should be ashamed.

Cayman was eventually taken to the hospital in the mid- morning, but by then he was in a coma and he never regained consciousness. Within days, his family was contacted through the British embassy, who asked for permission to remove his life support. Despite the heroic but impotent efforts of Arthur Porter and his cellmates to save him, Cayman lost his fight.

The British embassy had known that Mark needed a proper bed and the prison authorities had ignored our cries for help on his behalf. But somehow it was nobody's fault but his own that Cayman was dead.

Arthur decided to blow the whistle by speaking to the *Cayman Compass* newspaper after Mark's body was sent back home, and he told them exactly what had gone on. The *Compass* reported their scoop from La Joya in this way:

> *'Three of Mr Bodden's fellow prisoners, including Dr Arthur Porter, a high-profile physician wanted in Canada in connection with a bribery scandal involving Montreal's McGill University Hospital, have been in contact with the Cayman Compass to give their version of events surrounding the death.*
>
> *The Caymanian prisoner was left without access to proper medical attention for nearly 12 hours after sustaining serious head injuries when he fell eight feet from his "home-made bed space", according to an unofficial two- page medical report produced by Dr Porter.'*

In his best physician's formal style, Arthur gave the Panamanians both barrels: "I am of the opinion that if Mr Bodden had received a prompt transfer to a hospital with neurological competence, he would have had a substantial chance of making a complete recovery."

Leo and Ben also made their points with the *Compass*, and again, both were introduced to the readers with their criminal records uppermost for full disclosure. Leo was accurately described as a 'British drug dealer locked up for money laundering who has been representing foreign inmates in talks with prison officials and embassy diplomats to improve conditions.' They also dropped in that he was a 57-year-old former boxer and a 'drugs kingpin' who had seen 60 people die during his time in La Joya from accidents, stabbings, fights and disease. Which was also accurate.

Leo told the *Compass*:

> 'Mark was not a bad kid. He made a mistake, did something to make some money and he ended up here.
>
> 'What happened was an accident, but he didn't have to die. It could have been prevented if he had got medical care. He died because of neglect. There's no medical centre, there's not even any water. We have to buy everything we have. Mark had good people looking out for him in Cayman. His grandmother sent him money and the church was helping him out. You have to buy everything, you have to buy your bed, you have to buy toilet paper.'

Leo also told them about the overcrowding, with 506 foreign prisoners crammed into a 180-bed facility. Ben, who was serving a 112-month sentence for trying to smuggle cocaine, added his weight with WhatsApp messages describing Mark's final hours.

He related our frantic efforts to raise the alarm in vain, as well as Arthur's examination of Mark and efforts to help him.

> 'We carried him to the door. He was in a really, really bad way. We banged and banged on the door and at 8.30am. Sunday a policeman came and opened it and they took him away. Monday morning, we heard he had died. I believe he died because nobody came here to get him out and give him the care he needed to survive.'

The Panamanian authorities did perform toxicology tests on Mark and no doubt the readings for his blood alcohol levels were off the scale, but somehow this report went missing. An official document that showed prisoners getting blind drunk in La Joya would have been considered 'unhelpful' to the governing powers – especially if the liquor in question happened to be the President's own brand. Mark died a 'natural' death and that was that, as far as Panamá was concerned. Those of us who saw what really happened knew the truth, of course: that he was the victim of a whole catalogue of callous and preventable errors.

Armed with the information that Arthur fed them through the *Compass*, Mark's family in the Caymans decided to take the issue to court and pushed for an inquest. The Cayman authorities duly applied to Panamá for the post- mortem and toxicology reports, but nothing came back, despite repeated requests.

The deputy governor's office in the Caymans was advised of Mark's death by the British embassy, but once again, 'our man in Panamá' was found wanting when it came to even trying to get answers.

The official statement from the Cayman deputy governor ran: 'The circumstances of his death have not been confirmed, but we were advised by the family that it was accidental. We are now awaiting the results of the prison and police investigation. Our thoughts and prayers are with his family.' They could wait as long as they liked for those 'investigations' because they would never happen. The only thing the Panamanian authorities ever sent back to the Caymans in the matter of Mark Philip Bodden, deceased, was his body.

The coroner's inquest took place more than two years later in December 2016, and while the Cayman authorities had done their best to get to the bottom of his death, it was clear they were being stonewalled by the corrupt Panamá establishment.

Queen's coroner Eileen Nervik described the inquest as 'rather unique' given the circumstances and limited information. But sad to say there was nothing unique about Mark's death, as Arthur had told the *Compass* when he blew the whistle two years before:

> *'I have been incarcerated here for over 14 months and can attest that this is not an isolated incident... Not having any ability to contact authorities, transfer or even have basic resuscitation equipment represents a significant systemic flaw in the delivery of medical care in the Panamanian penitentiary system.'*

After considering the information that was available, jurors returned an open verdict – meaning that the evidence was insufficient for them to reach any other conclusion. They also found that the cause of death was unknown. The coroner explained that the inquest was being held because Mr Bodden's body was repatriated to Cayman and the family had requested an investigation and a second post- mortem examination.

"He was a member of our community, so we need to resolve the issue as far as possible," she commented.

The only witness to give evidence in person was government pathologist Dr Shravana Jyoti. Jurors were handed copies of the report written after an autopsy was performed in Cayman by pathologist Michaele Enghardt on September 5, 2014. Dr Jyoti explained that an autopsy had already been performed in Panamá, but a complete report from that procedure was not available. Cayman authorities did receive a post-mortem form from Panamá's National Directorate of Civil Registry. It listed causes of death to be oedema and brain haemorrhage, with severe head trauma, with pneumonia being a contributing factor. Not even a hospital record was available.

Dr Enghardt did not make a finding as to cause of death, but she did comment on the cause as found in Panamá. She said a small amount of coagulated blood in the cranial cavity might allude to a prior haemorrhage. Examination of the head showed no external marks of trauma or lacerations. There was no evidence of a skull fracture and no trauma to the neck. The coroner explained the possible verdicts the jury could reach, such as natural causes, misadventure, suicide, lawful or unlawful killing.

One of the jurors could clearly see right through the wall of silence from Panamá City and asked about a finding of negligence, but unfortunately the law of inquests doesn't allow that. The coroner emphasised that an inquest is a public fact-finding inquiry and not a trial; the jurors' role was to find facts as to the physical cause and manner of death, not to accord blame. It was up to them as to whether they accepted the findings of the autopsy performed in Panamá, she said. If they did not, they could say the cause of death was unknown. If the cause was unknown, they might ask themselves how they could know the manner of death, she observed. Cayman authorities had worked diligently to get more information from Panamá, she noted, but had been unsuccessful. "We did try," she told jurors before they considered their verdict.

Indeed they did, but could the same be said of the Foreign Office officials in Panamá? Not in my opinion.

Death came in many different forms. Before entering La Joya, I had never seen a corpse before, other than that of my much-mourned pet hamster. In prison, what I saw scarred me for life. In March 2014, things came to a boiling point when a Gillette razor blade was pulled out during a fight between inmates and faces were slashed. That was bad enough to witness but there was to be another incident that was far, far worse. This time it wasn't a razor being used as a weapon, but a machete that had been stolen from the landscaping crew and somehow made its way into our block.

At about 11.30pm, all hell broke loose between rival gangs over a kilo of coke destined for Building Six, which had been intercepted by inmates from Building Seven. The informant who had tipped off the thieves lived in cell B-12, and he paid a horrific penalty for his disloyalty. By the sunrise after the coke went astray, his arms and legs had been hacked from his body and his head had been severed. His limbs and head were then arranged on his torso as a graphic warning from the gang leaders to anyone else who might be thinking of double-crossing them.

The sight of his mutilated, dismembered remains will haunt me for the rest of my life.

The murder did not draw a line under hostilities; it raised the tension to an even higher level. This being La Joya, money was also to be made out of the feud. Depraved Panamanian individuals had filmed the killing as a snuff video and were hawking it around for five bucks a pop. The last one I saw showed the murderers holding up the guy's head as a trophy, while another inmate waved the severed arms high in the air.

Be warned. These images are on the site with a warning banner. They are not for the faint-hearted.

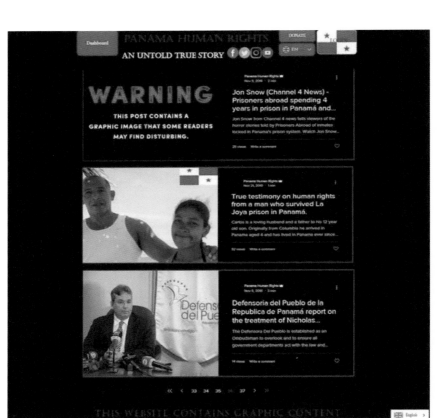

13

SMOKE AND MIRRORS

My letter-writing campaign with Arthur did not bring us the results we had been so optimistic about achieving.

No one capable of intervening or instituting change had responded to us. However, I was in daily contact with my attorney, Fidel, pressing him to get me a day in court that wouldn't be cancelled for some flimsy reason. By this stage, I confess that I was becoming sceptical about how hard he was really trying on my behalf. I had heard too many stories about how corruption flowed through the veins of Panamanian lawyers. Was I just another client who was being strung along? Fidel was becoming increasingly reluctant to return my calls and more often than not when I phoned him, I was greeted with a voicemail message. On one occasion, he came to La Joya to see another Building Six client and didn't even call me.

I came to the reluctant conclusion that he was a shark and that La Joya was a fertile hunting ground for him and his father, also an attorney. Penal cases were lucrative, and in our building there were Mexican and Colombian drug lords who were paying him hundreds of thousands of dollars. He often boasted about the money he made from them. My fees were comparatively paltry, and I guess that made me a lower priority.

Arthur's attorney, Ricardo, had questionable connections of his own. This former qualified pilot was also a convicted drug dealer, sentenced to 10 years in a US prison. (He served just over two of them.) He had links to various Colombian cartels. During the 1980s he passed millions of dollars in bribes to General Noriega – and later gave vital prosecution evidence at the former dictator's trial. On his release from prison, he returned to his home country to take up law again. Yes, even with his shady history, he was allowed to do so: anything seemed to go in Panamá.

Fidel was costing my family a fortune and I had to find some way to supplement their payments. I came up with a neat little deal that allowed me to make money on the inside as quickly as Fidel was taking it from the outside, and it involved an arrangement with my civil attorney, José. He often came to visit, as a friend and to deliver laundered cash for me, so that I could avoid paying a 10 per cent cut to the director as commission.

José and I decided to work as a team. He would print off 500 business cards for me to distribute on his behalf, and with every client I secured for him, I would receive a $500 commission. My patch in the gancha, close to the entrance and the commando's desk, gave me the perfect position from which to operate.

When disorientated new arrivals turned up after being captured at Tocumen Airport, most of them had no idea of how to hire a Panamanian attorney or where to look for one. That was my opening to offer a friendly face – and one of José's business cards. I also posted his details on the walls of the gancha. I saw the service as being a bit like posting the details of cab companies on the walls of a nightclub. Clients, and their down-payments, soon began to flow. Our first was an Israeli guy, Aryeh, who was charged with spying. Fidel's charges became far more palatable with this extra income stream.

I continued my covert filming. Some of the material was truly stomach-churning. I particularly remember a maggot-infested outdoor latrine trench that was covered in a green slime and humming with flies and mosquitoes. It was situated right next to the collection point for tap water via a hose pipe connected to a rickety standpipe. Therefore, in this same communal area of the yard where people had to piss and shit, they were brushing their teeth and washing themselves. It was also where the catering urns were washed after use. Predictably enough, this stinking corner was a breeding ground for diseases, a common one being the mosquito-borne dengue fever.

Those who were stuck in the gancha really got the short straw. The drain of the shower tray – there were no taps; you had to find your own water – was always clogged with pubic hair and used condoms. A shabby makeshift curtain provided some privacy, in theory, but it was constantly being opened by other inmates telling you to hurry up.

To add to the room's delights, some inmates used it as a 'conjugal' meeting place in the mornings and others just masturbated right up against the tiled wall, where they left globs of sperm. The Latino custom of blowing mucus out of your nose to mask the other deposit really didn't fool anyone, and it added an extra dimension of disgustingness.

My Trivago rating: minus 10 out of 10.

Here were the ideal conditions to harbour bacteria. Not one day passed when I did not suffer from some type of skin infection. Deep, painful boils developed all over my body to the extent that I felt about as appealing as Quasimodo. I noticed that even my friends used to stand their distance. In fact, I am still plagued by some of the skin problems that began in La Joya.

Those who could avoid sitting directly on the bowl did so by squatting over it instead. If their aim was poor, that was just hard luck for the next inmate, especially if he was blind. All I remember was the pain from the oozing sores in my crotch. (The sores were also under my arms). When I bent forward the pustules would burst.

I needed a course of heavy-duty antibiotics, but they were impossible to obtain. Instead, to treat the boils I had to resort to using a home-made knife. I used to heat the blade in a flame and then dig down to remove the root, and it had to be the whole root. If anything was left, the thing grew back like fungus on the side of my head.

The same people using the gancha facilities were, of course, serving up the prison rations. They used to trundle round on food carts left over from Manuel Noriega's era. When the cart needed a new wheel or an axel, all inmates were expected to contribute towards the repair costs. No cart meant no meals.

There were many other factors threatening our daily fare. Chief among them, the blatant theft of provisions. Inmates working to get time off their sentence became chefs in the kitchen, but they were also running their own scam. If, for instance, they were given 250 bags of chicken to serve for general consumption across the compound, they might sell off half of it at $25 per bag and then use the scraps and skins to make soup, without any meat. The chefs sometimes came into Building Six with wheelbarrow-loads of raw chicken to sell to the highest bidders. Those who could afford it cooked it in their makeshift ovens or, if they were drug lords, asked their personal lackeys to turn it into something tasty.

I wanted to prove the huge scale of the theft, and I devised a sting so that I could film what happened. This was back before poor Portugal killed himself, and he played an important part in negotiating the purchases and making it all work.

My first move was to buy three 15-pound sacks of whole chickens. I offered our guard five bucks to look the other way, and Portugal slipped the consignment past the checkpoints and into our building, where the most unfortunate inmates in the gancha would get the final benefit.

The captain of the wheelbarrow brigade was Globo 'Fat Boy Slim' Raul from Spain, a ballsy little bastard who was so greedy for cash that he would have sold his own mother, his father and all other remaining relatives if he could. He didn't give a toss about being caught. The

285

second person in the convoy was wheeling the genuine food cart as a decoy.

I stood at the gate with my watch primed. Action! Our boys did not even break a sweat as they sauntered casually past the checkpoints. Cut! That was a hell of a fantastic take. The video remains on my website as proof of Building Six's lax security.

Having directed one successful mission, I was keen to raise the bar and show the scale of the corruption. Judging from what I had managed to get into Building Six, the total value of the pilfered food from La Joya's kitchens must have run to hundreds of thousands of dollars over the course of a year. Money effectively stolen from the state. I decided to go for it again, but this time with a mammoth consignment. I sent out my new shopping order for two 80-pound sacks of rice and a 45-pound sack of powdered milk and waited for the volunteers to come forward, which they did (Fat Boy Slim had been caught the day before with a bag of cocaine so he was out of action, but replacements were soon found for $5).

The people in the gancha loved these unexpected free food deliveries, totally unaware of the reasons behind the bounty. I personally helped share out the spoils among those most seriously in need: the ones who had nothing, not even toilet paper.

My smuggling experiment taught me that audacity brought rewards. I began to wonder how easy it would be to smuggle in weapons, but thought twice about testing that one.

Yet ordinary, innocent civilians who could not afford back-handers to the cops were subjected to humiliating strip-searches both on arrival at La Joya and on departure. It was a particularly unpleasant ordeal for the women. A few of them were caught with pathetically small amounts of rice or powdered milk in sealed plastic bags: a mere fraction of the kilos of goods that went missing from the kitchens every day. The rich came out on top in prison, as elsewhere. It was grossly unfair. There were several inmates in Building Six who had so much money that they could buy whatever they wanted.

Just before my release, five major drug lords were unexpectedly freed, even though their rap sheets were as long as your arm and included multiple murders. I'd been awaiting a hearing for well over a year. These guys breezed in and out within six months. Most of them looked as if they'd arrived in the world with a full set of gold teeth, and their air of entitlement was galling to behold. Either they had a confident arrangement with God that He would release them early, or some less spiritual transactions were going on behind the scenes.

The drug lords acquired retinues of eager helpers the second they arrived in prison. They had their own chefs, cleaners and gophers, and their cells were fitted out with the latest technology. They nourished their beer bellies on tiger shrimp and steak and insane amounts of alcohol. The Claret they enjoyed was a local vintage, Chateau Lafite Building Six, and it tasted great, better than most of the stuff you could pick up at a supermarket. It was made from smuggled sugar and the Welch's Grape Juice the guards were happy to let us drink, unaware that it was being fermented by the ever-industrious Chinese prisoners at $7 a bottle.

Another pleasure available to those with the deepest pockets was sex, with women. Prostitutes advertised in the back of *La Critica* newspaper, and anyone who wanted to bring a girl in would call up her number and explain where he was. The girl would then appear at normal visiting time – every second Wednesday, for the record – and give her details as if she were a relative visiting the prisoner. While the cops and the guards were playing dominoes and poker, a mattress would be provided so that the girls could do their work.

There was a small room off the visiting area where this took place, and the girls generally brought in their own sheets. Normal family visits, meanwhile, carried on outside, near the administration building. Between four and five prostitutes dropped by each week. Everyone knew it went on and the authorities were prepared to turn a blind eye as long as they got their cut.

How exactly did you buy your way out of a Panamanian prison? I've captured every stage and I'll tell you.

The first step was to pay your dues to the fat mama, Luris, in the administration building. She charged $300 to lose a folder for three hours, during which time custodian Monroy brought it into Building Six, and you handed over another $600. The folder contained timesheets that were laid out in such a way that there were blanks between the names of genuine inmate workers. It was these blanks that were for sale. I saw at least five inmates released early using this method of falsifying working hours that were then offset against their sentences.

I filmed Portugal, who worked as a timekeeper as well as a doorman for the duty guard, filling in the timesheets with fabricated records of work done by lazy bastards who had never set foot in the kitchens or done a day's work. The profits that inmates made in this way were sent back to their families or used to buy their own early release dates.

The duty guard or commando oversaw the key for their gate and entry door, but gave the legwork to a proxy such as Portugal or Fat Boy Slim. These keys also opened other gates, including the alternative foreigner's quarters in Building Eight and the security block next door. The doorman was treated like a cross between the duty guard's waiter, nanny, housekeeper and handyman and would always be sent on errands when the fat – they were all fat – commando was too lazy to get off his own arse.

I filmed a hilarious segment that showed a squad of 100 cops dressed in armour and ready to enact a raid on Building Eight, which was situated right behind us. In an echo of our own experience when we were raided, the cops were made to look like complete idiots.

The platoon was kept waiting, their surprise tactic in tatters, because none of them could enter the building until Portugal ambled over with the keys. The prisoners in Eight found the situation just as entertaining as we did, and you could hear their euphoric cheers through the bars while they took advantage of the delay to hide their possessions. By the time Portugal rolled up, the cops looked more like bumbling Mr Beans than macho mean-machines and they were fuming.

On another occasion, Portugal forgot to lock up and the gates to Eight were left wide open. I remember that for different reasons, though. I had drunk a lot of moonshine and was standing in our yard looking through the fence. I swear I saw a horse canter up, then another, and they bent their heads to tell me in confidence that the keys were concealed between their teeth and their lips. I managed to fight my way back to reality, but it was a definite warning to stay off the booze, even if it was one of the few anaesthetics available to numb the pain and tedium of prison life. (Another of which was religion. I counted myself a Christian, but I wasn't one of the inmates who took to wandering around all day with a Bible under his arm, loudly praying to the Lord. Their belief was too often a kind of superficial comfort blanket that concealed deeper issues or mental health problems.)

Other film clips that I have show inmates from Panamanian-only cell blocks entering to sell stolen electric supplies like tattoo machines and drugs, or simply to braid their friends' hair. For certain individuals, there was a freedom of movement and business opportunities that would have been unimaginable in a UK or US prison. We were supposedly medium to maximum security, but the random levels of diligence, depending on who was on duty or how much he had been

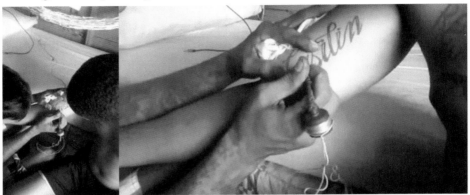

bribed, were laughably inadequate. This laxness put inmates and cops alike in danger when sieges developed, because some prisoners were able to defend themselves with some serious firepower: AK47s, grenades, pistols and hunting knives were all deployed. How these weapons got into the prison past five checkpoints never seemed to be questioned. Family visitors, allowed in for half an hour every two weeks, were thoroughly searched. If you didn't drop your pants and bend over, you weren't admitted by the police perverts, who got a thrill from humiliating civilians.

The majority of the contraband – the mobile phones, the weapons, the grenades – entered the prison via the police. Or else it was through the Super 99 food delivery trucks, which for many years were a supply monopoly owned by the previous president of Panamá, Ricardo Martinelli.

But the inmates had their own devious ways, too. Among the most impressive examples of their ingenuity involved some disappearing office equipment and some hijacked bathroom tiles.

The offices of the director, which were being refurbished, were located in the middle of the penitentiary compound, located on a second floor. The ground floor entrance was guarded 24 hours a day by armed national police, who checked everyone going in and coming out. On an evening in June 2014, after the administrative staff had left, opportunity knocked for persons unknown. The inmates were locked in their cells, or were supposed to be. Yet by the morning, every computer in the director's office had been stolen from the building that was the control hub and communications centre of the entire prison. It had to have been an inside job but a search of the prison yielded nothing.

This was not to be the end of the magic. Some inmates had nerves – and balls – of steel, and seemed impervious to fear.

A group of Colombians in the block decided to stick two fingers up at security again. Word was out that the director's office and the administration offices were being re-tiled. The washroom in cell B-12 of Building Six was also in need a of a makeover, and the game was on. Don't ask me how the guys managed to devise and execute their plan, but it was a blast.

Somehow, they passed through three commando checkpoints before the doors of Building Six swung wide open for them, and they entered with a wheelbarrow cavalcade that headed straight to cell B-12. They were the last ones into the block before the guard closed up for the night.

They now had 12 hours to perform a conjuring trick and convert their scummy, disgusting old bathroom into a show piece en-suite. Only God knows how they pulled it off, or from where they obtained two bags of cement and a range of cutting tools, but by the morning the transformation was complete. I was totally blown away by both the standard of the work and the sheer audacity. Their bathroom looked even better than mine back in Miami.

However, the contractors back on site in the admin building realised two days after the robbery that they were short of tiles for the last office. The alarm was raised and within an hour we had a visit from seven prison guards, who traipsed from cell to cell in search of the missing goods. In B-12, they found them, by then permanently cemented to the walls and floor.

Prisoners: 2. Director: 0. The score should have been enough, but these nutters would not give up.

Baiting the director had turned into a hobby, and he was regarded as an easy target. Building Six had a ban on freezers, because of the strain they would place on the already over-loaded electrical system, but that was no concern for our gang of ex-FARC Colombians. After years inside, all they wanted was ice cream, ice-cold beer and lollies.

By means never explained, they got a new Beko freezer delivered to cell B-14, and the excitement about this mod-con turned everyone a little giddy. The Colombians cashed in by selling bags of ice at 50¢ a time.

It was a sad, sad moment when the guards caught the prisoners red-handed within 24 hours and removed the freezer, which was no doubt destined to end its days in a cop's house.

Smoke and mirrors were part of the emergency pack you needed to survive inside jail. In our building, some inmates practically made a career of it. We all had to turn a buck to survive, even if that meant selling your body or soul. At the far end of the block, in cell B-18, there was a master in the making. His name was Virgil, but he was known to everyone as Rasta from Jamaica.

He was a skyscraper of a guy. Full-on dreadlocks dangled from his head, and he was blessed with the kind of six-pack that lesser men would spend hours in the gym failing to achieve. He loved reggae music, as did I, and whenever I walked past the cell he shared with other Jamaicans and heard Bob Marley's 'No Woman No Cry' blaring out, it lifted my spirits.

When I arrived, he had already been in La Joya for years and was living a hard life. I thought he was a cool guy, but I had a beef with him: he was always trying to ponce a fag or two from me. In stature, he was Goliath and I was a limping David, but I used to stand my ground and say no, otherwise I wouldn't have had a cigarette left to myself.

Tired of the constant requests, I offered up a suggestion that would exploit his natural assets and make him enough money to buy his own supplies. The idea required some input from Rasta's tech-savvy friend Soko-Soko, who helped him to open a Facebook account. Then, all we needed were some sexy pictures.

The lighting for the photo-shoot was adjusted by draping a sheet around one side of the cell's bare bulb to achieve a romantic glow. One of the gay guys who lived in the attic space above the cell gifted Rasta some baby oil to polish his muscles until they looked suitably jaw-dropping, and then his new career as a professional model was ready for lift-off.

I have to give praise for their efforts; the pictures looked great. I even admit to a twinge of jealousy. The girls were going to wet themselves when they saw him (I'll just add that I had bigger feet). Not one of the Facebook users drooling over the shots would have guessed they were taken in a grimy shower area of cell B-18, Building Six, La Joya State Penitentiary.

After the profile was posted, Soko-Soko added a paragraph or two of glossy content about Rasta's history, and most importantly, his status. Single. Now it was down to Rasta to do the work: he was going to have to sell his body if he wanted to climb out of poverty. He needed to offer extra, uncensored library pictures that were not listed in his post. Within minutes of the bait being set, the first girl responded online and Rasta's confidence started to climb. The Europeans loved him.

It did not take long for him to gather an international clientele of girls, all gagging for his bits. He operated on an auction-only rather than a buy-now basis, offering himself to the highest bidder. The only drawback of his success was that he needed to be online 24/7, which was far from easy when you had worries about keeping your data signal going, or about your phone being confiscated during a raid.

His first Western Union deposit of $300 arrived from Spain. Rasta had used the story that if she sent money to 'my agent in Panamá', he would then be able to buy a ticket and get a plane to Madrid. "I promise to pay you back when we meet, my darling," he messaged. Yeah, right.

It wasn't honest, but it was profitable. Rasta's sideline as a porn star and scam artist was soon making him $1,000 a week. The best consequence of his success, from my point of view, was that he stopped trying to take my cigarettes.

He and Soko both left La Joya in 2015, and continue to pull the same stunts to this day. Thanks to the wonders of internet connectivity and the La Joya escuela education, Rasta works from Jamaica and Soko, his spin doctor and PR mastermind, works from Colombia, busily tweaking the profile of their online creation to make it more enticing.

At least a few, if not many, people managed to come out of Building Six with new skills and career opportunities. Good luck to them both. They sure as hell deserved a break after Building Six.

14

WHERE ARE THE MEDICAL PLIERS?

Whatever the privileges money could buy inside La Joya, there was one fear that haunted drug barons and drug mules alike: illness. Getting sick was a problem whatever your resources.

The dread of contracting a serious disease made us all equal because, without specialist care, it was as good as a death sentence. HIV and AIDS, hepatitis, tuberculosis and typhoid were rife among the inmates – the virtuous and the reckless – crowded together in the perfect conditions to incubate and spread infection. Our filthy surroundings allowed bacteria to thrive on every surface. The humidity from ever-present damp laundry did not help,

The inmates who suffered most from rodent and insect- infested conditions and the grossly inadequate drainage system were the poorest of the poor, the men desperate enough to accept the job of maintaining the cell toilets for a few cents a day. They regularly had to wade through raw sewage, in bare feet, and handle used needles and condoms, without gloves. Of course, they succumbed to sickness. Panamá failed to provide us with qualified maintenance engineers, which meant that either prisoners fixed blockages or no one did.

Lucky though I was to escape the very worst La Joya had to offer, the prison inflicted lasting mental and physical damage on me, as on many others. The skin lesions that plagued me while I was inside have left me with a legacy of poor health and scars.

I am delighted to report that Building Six was demolished in 2014, after I left Panamá, when it was condemned for human rights violations – the only block out of the 15 in the prison compound to be destroyed (La Palma prison, described by the International Human Rights Commission as inhumane, has also been demolished). The coming chapters will show that this was not a coincidence: Arthur and I applied the pressure to make it happen.

I have already described the near-impossibility of seeing any kind of doctor in prison, but the quality of those doctors was an issue in itself. Among the reasons why so many qualified medics refused to work at La Joya was that it was an hour's drive from Panamá City and government employees were only paid for time worked, not travel time. Busy, successful professionals didn't want the hassle of a 60-mile round-trip, which is why we got the leftovers. The state plugged the shortage with student doctors, who earned credits towards their degrees by practicing on us.

They would prescribe blood pressure pills without bothering to check patients' blood pressure readings. Chest and lung conditions were diagnosed without the aid of a stethoscope. Pharmaceuticals were invariably out of date because La Joya's medication was expired inventory off-loaded by Panamá City's Santo Tomás hospital. When Arthur visited the Merced clinic, he was forced to give these kids a tutorial on cancer care because they were clueless about how to treat him.

It would be foolish to believe that when three doctors just out of puberty were responsible for 17,000 inmates, mistakes did not happen. Non-Spanish speaking inmates were especially vulnerable to prescription errors or misdiagnoses, and you can bet that if failings came to light, they were denied or blamed squarely on the prisoners. The culture was that doctors always covered for each other and the rotten system that paid them, irrespective of the facts.

My own case made the point. When the British embassy asked Merced for information on my condition, it got back a convincing report of the medication I was being prescribed. In fact, I had not visited Merced at that point and I never received any meds. The embassy nonetheless chose to believe the clinic (fortunately for my records, I have a copy of the fictitious case notes).

The web of lies was extensive. Vitamin supplements were an essential extra in La Joya and the embassy was given specific funding to supply them to British nationals, to compensate for the nutrients missing in our prison diet and the ban on fruit and vegetables. The money came from a UK non-profit charity called Prisoners Abroad. According to an FOI request I later made, I had been the happy recipient of monthly free vitamins, but that was absolutely not the case. I visited Prisoners Abroad when I got home, and they were very unhappy to hear that charity money was being misused or mislaid by the embassy.

My case regarding the embassy's widespread and general maladministration was taken up by my MP and the human rights charity Redress. It was brought before the parliamentary ombudsman and upheld in October 2019. Below is the ombudsman's verdict:

'The embassy's actions in relation to the mistreatment/torture allegations were not consistent with FCO guidance, and that was maladministration.

The embassy's handling of the January 8, 2014 letter was not sufficiently sensitive, and did not take account of Mr Tuffney's circumstances: and that was maladministration.

The embassy's decision not to visit Mr Tuffney between May 28, 2013 and July 10, 2013 whilst he was chained 24 hours a day was maladministration.

The embassy could, and should have, done more to ensure he had a bed at La Joya prison.

The embassy staff failed to act on seeing Mr Tuffney handcuffed to a hospital bed on May 24, 2013.

The FCO provided inadequate information about what detainees might expect. The FCO did not attempt to contact immigration authorities in relation to his impending deportation.

We find that in some areas of Mr Tuffney's complaint, FCO's actions were not consistent with the expectations of relevant guidance, and that was maladministration; as that caused an injustice to him that has not been remedied, we therefore uphold the complaint."

Given that dentists were even rarer than doctors, Aspirin was often the only relief available to those with toothache. The ultimate remedy was a shot of cocaine and a strong- armed friend who could use a pair of utility pliers to remove the troublesome molar. Gum infections and abscesses were tougher to cure, and they could reduce the most fearsome guys to whimpering invalids.

A British friend who visited the clinic for an urgently needed filling was told, "Wait until you get back to your rich country and let them sort it out."

There was a distinct shortage of Hollywood smiles in La Joya. People were more likely to flash you a mouth full of tree bark, with breath that smelled as if it had wafted from the depths of a garbage can. Not even mouthwash was available (another unwelcome reminder of my time in prison is that my taste buds have been permanently affected by the poor hygiene on offer).

To ease the load on the medical clinic, a first alert and assessment station was set up within the prison compound, on the ground floor of building seven. This unit also provided an isolation ward for highly communicable diseases, such as scabies, TB and now Covid-19. The faculty was so disgusting that it was a solid bet that if the disease didn't kill you, the conditions would.

Redundant electric cables hung from the ceiling where lights had once been, which meant there was pitch darkness inside once the day faded. The bed frames had only banded metal straps, not mattresses, to support the weight of your body. A trough in the floor was used as a makeshift urinal and you had to flush the waste outdoors through a hole in the wall. Food, or should I say swill, was delivered in buckets from the kitchens and left outside the ward, to be retrieved once the delivery person had left.

The station's approved employees looked the part, dressed as they were in nurse's uniforms with the state's medical logo embroidered on their chests, but they were playing at the role. In reality they were two inmates from our cell block, working time off their sentences. One was a former taxi driver from Venezuela, the other a builder from Colombia, both convicted of drug trafficking and neither with the slightest training in first aid. They were, however, smart enough to take full advantage of Panamá's asinine system, which was partially funded by the US Aid program.

Their job came with many perks. Chief among them was use of the office computer, which gave them access to classified medical information they could sell as requested, and to a steady stream of porn. They would download it onto multiple memory sticks and then rent them out at three bucks a pop when they returned in the evenings. Pizza Sluts was the inmates' favourite, closely followed by Gays Come with Me.

The first step in capturing this shady operation on film was to make an appointment. I caught Ernesto, the taxi driver/nurse, as he left our block for his job one morning and offered him $5 in return for a consultation. He could see I was walking with difficulty and, having pocketed the money, agreed to see me at his clinic at 11am.

His considered professional opinion was that I was suffering from malnutrition — a safe assumption for 90 per cent of La Joya's population – but, not to worry, he had the perfect cure. He flourished a packet of pills. They turned out, when I checked them on my phone, to be medication for schizophrenia, with a long list of side effects and contraindications.

It was incredibly irresponsible for the state to allow people with no expertise or training to prescribe medicines. I could well imagine my 'cause of my death' had it resulted from being given unsuitable tablets: 'natural causes' or 'unknown'. Or perhaps the verdict would have been left open, as it was in Mark Bodden's case.

Worse was to come on my tour of Ernesto's domain. I asked him what he would charge for a copy of my medical records and a print–out of other La Joya prisoner and staff records held at Santo Tomás hospital. He soon settled on

$20. I left the clinic with damning proof that he was willing to sell what should have been confidential information, and a list on my WhatsApp that included the details of 50 cops and their family members.

CELDA B-10

#	Primer apellido	Segundo apellido	Primer Nombre	Segundo nombre	Cedula	Delito	Nacionalidad
1	CASTRO	POCE	MARIO	ERIQUE	7533989	DROGA	GUATEMALA
2	CASTILLO		RAMIRO	Áñez	16472623	DROGA	COLOMBIA
3	CUERO	GONZALEZ	ARNALDO	CSAR	11-886149	DROGA	COLOMBIA
4	GOMEZ		WILMAR	PLAÑOS	16779208	DROGA	COLOMBIA
5	LEON		ALEXIS	ENDEZ	16886030	DROGA	COLOMBIA
6	MOSQUEDA	RUEDAS	BLASS		6160237650	DROGA	MEXICO
7	PINEDA	DOSAMANTE	ISAI	AVID	G05386276	DROGA	MEXICO
8	TORRES	HERNANDEZ	JEFFERSON	YNATAN	RN15494808	DROGA	COLOMBIA
9	VALENSUELA		JAVIER		7140006590	DROGA	MEXICO
10	VIVEROS	QUIÑONES	DENIS	JSE	1-6864295	DROGA	COLOMBIA

CELDA B-11

#	Primer apellido	Segundo apellido	Primer Nombre	Segundo nombre	Cedula	Delito	Nacionalidad
1	ADRIAAN	GUSTINA	OTWIN A		N.H.4812701	DROGA	HOLANDA
2	BARRERA	BARRERA	JAIME	AELCAR	556145	DROGA	GUATEMAL
3	CARDALES		EFRAIN	MARTIN	C1031815	T. HOMICD	COLOMBIA
4	CASTRELLON		DANIEL	TIROCO	8-724-242	DROGA	PANAMA
5	HERRERA	RODAS	JOSE	GEOVANY	9873586	DROGA	COLOMBIA
6	HERRERA	Núñez	JAIME	ALBERTO	94364980	DROGA	COLOMBIA
7	MEDINA		MIGUEL	FERNANDO	71716472	DROGA	COLOMBIA
8	PAUTT		CARLOS	MARIO	107857650	LABADO	COLOMBIA
9	RAMOS	REYES	JOSE	LUS	16484448	DROGA	COLOMBIA
10	SERNA	VALENCIA	JHON	FREEDI	E-8-72-158	DROGA	COLOMBIA
11	VALENCIA	MURILLO	JEFFERSON		4849383	DROGA	COLOMBIA

CELDA B-12

#	Primer apellido	Segundo apellido	Primer Nombre	Segundo nombre	Cedula	Delito	Nacionalidad
1	NAVEROS	MARULANDA	JUAN	DAVID	111275-8738	DROGA	COLOMBIA
2	ACOSTA	PEREIRA	ABDON	EMILIO	71350412	C.S.C.	COLOMBIA
3	ANGULO	ARANGO	WILSON		94307692	DROGA	COLOMBIA
4	Ávila	GALLEGO	Iván		AAC849364	DROGA	ESPAÑA
5	CRUZ	ALSATE	FREDY	ALEXANDER	A0220631	DROGA	COLOMBIA
6	GILI	MOLINA	RAUL		AAG9117264	DROGA	COLOMBIA
7	ORDUZ	HERNANDEZ	PEDRO	JOSE	86257721	DROGA	COLOMBIA
8	QUINSENO		LUIS	GONZALO	10136154	DROGA	COLOMBIA
9	ZULUAGA	GIL	CARLOS	ANDRES	10007264	DROGA	COLOMBIA

CELDA B-13

#	Primer apellido	Segundo apellido	Primer Nombre	Segundo nombre	Cedula	Delito	Nacionalidad
1	CARILLO	GOMEZ	MARIO	ESTUANDO	1246931	DROGA	GUATEMALA
2	CASTRO	CAICEDO	JOHN	JAIRO	4701772	DROGA	COLOMBIA
3	CRUZ	SALAZAR	AGUSTIN		87111772	DROGA	COLOMBIA
4	JIMENEZ		JULIO		P046194163	DROGA	VENEZUELA
5	LOPEZ	MINAYA	CARLOS	JOSE	E-800-038	DROGA	DOMINICANO
6	MATEUS		MAURICIO	ROMERO	CC13953062	DROGA	COLOMBIA
7	POLO		CANDELARIO		E-8-92010	DROGA	COLOMBIA
8	TORO		JORGE	Iván	71629365	DROGA	COLOMBIA

CELDA B-14

#	Primer apellido	Segundo apellido	Primer Nombre	Segundo nombre	Cedula	Delito	Nacionalidad
						DROGA	
1	ARREGUI	GUEVARRA	FAUSTO	PEDRON	6350040393	DROGA	MEXICO
2	CARRILO	ESPERICUETA	RODOLFO		G 02372483	DROGA	MEXICO
3	CERVANTES	HERRERA	HECTOR		G03853406	DROGA	MEXICO
4	GARCIA	RAMIREZ	JUAN	CARLOS	F-02715776	DROGA	MEXICO
5	IÑIGUEZ	GAVIÑO	LINO		2006829	DROGA	MEXICO
6	LOPEZ		FABIAN	RAMON	G-03185415	DROGA	MEXICO
7	NAVA	CASILLAS	JUAN	ENRIQUE	G-02536061	DROGA	MEXICO
8	TORRES		EDGAR	JAVIER	G-02753035	DROGA	MEXICO
9	VELASQUEZ		DAVID	ALEJANDRO	9690686	DROGA	MEXICO

CELDA B-15

#	Primer apellido	Segundo apellido	Primer Nombre	Segundo nombre	Cedula	Delito	Nacionalidad
1	AMAYA		OSCAR		8-726-17	DROGA	PANAMA
2	BERMUDES		CESAR	RODOLFO	G10462521	DROGA	MEXICO
3	BERMUDES		JOSE	ARMANDO	G-10614810	DROGA	MEXICO
4	CASTAÑO	VALENCIA	ANDRES	FELIPE	CC1088010413	FE. PUB.	COLOMBIA
5	CELIS		LUIS	FERNANDO	79590025	ARMA	COLOMBIA
6	MONTOYA		JULIAN	FERNANDO	1017133872	DROGA	COLOMBIA
7	QUINTERO	AMAYA	LEONARDO		1127533867	SECUESTR	COLOMBIA

CELDA B-16

#	Primer apellido	Segundo apellido	Primer Nombre	Segundo nombre	Cedula	Delito	Nacionalidad
1	ASANTE		FELIX		NJ0163770	DROGA	HOLANDA
2	BASIL		JACOB		A-02663772	DROGA	NIGUERIA
3	FLORES	HINEZTROZA	JESUS	ABEL	6164000	DROGA	COLOMBIA
4	LAMBERT		JEAN		PSUK339639	DROGA	CANADA
5	PINNOCK		DELROY		242880	DROGA	JAMAICA
6	RICHARDS		STEVEN		E-2980069	DROGA	JAMAICA
7	SANTAMARIA		CARLOS		SC0234342	ESTAFA	DOMINICANO
8	SIMPSON		ANTONI		A2393465	DROGA	JAMAICA
9	WHITTE	ORAL	TIMOTHY		A2408217		JAMAIQUINO

My drive to expose the truth, then and now, was inspired by Arthur and I always remember that he was equally eager to tell his story. Before his death in 2015, he was able to complete the memoir he began in prison. The book was called *The Man Behind the Bow Tie*, and he wrote it with help from T.R. Todd, a good and trusted friend of his, living on the outside. It was a therapeutic exercise for Arthur that helped to make prison more bearable.

Panamá seemed to generate colourful tales about foreigners with criminal records. It was considered rich enough in material to merit an episode to itself in the docu- drama TV series *Banged Up Abroad*.

British canoeist John Darwin, who faked his own death in 2002 so that he and his wife, Anne, could claim the life insurance, bought a house near the Caribbean coastal city of Colon in 2007. They went to prison in the UK the following year when their elaborate ruse unravelled. They both subsequently produced memoirs: his was called *The Canoe Man: Panamá and Back*, and hers was *Out of My Depth*.

William Holbert, aka 'Wild Bill', inspired *The Jolly Roger Social Club*, published in 2016. Journalist Nick Foster's book tells the unlovely tale of how Bill, a scam artist and former white supremacist on the run from a previous fraud charge in the US, murdered five people on the Bocas del Toro archipelago so that he could steal their properties. He shot them in the back of the head and then buried their bodies in shallow jungle graves. One of his victims was a teenage boy.

Panama prisons gave rise to many new authors

My unnerving cannibalistic neighbour in the gancha, Sandy Patric Luzer, came out with a book in 2018: *Evangelios De La Oscuridad*, which translates as *Gospels of Darkness*. He (or, as he claimed to prefer in prison, 'she') described how he and his brother had murdered a girl during a satanic cult ritual in Panamá. On his release after serving 20 years, he did a national publicity tour and posted videos on YouTube to promote the work. His coldness in describing the details of Oristela Batista's death is striking. I still have his number, but something tells me we won't be meeting for cocktails any time soon.

'Fat' Tony Galeota, an American hustler who served time in La Joya from 2011 to 2013 on charges that were later dropped, did not produce a book but he gave extensive interviews to the *Miami Herald* and the *Miami New Times*. His trajectory from small-time gangster to strip club entrepreneur and pimp, to bit-player in a bizarre attempt to smuggle Colombian drugs into Russia via submarine, is certainly a pacey read. Once the brains behind an infamous Miami strip, drugs and sex joint called Porky's, Galeota moved to Panamá City in an attempt to run a legal brothel. There he fell foul of visa requirements for his workers and ended up awaiting trial in La Joya Building Six for almost two years before a judge dismissed the case. He also spoke publicly about the violence, overcrowding and filth of his incarceration.

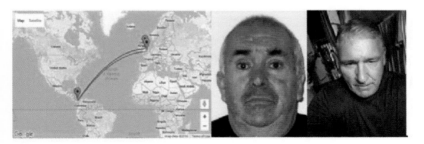

Birmingham drug dealer ran international cocaine ring from jail

Leo on the right, George on the left

A vast number of untold stories from La Joya would be just as gruesome or eye- popping. In 2009, Leo joined heads with a prisoner called George Moon, who was detained at Her Majesty's Pleasure in Yorkshire, to orchestrate a million-dollar drugs deal by mobile phone. The plan was to use DHL and Royal Mail to smuggle drugs into the UK, but it didn't quite work out and Leo is still in prison.

The narrative of daily life was less about murder (though that happened often enough) and heists, and more about satisfying basic human needs in stressful, restricted surroundings. Many long-term inmates who wanted affection and release became 'gay for the stay', even when they had wives on the outside. A side effect was the high rate of chlamydia and genital warts – also untreated, of course.

When transvestites Aleska and Brenda arrived on the scene as inmates, other prisoners starved of female company could not believe their eyes, or their luck. Here were what looked like two girls who had wandered in off the back streets of Soho. They wore mini dresses, makeup and stiletto heels and they even had cleavage, courtesy of boob jobs. The frequent catfights, complete with scratching and hair pulling, that broke out between them added to the effect that there was suddenly a whole different gender in our midst.

Aleska and Brenda handled, quite literally, all the grabbing guys with aplomb. They had such a trade going with their captive audience that on early mornings when I headed to the back of the building to have a cigarette and gather my thoughts, I would often see one of them sitting on a stool with her cell phone in one fist and whichever gent was at the front of the queue in the other. She would be so intent on the screen that she wasn't even looking at her client.

They were paid a few bucks a time or in cigarettes for the valuable service they provided, and I shudder to think of the infections they must have helped to transmit.

The air of Building Six – of the entire prison compound – was overlaid with the stench of stale sex. Hundreds of pumped, sweaty guys, shirtless in the heat, trapped in a man cave… it was oppressive. Just brushing past them made you wonder what you might have contracted.

The richer prisoners could buy themselves the hottest chicks in Panamá, with the help of a few bent cops and a couple of prison guards.

Sex between inmates and visitors was allowed in Panamá, under the term of 'conjugales', but the law seemed crazy to me. You were risking an STD or more emotional damage to your family if you used a prostitute, and what if your wife or girlfriend got pregnant while you were serving a 45-year stretch?

Anyway, back to the ABC of prison sex. Once you had chosen your girl, you arranged for the guard to pay all the people in the chain of bribery that ran from the exterior gate to the so-called 'sex room' in Building Eight. This was a segregated and air-conditioned area divided into two, and it boasted a skanky mattress that must have bred bacteria faster than the average petri dish.

That mattress went through a lot. Being hammered seven times a day from Monday to Friday must have been hell on the springs. The girls used to arrive with their own crisp white sheets, newly washed pillows and large bottles of perfume to disguise the horror, but the snowy linen soon turned a nasty shade of umber. The inmate had 30 minutes to prove his manhood, as the guard looked on and edged just a little too close.

At the weekend, the mattress was at least aired and given a chance for the accumulation of pubic hairs to blow away in the prison yard breeze, which – now I think about it – counts as more consideration for welfare than was shown to most inmates.

I have what I consider the ultimate exposé of Building Six on my website: true and uncut and not glossed with any Wild Bill style bullshit. It gives the best account I can muster of my journey through the Panamanian penal and judicial systems.

It was surreal in many ways. I had been a business and family man, leading a privileged life, who suddenly found himself surrounded – with exceptions – by a grab-bag of scumbags and lunatics. I had wanted my son, that was all. My ex-wife had pulled every stroke she could to keep us apart and the ultimate trick was landing me in prison. As well as separating me from my hard-won material assets, she even had the petty satisfaction of separating me from my dog, Skippy, who died while I was inside.

Below, to give a range of additional experiences of Panamá's dark side, is a collection of headlines and stories that reflect a still wider view of the crazy, fractured reality.

BLOOD AND GUTS:
A WARNING TO CHILDREN AND PARENTS

A notorious trafficker in children's body parts was extradited to Costa Rica on Thursday from La Joya's Building Six, to serve a sentence of 10 years in prison.

The 72-year-old Levy Berger, using the false identity of Rolf Salmon, was caught in Panamá, in November 2012, after the justice courts in Costa Rica issued an international arrest warrant for him.

Berger had been on the run since he was sentenced in 2006 for kidnapping children and illegally operating on them to sell their corneas and organs for transplant. He exported the body parts across the globe, to countries that included Israel and China.

Costa Rica requested his extradition after he was captured by the authorities in Panamá. He was taken to Palmar Sur de Osa in Puntarenas, and then to Base Dos in the international airport, Juan Santamaría.

When he arrived in Building Six, he was a marked man. In the view of the other inmates, he already had a death sentence for his vile crimes. Opinion was that he would be dismembered on his first night in custody but he somehow survived.

Child killers and molesters do not generally last long in La Joya, where the prisoners regard themselves as judge and jury in lieu of a fair national justice system.

23-YEAR-OLD WOMAN
ABDUCTED AND GANG-RAPED BY PRISON INMATES DURING VISITING HOURS IN COLON

"I just asked God for it to be over quickly," said the young woman, who was raped by eight inmates in the Nueva Esperanza prison in Colon last week, during visiting hours. The 23-year-old said she arrived at the scene in order to give money to an inmate, as a favour for a friend who could not go to the site. She explained that when she entered the site, some inmates threatened her with a knife and forced her walk to the cell area. The guards on duty either failed to intervene or did not notice.

From hospital, she recounted in tears how she was violently raped and abused.

She demands that the authorities investigate the matter.

MAN ARRESTED WITH FAKE POLICE UNIFORM

A police impersonator was arrested in his car by genuine officers at a checkpoint in Santa Cruz, Curundú.

During verification, the man was found to have a counterfeit police uniform and was in the process of installing fake police checkpoints in order to commit his crimes of extortion. The suspect was taken to the police station in Curundú for interrogation.

ROGELIO CRUZ INSISTS ON HIS OWN INNOCENCE IN LAWYER MOBILE PHONE

SMUGGLING CASE

Top lawyer Rogelio Cruz, who is defending the alleged murderer Fermin Antonio Taveras Ramirez, insisted that no rules were violated when he gave his client a wristwatch with an integrated cell phone while visiting him in prison.

Ramirez is a suspect in the kidnapping and murder of five young people from La Chorrera. National police caught him and four associates in El Dorado, in possession of weapons that included two .38-calibre pistols, when they were preparing to rob a store.

Cruz insisted that by passing over the watch, which had been bought by one of Ramirez's relatives, during visiting time in Ancón jail, he did not break the rules.

Cruz insists he was unaware that the watch had an integrated cell phone. He says that the police at Ancón are themselves guilty: of inappropriate behaviour and arbitrary attitudes to enforcement.

FOUR ARRESTED AS 'HITMEN FOR HIRE' IN BOCA DEL TORO

A gang of four suspected assassins was captured early yesterday, Sunday 23 September, in Changuinola, Bocas del Toro province.

Some of them confessed their involvement in the murder of the customs official Virgilio Abrego, 32, whose funeral was by chance taking place at the moment his killers were caught.

Roberto De Arco, the prosecutor of Bocas del Toro, said this was a case of murder for hire. According to De Arco, they were sent to kill the customs officer to settle an account, but he did not specify the reason

Regarding the case of the nine-year-old girl who was found dead in a bag under a bridge on the Oeste Arriba in Almirante, he said the investigations were continuing.

INMATES SHOT AND INJURED IN LA JOYA PRISON RIOT

A gun-battle and riot in Pavilion Nine of La Joya Prison has resulted in injuries to seven prisoners. Early reports indicate three of the prisoners were shot and four were injured with illegal, improvised weapons.

The inmates were first attended at the hospital in 24 de Diciembre and the Regional Medical Centre in Chepo. However, two of the most badly wounded have been taken to the Santo Tomás Hospital in Panamá City.

15

A New Dawn

On July 24, 2014, a full 15 months after my arrest, my day in court finally arrived. It was at long last an opportunity to prove that I was innocent of the ridiculous charges against Angel and me.

I had, as convention dictated, paid the guards in advance to make sure they would be up on time to get me to La Palma for the 11am hearing. After so many disappointments and false starts, I allowed myself to feel some optimism. The signs were, for once, encouraging: the minibus was ready and there was even enough gasoline in its tank for the journey.

The night before, I had taken calls from my family and friends and their support was exactly the morale boost I had needed. Arthur and I had found a quiet moment to pray together that I would be blessed with a just result.

Now here I was, more buoyant than I had felt for months, having my first smoke of the morning in the prison yard. The sun had not yet risen, everyone inside the gancha was asleep, and in the silent gloom I looked for what I hoped was the last time at the wire fences, the lines of buckets and the stinking latrine, and made a silent goodbye to La Joya. Much longer confined within its walls would kill me, I was sure of it.

My attorney, Fidel, was confident that this time the hearing would not be cancelled. He had promised to track down Angel, my co-defendant, and personally bring him to Darién.

I was grateful for entirely selfish reasons that Angel was ignorant of the affair going on between his partner and Fidel, whose sexual adventure broke every code of ethics in the attorneys' handbook. Another worry was the national capture warrant issued for Angel's arrest. How on earth was Fidel going to get him through all those police checkpoints and avoid his being taken into custody before they reached La Palma?

My faith in the judicial system was minimal, but I worked on the fatalistic principle that a good result was like betting on just two numbers on the national lottery; wait long enough and your combination was bound to come up. I reckoned that the rest of my life was going to be based on guesswork and lucky dips in any case.

I had prepared by asking Mikey for some diarrhoea tablets and anything from his stock of second-hand clothing that would make me look more respectable. I didn't care if it had been peeled from the back of the recently deceased. He found me a jacket in dark slate blue, with a suede finish, that was a miraculously good fit: a mere $15 and no blood stains! I concealed some money in the lining for my journey. Any privileges along the way would need to be bought.

Assuming the Imodium tablets did their job of bunging up my insides, I was ready to leave. Urgent trips to the toilet are never a good idea when you're bound in chains.

The guard's shout of "Tuffney!" cut through the still air. He escorted me to the administration block, and for the first time I walked down its corridors without hearing a cacophony of shouting from the nearby prison buildings. I cleared the pat down and, at the front desk, was shackled in preparation for the long ride to Darién.

The guards had to support me under my elbows to get me into the minibus because my legs were too weak to manage the step. As I was shoved inside my only concern was that the driver would make it beyond the last prison barrier and onto the national highway. Any other discomfort or humiliation was irrelevant. I willed us past every checkpoint, and the moment when we turned towards Darién felt sweeter than I can say.

My next move was to try and befriend the guards in my broken Spanish. My experience was that small talk built invaluable connections. It took half an hour to get the first laugh out of them: another good sign. I asked if any of them had eaten breakfast, or desayuno. The answer was no, and they were happy for me to provide it. We pulled up at Agua

Dulce and I asked for my chains to be released so I could extract a 50 from my lining to give to a guard.

I knew I wouldn't see any of the change, and added a request for a pack of Viceroy and a lighter in the spirit of if you don't ask, you don't get. We stopped for long enough for me to enjoy my second smoke. As I put it to them, what harm could it possibly do?

And what harm, indeed, could numbers three, four, five or six do either? For the next four and a half hours, all you could see billowing from the back of the minibus was a cloud of tobacco fumes. I burnt through cigarette after cigarette, the adrenaline and the nicotine coursing through my veins. The feeling of imminent freedom was intoxicating, and the simple pleasure of travelling to somewhere gave me a high. (I still relish the thrill of being able to drive wherever and whenever I want.)

At 10.30am, we arrived in the jungle of Puerto Quimba, ready to cross the Rio Tuira, the same river into which I had contemplated jumping on the way to La Joya. None of that despair touched me today, thank God, even when I saw the La Palma police arriving by boat to pick me up from Puerto Quimba with AK47s at the ready, just in case I misbehaved. To my immeasurable relief, I saw Angel with Fidel having a coffee in the restaurant. Our eyes met as they up stood from the restaurant table, and Angel's jaw fell open as he took in for the first time my manacles and chains. He remembered me only as a free man, having missed my capture at Tocumen Airport on that day – it seemed decades ago – when we were supposed to meet in the arrivals hall.

I would have hugged him in gratitude if I'd been allowed to. Angel, charged like me, was a key figure in the hearing.

We shuffled slowly down the slippery ramp to the waiting boat. A guard placed a life jacket, more like a strait jacket, over my head and I was positioned on a central seat. The crossing was rough; if I'd fallen in on this occasion, it would have been a genuine accident.

A little under an hour later, we pulled up at the rear of La Palma police station, at exactly the same spot where I had been chained like a circus exhibit. I tried to resist the bad memories, but they threatened to sabotage me. All the horrific things that I had buried in an effort to keep my sanity began to rise to the surface again.

The antidote was the sight of the familiar faces who, I was touched to see, had arrived to watch the hearing. These were the people who, when I was at my most abject, had taken the trouble to bring me some fruit or a drink of apple juice. I wanted to thank them, every one of them, for their kindness and loyalty. It meant a huge amount to me. Whether they had offered to wash my soiled clothes or given words of encouragement, they had quietly provided support that I still treasure. I caught a glimpse of several Emberá friends on the court steps, and their smiles were a kind of balm that soothed the bad thoughts and increased my hope that this experience would soon have a happy conclusion.

We entered the courtroom, tensed for the hearing. We discovered all the seats apart from our own were empty. My accusers, who I'd so wanted to berate, were not there. They had no legal representation. Fidel was the only attorney present. Flat silence. Angel and I, bewildered, wondered if we had somehow arrived at the wrong time.

The squat little prosecutor started his spiel and showed the judge a letter from the accusers' attorney, who said that he had resigned from the case, and then went on to announce that the accusers had retracted their testimonies and would not be attending. His anger evident, the prosecutor finally admitted that he had not one shred of evidence against us.

Within 10 minutes, the female judge has dismissed all the charges against Angel and me as totally unfounded and without evidence.

It was a moment that combined elation at her verdict with fury at the way I had been treated; relief and disbelief; a burst of euphoria and also long-suppressed exhaustion. I thought the nightmare was over at last.

The minors in the case had previously admitted that their parents were paid to participate in Laura's conspiracy. In fact, they had withdrawn their testimonies some three months beforehand. Did I want them put before a judge for perjury with everyone else who had colluded in this farce?

You bet I did!

A girl called Jocelyn was apparently the star witness for the prosecution and had been the only one not to withdraw her testimony, but she had sadly passed away. Her word would have been thrown out even if she were alive because she was so ill, effectively in a vegetative state, with a brain tumour. There is no doubt her frail state was exploited by the Gallardos and the prosecutor.

A video of Jocelyn taken in 2012, two years before the prosecutor extracted his highly dubious statement from her, can be seen on my website and it shows how ill she was even then. Friends have told me that she had been moved from Darién to Cabima, near Panamá City, to undergo extreme surgery on three tumours. My mother was also a close friend of this family, and wired money to them to cover essentials. She was the one who asked me to visit the family and send them the video. It was heart-breaking to see this youngster, around the same age as my own kids, a girl who had dreamed of working in tourism, reduced to a shell. She believed that she had been possessed by demons sent by the Gallardo family, and it was clear that her mental faculties were slipping away.

In total, 15 months of my life have gone to waste. 15 months awaiting trial, while everything I'd worked for was taken away. 15 months enduring the same travesty of justice as Arthur and many others in a shitty prison. Maybe I should have been filled with more forgiveness, but

I sincerely wished comparable suffering on the people who had caused my misery.

Angel walked from the court a free and happy man, in tears of joy. He had been through his own torment caused by the Gallardos and he deserved to enjoy every second of his life now that there was no longer an arrest warrant hanging over him. All he wanted was to head back to his family in Sona, Veraguas, and settle down peacefully. The trip back home must have been the best 12-hour bus ride of his life.

I, on the other hand, had to return to La Joya. I said goodbye to Angel believing that we would soon be able to meet again. I had no idea that it would be the last time we would see each other.

Fidel advised me that the necessary paperwork would need to be completed before my release. Then, after taking a breath, he detonated a massive bombshell.

"You do know, Nick, that when you're released, you will be deported from Panamá and expelled for life?"

I still remember the exchange exactly. "What? Why?" I asked.

He hung his head. "The law says that any international who has been imprisoned will be deported, regardless of the verdict."

Having officially committed no crime, I was to be treated like a guilty man all the same. What a result for justice – and for Laura!

Over the next week in La Joya I frantically lobbied both the UK and US embassies to intervene on my behalf, in the mistaken belief that someone would be able to wave a magic wand that allowed me to stay: that, crucially, allowed me to resume my fight for my son Jason.

It was no good. The clock was counting down to my longed- for freedom and finally the notification came through from the administration building. 'Libertad-Innocent' jumped out from the second paragraph. At the bottom of the page was the word 'expulso'. By the end of that afternoon I would be released from the prison's control. I decided to do one last good deed before I left. I arranged for 100 cans of soda to be smuggled in.

I used the tannoy system to say goodbye and to thank the real friends I had made in La Joya for their support. I found myself gulping back tears as I announced, "Carlos has a hundred sodas for you, my brothers!"

The most difficult and emotional goodbye was to Arthur. I climbed into his attic space as best I could for one last time, and we exchanged hugs. The moment was like a bereavement. I was leaving behind the best friend I had ever made.

"See you later Arthur," I said. "God bless you, and we will soon fish together in Nevis."

I left the gancha to cheers and applause with my single item of memorabilia, one of the meticulously crafted hammocks made by an inmate from discarded ice bags.

16

ESCAPING HELL

I was ready to leave Building Six and all its memories, good and bad, behind. The saddest part for me was the thought of what would happen to my less fortunate friends, the people who had protected me and whom I had helped in turn. We had grown to rely on each other and now I felt as if I was abandoning them.

"Adios mi amigos," I told them. That moment when I heard the creaking front door, a sound that had formed a backdrop to my life for more than a year, close for the last time will stay with me forever. It has imprinted itself on my memory so deeply that even today, the same noise instantly takes me back to my final day in La Joya.

I was to be transported in chains once more; this time to the migración lock-up in Curundú at the rough end of town, where Noriega was imprisoned in the days before his death. It was an interesting thing to have in common, if the only thing, with a ruthless dictator.

I was in a state of shock. Throughout the trauma of my imprisonment, my focus had been on release. Yet this was not the exit I had imagined. Instead, it snatched my choices from me and imposed an ending I had never imagined. All my efforts in Panamá to find Jason suddenly looked puny and hopeless. The battle had started when he was six years old and I wondered what of me he would remember or believe if I was forced to leave the country without him.

Arriving at the facility, Iwaspatteddownby an immigration guard. He took $50 out of my pocket but failed to check the lining of my jacket, where I had hidden a few more dollars for safety's sake. I was next thrown through a cell doorway to be greeted by yet another jeering, chanting crowd, which was becoming a familiar part of any Panamanian detention experience. This time I had no need to drop to the floor like a sack of spuds.

This particular bunch was made up of captured illegals, not convicted felons. Fuck me, but by some bizarre chance, my mate Pedro loomed out of the throng to calm things down. I knew he had left prison the week before, but I thought by now he would be back home with his kids. The migrants were extremely scared of anyone from La Joya, as it had a reputation for breeding killers. Once they knew where I had been locked up, they meekly backed away. The initiation ceremony was over in a heartbeat.

Pedro took me down a corridor behind the cell, into one of many small rooms, and I was astonished to see at least 15 familiar faces. The space was reserved exclusively for ex- prisoners of La Joya who were awaiting their deportation notifications. At least now there was safety in numbers.

Pedro told me that although he had lived in Panamá since he was three, he was being deported to the country of his birth, Colombia. He had no relatives or connections there, but his prison record had sealed his fate. The authorities gave no weight to his Panamanian wife and two children.

I contacted Pedro in the process of writing this book. Since leaving Panamá he has been unable to see his family, and I really feel for his predicament. He is now in Peru because there are better job opportunities, and is saving his money for attorneys. Despite attempts to lobby the Panamanian government through their embassy in Peru, he has drawn a blank.

For foreign nationals with family ties to Panamá, release from prison just marks the beginning of another sentence, separated from the people we love.

My aim now was to fight, and I meant fight, to stay in the country. I was not willingly going to leave without Jason, knowing that I would never be allowed back. I felt desperate enough to think I'd die for the cause.

The immigration detention facility was overcrowded and full of dodgy people, but it was a slight improvement on La Joya. I reflected, as I looked at the iron bars still surrounding me, that at no point since I had been found innocent by a judge had I actually been free. It took until day four for a representative from the British embassy to come and see me, and I pleaded with him to intervene against my expulsion or to contact the director of immigration. I even asked, knowing what the response would be, for help from the US embassy. For all the good it did, I might as well have sent them a message in a bottle. They could see my human rights were about to be blatantly violated and they didn't give a toss. 'Right to a family life', indeed!

The Foreign Office may proclaim itself a proud advocate of international human rights, but at embassy level that is a fig leaf for weakness. If they really cared about British nationals abroad, I wouldn't be telling this story, I would be with my son in Panamá. I remain committed to bringing their failures to light because they have real human consequences. They destroy lives.

All I had heard from them was the same bleating response: "We cannot get involved in the politics of a foreign state, as we are only guests." Human rights agreements signed and ratified, between Panamá, the UK and USA, are surely worthless unless someone has the balls to uphold them. The sad fact was that the embassies in Panamá believed that trade came before citizens. The UK and the US were two of the largest investors in the country and they weren't going to jeopardise billion-dollar deals over one individual who was bitching about his kid. Far easier just to ship him out, as soon as possible.

Jason was born, raised and schooled in the US and UK up to the age of six, and was an American citizen. The US embassy was not only legally responsible for my care in immigration, as I was first captured with my US passport, but also had a duty of care towards him. They should have been concerned with protecting his human rights under the Rights of a Child ruling, yet once he was taken to Panamá by Laura, into what was an alien culture, they did nothing to get him home. Absolutely zero. It seems child abduction is classed as a mere misdemeanour in their eyes.

At least the UK embassy sent someone to see me, once. He promised to return with medical supplies and toiletries but failed to do so. It was a poor response given that I had worked for them as a warden for many years, but I suppose it was a token effort. Not a single person from the US embassy even turned up at the immigration facility. The lack of compassion was astounding and disgraceful.

I voted for Donald Trump at the time because his pledge to give priority to all American individuals resonated with me. I think it's worth quoting him in full on this subject.

The forgotten men and women of our country will be forgotten no longer. We assembled here today are issuing a new decree to be heard in every city in every foreign capital and in every hall of power. From this day forward, a new vision will govern our land. From this day forward, it's going to be only America first, America first.

Every decision on trade, on taxes, on immigration, on foreign affairs will be made to benefit American workers and American families.

Finally, we must think big and dream even bigger. In America, we understand that a nation is only living as long it is striving. We will no longer accept politicians who are all talk and no action, constantly complaining, but never doing anything about it. The time for empty talk is over. Now arrives the hour of action. Do not allow anyone to tell you that it cannot be done. No challenge can match the heart and fight and spirit of America. We will not fail.

We all enjoy the same glorious freedoms. And we all salute the same great American flag. And whether a child is born in the urban sprawl of Detroit or the wind-swept plains of Nebraska, they look at the same night sky. They fill their heart with the same dreams, and they are infused with the breath of life by the same almighty creator.

So, to all Americans in every city near and far, small and large, from mountain to mountain, from ocean to ocean, hear these words, you will never be ignored again."

Well, President Trump, make good on your word. Get me my boy back. Your actions and speeches to date have not helped.

How can a foreign national ever feel safe abroad in the knowledge that trade interests will always take precedence with his government over individual human rights? We elect politicians on trust. Well, there is an obligation in return to look after ordinary citizens, the ones who actually pay taxes. At embassy level, that money funded ambassadors' jollies but didn't trickle down to helping people wrongfully imprisoned in La Joya. My sad experience was that 'ignored' was exactly what citizens were when they proved to be inconvenient.

More than a week after I was locked in the immigration facility, an official beckoned me into a cramped, dingy room where the desk was spread with pieces of paper. He fired rapid Spanish at me, which I could not understand, and then pointed to the forms lying between us. I saw 'firma', meaning signature, written there and, in big letters, the word 'Libertad'. I thought that at last I was going to be freed. Bear in mind that my health had continued to deteriorate since leaving La Joya. I barely had the strength to walk. I was wrung-out mentally and physically and an awful, heavy despair had settled over me. After the temporary high that followed the hearing in La Palma, I had realised how little had really changed and, despite my unceasing efforts, just how powerless I was.

I started to self-harm, something I had never done before, even in prison. As I sat in that room, waves of exhaustion crashing over my head, my arms were scarred with razor cuts and cigarette burns.

All I wanted to do was sleep. And yet the official kept pointing and talking in ever more agitated Spanish. In the end, like an idiot, I put my name on the documents he told me to sign. I didn't know it, but I had just agreed to my own permanent deportation.

On my last day in Panamá I was summoned at first light by a guard who did not explain where I was going but did take pains to lock me in manacles again: always the prelude to transportation, whether you were innocent or not. I was given my scant possessions and escorted to another minibus. I assumed I was being taken for an interview about my application to stay in Panamá. As we pulled up at the back of the central immigration offices, I was rehearsing my arguments and my lines, aware that Jason's future depended on how well I presented my case. "It is your right," I kept telling myself. "Yours and his. Stay focused."

10. .silent minutes passed. This did not feel right. Then I heard the driver being given instructions: "Tocumen. Aeropuerto de Internacional Tocumen. Rápido!"

It was 9.30 am on September 9, 2014, and I was being taken back to the place where my nightmare had begun. It was time to be processed for removal, along with my former comrades from La Joya. When I saw them again at the airport, I didn't notice a single one of them being given a medical examination. I certainly did not get examined myself. I knew from seeing their medical records in prison that three out of the 15 in Corundú had tuberculosis and hepatitis C.

I was stunned that these highly infectious people were going to be placed on commercial flights out of Panamá alongside unsuspecting passengers. The relevant embassies should surely have sent representatives to oversee the deportations and ensure that checks were carried out.

Staff at the US embassy knew I was being shipped out.

They knew full well about Jason. In fact, the US embassy had conducted a welfare and whereabouts visit back in August 2013. So where were they now? It was a question that has never been answered.

I was put in a wheelchair, still in chains, and pushed straight past all the usual security checkpoints because my minders were so keen to guarantee that I caught my flight back to Miami. The announcement, "Boarding flight! American Airlines flight AA-982 bound for Miami", came too soon. I was next escorted onto the plane itself. Clearly, as a semi-crippled middle-aged man acquitted of all charges, I posed a grave security risk. Only once I was buckled into my seat was I trusted to remain there.

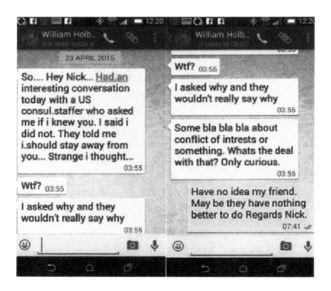

I cried for the entire length of that three-hour flight. I knew with a sickening finality that I was leaving Jason behind forever. Today, as I write, it is 10 years since I last saw him.

I believe that an order had been issued from on high to get me out of Panamá as quickly as possible. Maybe because I was rash enough, back in June, to tell consuls from both embassies about my video evidence of human rights atrocities in La Joya. The political hassle such publicised evidence could bring them was something all the governments involved wanted to avoid, and therefore I think it's reasonable to assume a degree of collusion between them.

Not that I'm eager to compare myself to serial killer Wild Bill Holbert, but I do know that the Panamanian government came down hard on him for running a website out of Colon prison, on which he detailed human rights offences. He made the state look pretty stupid by posting blogs from his mobile phone – and continuing to do so after repeated raids that were supposed to shut him up. He was beaten by the guards for forming Panamáhumanrights.com, and eventually backed down. (He failed to renew his Go- Daddy web registration subscription after all this and, in 2015, I purchased it off the shelf for 99¢.)

On arrival in Miami I was decanted into another wheelchair to get through immigration. An old incident when a stranger had stolen my identity, expunged at state level but for some reason still registered on federal computers, flashed up as it always did, and I was pulled over by the immigration officers. They were my saviours. They could see from my bloodshot eyes and haggard face that I had taken a battering somewhere, and they offered me my first taste of pure human kindness in a long time. It wasn't much, just a cup of coffee and a chance to sit quietly for five minutes, but it steadied me and was a timely reminder that not everyone in uniform was an enemy.

My mother and stepbrother were waiting for me kerbside at the arrivals hall. It was the first time since the horror of my detention that I'd seen any member of my family and a rush of love, gratitude and relief overwhelmed me. We all burst into unstoppable tears. They were crying for me and I was crying for a hundred reasons. Chief among them, the son I had left behind in Panamá and a recognition of the terrible waste, the loss, the cumulative stress, of the past 16 months.

What should have been a celebratory first day of freedom was marred by many shadows. Worse was to come. I was in an extremely frail condition and the emotional shock of my return triggered a seizure. I was rushed for treatment at the Cleveland Clinic emergency room, where doctors diagnosed me with severe malnutrition. On my discharge, their $7,000 bill nearly gave me a heart attack as well.

It did occur to me that my death at this point would have been a neatly symbolic ending to the story. What better way to underline my crash in fortunes? I no longer had a house, in Miami or in Panamá, having lost all my assets while I was in La Joya. Losing my boy as well would surely be good enough to drive me to the grave.

I had arrived in America with one bag and I was leaving the country in the same way. The difference was that in 1996, I had been full of energy and excitement, in pursuit of a dream. Maybe I was so keen to create a perfect, successful life that I neglected to heed my own warning instincts about Laura or Darién,

Before I completed the final leg of the journey back to London, I needed to say some goodbyes that had been impossible when I had disappeared into Panamá's prison system. I stood at the gates that lead to my former street, my former house, and let the good memories flood back for a while, as I held back my tears. The place had new occupants, who'd put up fresh blinds and repainted the woodwork, and I wished them as much happiness as I had once enjoyed there.

There was just one last person I needed to see: my old friend, Willie. We met in an I-Hop on US-1. To say he was gobsmacked by what had happened to me, especially my struggle to get Jason back, was an understatement. You never saw a man so apologetic for his actions in setting me up for that one, fateful blind date. We left on good terms and he remains a friend to this day.

On September 14, 2014, I departed for London. As the plane climbed into Miami's night sky, I looked down at the receding city and thought how beautiful it looked. But the lights and the glowing neon belonged to my old life, and my past. My new life would be far from the one I had left behind.

I was on a different path now. I had a duty to turn the chaos and cruelty of La Joya into something positive: a duty that I owed to more people than just myself. Wish me luck.

EPILOGUE

Panamá's corrupt and broken justice system robbed me of my freedom and of much else besides.

But Panamá has also given me something: the determination to fight. Anger and a need for revenge are great motivators, and I feel them not just on my own behalf, but for the thousands who are treated appallingly in Panamanian courts and prisons.

My story illustrates a bigger truth, and by telling it I am honouring my promise to Arthur, who died – still chained and in custody in his final moments – at the National Cancer Centre in June 2015. I am also respecting my personal integrity.

I believe that my ex-wife, her family members and the prosecutor in Darién should be charged for their cynical and criminal manipulation of the law. The Gallardos lied in pursuit of a vendetta against Angel and me, defamed my character on national TV and swindled me out of all my properties. Worse, they conspired to take my son from me and his family, and deliberately kept us apart.

I hold the Panamanian government responsible for my incarceration in the cesspits of Ancón, La Palma and La Joya. Officials were well aware of my case but did nothing to expedite it, and may have conspired to delay my hearing.

Although all charges against me – and Angel – were dismissed as groundless, I have been deported for life on the grounds that I am a threat to national and public security.

341

Jason remains beyond my reach. Having asked the US and UK embassies in Panamá to carry out a welfare and whereabouts inspection so that I could check whether he was, at least, OK, the American embassy wrote back with the non-response of. "...your ex-wife did not allow us permission to visit Jason." I have since had informal word that Laura has abandoned him and now lives in the States.

My son is an American citizen, yet the embassy in Panamá City has effectively washed its hands of him. It seems more concerned with entertaining dignitaries and boosting trade than in the welfare of vulnerable individuals.

Panamá, ACS <Panamá-ACS@state.gov>

Mon 12/09/2016 18:13

Good Afternoon, Mr Tuffney,

You are correct that your ex-wife did not allow us permission to visit Jason. As you know, unless we have her permission, we are not able to visit. If you would like to talk to someone about the legal options you can pursue, below is the contact information from the Children's Issues Officer at the State Department that covers Panamá. I am sorry that we cannot be of further assistance but the Embassy is extremely limited in what we can do in this case.

Kimberly Lopez

Lopezk2@state.gov

1 (202) 485-6328

What the Law Says

Since 2010, when Laura took Jason, I have been granted no opportunity to contact him. The onus is on the state of Panamá to respect bilateral agreements that apply to children removed in this manner. Panamá, the US and the UK should have co-operated in accordance with The Hague Convention in pursuing my complaint.

My rights as a loving parent were simply not taken into account. I feel as if I have been criminalised, though I have never voluntarily neglected my responsibilities towards him or committed any kind of abuse.

At the time of my deportation I was the subject of a court order for Jason's financial support, and for that reason alone I should not have been flown out: people with current court orders are banned from leaving the state. Yet I am now prohibited from entering Panamá, and therefore can neither find nor see my son. A court order initiated by Laura prohibits Jason himself from leaving the country.

When I decided to test the validity of my deportation, I asked my Panamanian lawyer if there was any way I could expunge my immigration record and re-enter Panamá to which the answer was yes. Later, the director of immigration, Maria González, would resign her post amidst numerous charges of alleged corruption. The new director, Javier Carrillo, purged 40 immigration officials from one of the most lucrative ministries of everyday corruption. My deportation, however, was ordered by government officials, who are much higher up the ladder.

Shortly before his death in 2015, Arthur contacted his barrister, John Jones QC from Doughty Street Chambers, and arranged an introduction. I was very fortunate that John took up my case, as he had successfully represented Arthur and won a verdict from the UN Special Rapporteur on torture that Panamá was guilty of cruel and inhumane treatment. The 600 hours of video evidence I had collected, along with my documentation and unanswered letters to the authorities, strengthened my case, which was filed with the United Nations in Geneva.

In October 2015, the UN Special Rapporteur on torture wrote to the president of Panamá, Juan Carlos Varela, to say that his findings indicated that I had been kept in debilitating and insanitary conditions. He detailed the lack of sleeping space, the extreme overcrowding and the generally poor living conditions, which were exacerbated by the inattention to mental and physical integrity and the lack of obligatory medical care.

His report further detailed the abuse I had suffered in the Ancón and La Palma detention facilities, including torture, harassment and intimidation. The state had failed to separate the inmates by category, resulting in dangerous and convicted criminals being housed with those presumed innocent and awaiting trial.

The Special Rapporteur asked for a response to these allegations within 60 days, specifically pointing out the various conventions to which Panamá was signatory but appeared to be in violation. The letter further pointed out that it was the state's responsibility to rectify deficiencies and punish offenders.

Direct questions of clarification were made to the president, whom the Rapporteur said would be heard without prejudice. However, neither the president nor any of his ministers responded.

In February of 2016, the Special Rapporteur concluded that Panamá had indeed failed to fulfil its responsibilities and obligations to protect my physical and psychological integrity and that conditions within the prison constituted inhuman or degrading treatment, under articles one and 16 of the Convention Against Torture. The Special Rapporteur urged the government of Panamá to publicise the developments on this case and called on it to begin the investigation, prosecution and possible conviction of those guilty of abuse and make reparations to me. Once again, Panamá was silent.

HAUT-COMMISSARIAT AUX DROITS DE L'HOMME • OFFICE OF THE HIGH COMMISSIONER FOR HUMAN RIGHTS

PALAIS DES NATIONS • 1211 GENEVA 10, SWITZERLAND

www.ohchr.org • TEL: +41 22 917 9359 / +41 22 917 9407 • FAX: +41 22 917 9008 • E-MAIL: registry@ohchr.org

Mandate of the Special Rapporteur on torture and other cruel, inhuman or degrading treatment or punishment degrading

REFERENCE: AL

PAN 2/2015:

October 26, 2015

Excellence,

I have the honour to address you in my capacity as Special Rapporteur on the torture and other cruel, inhuman or degrading treatment or punishment in accordance with resolution 25/13 of the Human Rights Council.

In this context, I would like to draw the urgent attention of the Government of Excellency the information I have received regarding the conditions and treatment during the arrest of Mr. Nicholas Tuffney. The allegations indicate that conditions within penitentiary centres, such as overcrowding and others, would have led to a series of cruel, inhuman, degrading treatment and even torture against Mr. Tuffney, on the part of others deprived of their liberty, as well as on the part of authorities of the three penitentiary centres where he was detained, impacting negatively on the physical and mental integrity of Mr. Tuffney.

According to the information received: Mr. Nicolas Tuffney was arrested in April 2013 by forces police at the Tocumen International Airport. Subsequently it would have been transferred to Ancón, Police Detention Centre; once in this centre, where remained for a period of two weeks, Mr Tuffney would have suffered from abuses, harassment and intimidation by others deprived of their liberty, as well as by the authorities of the penitentiary centre. Fear of abuse of the other persons deprived of their liberty would have caused Mr. Tuffney not to leave his cell, not even to make use of the bathroom. Also during this Ancon, Mr. Tuffney would not have had a place to sleep and he would have had to sleep on the concrete floor.

Mr. Tuffney would have been transferred to the San José de la Palma Hospital in Darien, where he would have been hospitalized for a period of two weeks due to deterioration of their health conditions. Subsequently, and against the recommendations of the doctor, he would have been transferred to the La Palma prison on 8 of June of 2013 where it would have remained until the 16 of July of the same year.

During the almost two months of imprisonment in this penitentiary he was kept handcuffed every day and would not have been allowed to stand move freely. He would also not have been allowed to exercise and, although condition of their joints continued to deteriorate, they would not have offered any medication. On several occasions, and due to the poor and inadequate water drainage conditions in the prison, Mr. Tuffney was allegedly damaged by flooding. You would not have been personal hygiene products, including toilet paper, drinking water.

Then, for no apparent reason, he would have been transferred from La Palma prison to the La Joya prison on 16 July 2013 where he would have been held until August 27, 2014. Their evaluation for infectious diseases was not practiced by the fact that on their arrival the change of authorities of the penitentiary would have been unfinished.

In the building where Mr. Tuffney was held would have been found between 430 and 520 persons deprived of their liberty, when the building has the capacity more than 240 people. Mr. Tuffney would have slept on the concrete floor. In terms of health conditions, those deprived of liberty would have had to improvise with bottles to collect water from the rain or to place tubes in the patios to rinse the water from the toilets. However, in the drought, water would have been insufficient or non-existent. For a period of 10 days, the deprived of their liberty, including Mr. Tuffney, would not have had access to water, nor even to water that they could buy inside the detention centre.

In addition, inmates within the penitentiary they would have been categorized as pre-trial or sentenced. Together to overcrowding, excessive heat, restrictions to move within imprisonment and the absence of activities would have led to acts of violence among inmates.

As for hygiene and health treatments, the medicines would have been sold by the authorities or by the inmates themselves. In addition, Mr. Tuffney would have asked the Director of the Prison psychological evaluation, which was ignored. After staying in this detention centre for more than a year, it would have been transferred to the Centre for the Detention of Migrants since August 27, 2014 until September 9, 2014. The centre would have had mattresses thin on the floor, but only two of the rooms had windows, these they would have been the only entrances of fresh air. So the centre would not have basic needs of hygiene and cleanliness, nor would it have counted with immediate medical assistance within the Centre.

After being released from prison Mr. Tuffney's mental capacity would have been seriously affected. His mobility would be severely limited due to the progression of osteoarthritis caused by their arrest. I would also experience anguish and suffering because of his detention.

Without wishing to prejudge the truth of these allegations, I would like to express my concern for these facts. I would like to appeal to the Government of your Excellency to seek clarification to ensure that violations of the right to physical and mental integrity of Mr. Tuffney, as well as of the detainees of La Joya and of the other detention centres mentioned previously do not continue to occur. I would like to emphasize that the Government has the obligation protect the life and integrity of individuals, are under his custody, as are those deprived of liberty.

These rights are enshrined in Articles 3 and 5 of the Declaration Universal Declaration on Human Rights, Articles 6 and 7 of the International Civil and Political Rights, ratified by the Government of Panamá on March 8 1977 and Articles 2 and 16 of the Convention against Torture and Other Forms of cruel, inhuman or degrading punishment, ratified by Panamá on August 24, 1987.

In relation to the above allegations, please find enclosed the Annex of references to international human rights law which summarizes the relevant international instruments and principles.

It is my responsibility in accordance with the mandate given to me by the Human Rights Council; try to clarify the allegations brought to my attention.

In this regard, I would be grateful to have the cooperation and comments of Your Excellency on the following matters:

1   Please provide all the information you have about the claims.

2   Please provide detailed information as well as the results if available, from any investigation, medical and judicial examination or other type of research that has been carried out in this case. If these have not taken place or have not been concluded, please explain the why.

3   In the event that the alleged perpetrators of the offenses have been identified and arrested, please provide detailed information on the judicial and administrative proceedings. Have you imposed any penal, disciplinary or administrative sanction to the alleged culprits /perpetrators?

4   Please indicate what compensation, repair and rehabilitation have been taken in favour of the victim on account of these events.

I would be grateful if you would receive a reply from Your Excellency's Government to these questions in a maximum period of 60 days.

Pending its reply, I would like to urge the Government of your Excellency to take all necessary measures to protect the rights and freedoms and to investigate prosecute and impose sanctions person responsible for the alleged violations. I would also urge you to take the effective measures to avoid that such facts, if they occurred, are repeated.

I guarantee that the response of Your Excellency's Government will be included in the report to be submitted to the Human Rights Council. Accept, Excellency, the assurances of my highest consideration.

Juan E. Méndez

Special Rapporteur on torture and other cruel, inhuman or degrading treatment or punishment

Annexed

References to international human rights law

With regard to the allegations, I would like to appeal to the principles applicable in accordance with international law in this case.

I would like to draw the attention of your Government to article 6 of the Covenant International Covenant on Civil and Political Rights (ICCPR), ratified by the Government of Panamá on March 8, 1977, which provides that every individual has the right to life and personal safety. When the State detains an individual is found obliged to maintain a high level of diligence to protect the rights of that person.

I would like to remind the Government of His Excellency of the absolute and of torture and ill-treatment as set out in

Articles 7 of the ICCPR and 2 and 16 of the Convention against Torture and Other Cruel, Inhuman or Degrading Treatment or Punishment Cruel, Inhuman or Degrading Treatment or Punishment (CAT) ratified by Panamá on 24 August 1987.

I would also like to reiterate to the Government of your Excellency the Principles for the protection of all persons subject to any form of detention or imprisonment (adopted by the General Assembly in its resolution 43/173 of 9

December 1988). The Committee against Torture and the Human Rights Committee have concluded that conditions of detention may constitute inhuman or degrading treatment or punishment.

I remind the Government of your Excellency of the Minimum Rules for Treatment of the Prisoners, provision

22 (2) of which provides that "The transfer of patients whose condition requires special care, to prisons specialized hospitals or civil hospitals. When the establishment has services hospital, they will be provided with the material, instruments and pharmaceutical products necessary to provide sick prisoners with the necessary care and treatment. In addition, staff must have sufficient In this context, I would like to refer to Recommendation E / CN.4 / 2003/68, paragraph

26 (j) of the former Special Rapporteur on Torture, which states that "the countries should take effective measures to prevent violence among prisoners by investigating reports of this type of violence, prosecuting and punishing those responsible and offering protection to the people without marginalizing them from the penitentiary population more than what the needs of protection demand and without subjecting them to new risks of bad treatment. Training programs should be considered to sensitize official's prisons about the importance of taking effective measures to prevent and stop with abuses among prisoners, and equip them with means to do so. In accordance with Set of Principles for the Protection of All Persons

Subject to Any Form of Detention or Imprisonment, prisoners should be divided by sex, age and severity of the crime allegedly committed, and to separate those who have committed for the first time and the recidivists, and those detained in pre-trial detention and those convicted. "

Finally, I would like to refer to the Minimum Rules for the Treatment of prisoners, adopted by the Economic and Social Council in its resolutions 663C (XXIV) of July 31, 1957 and 2076 (LXII) of May 13, 1977 which establish certain criteria for the cells of persons deprived of liberty in principle 9 (1) and (2) provides that: "Cells or rooms intended for night-time isolation shall not be occupied by more than one prisoner. If for special reasons, such as excess of the prison population, it would be essential that the administration prison system should make exceptions to this rule, it should be avoided that two inmates in each individual cell or room. 2) When resorting to dormitories, these should be filled by carefully selected prisoners suitable to be housed in these conditions. At night, they will be subjected to a regular surveillance, adapted to the type of establishment concerned. "I would also like to remind the Government of your Excellency of articles 7 and 12 of that Convention, which requires, respectively, that any State Party ensure that, provided that there are reasonable grounds to believe that within its jurisdiction there has been committed an act of torture, the competent prompt and impartial investigation and that any State Party prosecute alleged perpetrators of acts of torture.

In this regard, I note Human Rights Council Resolution 16/23, paragraph 7 (b) which urges States to hold those responsible who perpetrate acts of torture, but also that: "(those persons who) encourage, order, tolerate or to commit acts of torture are held liable and punishable by penalties proportional to the gravity of the offense, including officials in charge of the place of detention in which the prohibited act took place. "

I also recall the thematic report of the Special Rapporteur on torture and other cruel, inhuman or degrading treatment or punishment (A / 69/387), in which the Special Rapporteur stresses that the CAT provides three fundamental pillars in the fight against torture, which are the obligation of States to ensure justice, to prevent all acts of torture and ensure the repair by them. The obligation to investigate is essential to achieve those three main pillars (paragraph 21). Moreover, the fact that it is not investigated, together with lack of accountability, perpetuates the practice of torture and other ill-treatment (paragraph 20).

I would like to draw Your Excellency's attention to article

14 of the Convention against torture and other cruel treatment or inhuman and degrading punishment, which provides that victims of such cruel, inhuman or degrading treatment or punishment have the right to a reparation and just compensation. In this regard, I would like to recall paragraph 7 (e) of the Human Rights that urges States to "ensure that the victims of torturer other cruel, inhuman or degrading treatment or punishment obtain reparation and receive fair and adequate compensation, as well as social, psychological and medical services and other relevant and specialized rehabilitation services, and urges States to establish, maintain, facilitate or support centres or facilities of rehabilitation where victims of torture can receive such treatment and take effective measures to ensure the safety of their staff and patients.

Finally, I would like to recall that Article 12 of the International Covenant on Economic, Social and Cultural Rights, provides the right of everyone to the enjoyment of highest attainable standard of physical and mental health. This includes the obligation for all States to guarantee access to health, with goods and services accessible to all, especially for those segments of the population in situations of vulnerability or marginality, without any discrimination. I would also like to refer the Government of your Excellency General Comments No. 14 of the Committee on Economic, Social and Cultural Rights, which states that: "States have an obligation to respect the right to health, in particular by refraining from denying or limiting equal access to all persons, including prisoners or detainees, representatives of minorities, asylum-seekers or illegal immigrants, preventive health services,

Curative and palliative care [...] "(paragraph 34).

While awaiting further news, John made several approaches to try and find a solution. Ms Ana Delgado, the ambassador to London under president Martinelli, was aware of Arthur's case and my own. John arranged a meeting with her at the private Lansdowne club in Mayfair, at the Panamanian embassy's expense. Ms Delgado said that for a pre-payment of $30,000, she would intervene in my case. She emphasised the importance of commencing a legal case against her country immediately, as Panamá was hosting the Summit of the Americas and would be in international spotlight.

John Jones

Tue 07/04/2015 18:27

Dear Nick,

Please see the message below from Ana Delgado. As you can see, she is asking for advance payment of fees of USD 30,000 to work on your case. I explained to her that, as I understand it, you are not in funds but would be willing to work on the basis of a conditional fee agreement (success fee). So I have repeated that to her just now.

To be candid, even if you were in funds, I could not advise you to forward such a large sum of money without better information as to what the likely yields would be for such an outlay.

In any event, I promised to convey her terms to you, and to revert. So please let me know your thoughts.

From: Ana Irene Delgado <anaidelgado@solendeg. com>

Date: 7 April 2015 19:28:14 CEST

To: 'John Jones' <j.jones@doughtystreet.co.uk>

Subject: RE: Follow up

Dear Mr Jones,

Just finished a meeting in Panamá regarding Ambassador Porter case with my team here in Panamá. It is important we start working as soon as possible with media, to get right momentum, BEFORE summit of the Americas starts which will start tomorrow in Panamá.

Regarding Ambassador Arthur Porter's case, to work out media and journalists it is:[...]. And for Nick Tuffney, USD 30,000 for advancement of legal fees. We can guarantee that right momentum is now before Summit where all media will be focused in Panamá.

Please confirm, and if you have any inquiries, I can coordinate teleconference today.

Ana Irene Delgado

Solis, Endara, Delgado & Guevara Abogados - Attorneys at Law London, UK

John Jones, having had no success in pressuring Panamá to release Arthur, was sceptical. He was also astounded by the enormous upfront fee being demanded. He advised me not to pay, and that was when Ms Delgado's interest in the case fizzled out.

BREAKING: DEATH OF WIKILEAKS LAWYER, JOHN JONES QC, RULED NOT 'SUICIDE'   NEXT NEWS NETWORK

Just prior to the Rapporteur's decision against Panamá, I launched a criminal complaint formally denouncing the government of Panamá and its public officials for violations of my human rights (as defined by the American Convention on Human Rights ratified by Panamá in 1977). John passed it over to the charitable organisation Redress, which seeks justice for torture survivors by combatting government and individual impunity to international human rights standards. Redress engaged the Panamanian attorneys Barrios and Barrios to represent me. They filed the case in August 2016 and the courts held it until April 2018 – at which time the court suspiciously dismissed the complaint against their government, despite the video evidence.

Barrios and Barrios did not inform me or Redress of this dismissal, as was their professional obligation to their client. Strangely enough, that lack of notification allowed the statutory period for appeal to expire.

Back in April 2017, Barrios had also agreed to launch a lawsuit against TVN-2, the station that made the ridiculous documentary, *Terror en Darién*, about me being a practising witch. TVN-2 happened to be owned by one of the most influential businessmen in Panamá, who was an avid supporter of the incumbent government. Instead of pressing ahead, Barios merely wrote a letter to TVN-2 soliciting 'more information' over the production of the film, and never dug any deeper. I saw this as a stalling tactic to string me along until my statute of limitations ran out.

The film had represented me as a weird, black magic-worshipping corruptor of minors and was highly defamatory. Broadcast on national TV with the collusion of the Gallardos, it destroyed my name and reputation. It was lurid sensationalism, with no basis in truth.

Since Barrios and Barrios dropped the ball in my previous case, I found another attorney to bring TVN-2 to account. The case was re-filed by May 8, 2019 and is awaiting a trial date.

Mr Tuffney seeks justice for the wrongs that were done by TVN-2 and others. Mr Tuffney with the help of Mr Giann Carlo Mascarin, barristers in penal law, Republic of Panamá.

Mr Tuffney seeks damages from his accusers in the amount of $10 million for damaging his good name and his family reputation.

Accused perpetrators:

Juan Carlos Heilbron, Roberto Pascual, Janette Poll, Haralambos Tzanetatos, Elsa Gnzzo, Stanley Alberto Motta Cunningham, Alberto Cecilio Motta, plus others who were involved in the filming of (*Lo Desconocido:Terror En Darién*).

GIANN CARLO MASCARIN
Abogado–Attorney at law
LITIGACIÓN–LITIGATION SOLICITOR AND BARRISTER
ESPECIALISTA EN DERECHO PENAL, PROPIEDAD INTELECTUAL
DERECHO ECONOMICO COMERCIAL
Calle I, El Cangrejo nº 27, apto #6
teléfono 64907137

PROCESO _____ PENAL

FISCALIA METROPOLITANA
CCIÓN DE ATENCIÓN PRIMARI

RECIBIDO
08 _____ Mayo _____ 20 __

QUERELLA   FORMAL.

QUERELLA PENAL, EN CONTRA DE LOS SEÑORES JUAN CARLOS HEILBRON, ROBERTO PASCUAL, JANETTE POLL, HARALAMOS TZANETATOS, ELISA GNAZZO, STANLEY ALBERTO MOTTA CUNNINGHAM, ALBERTO CECILIO MOTTA Y OTROS, DENTRO DEL PROCESO PENAL, POR LA SUPUESTA COMISIÓN DE UN DELITO CONTRA EL HONOR DE LA PERSONA NATURAL, EN SU MODALIDAD DE CALUMNIA E INJURIA, COMETIDO POR PARTE D ELA EMPRESA TVN MEDIA, TELEVISORA NACIONAL CANAL 2, Y CONTRA SUS DIRECTIVOS, DIGNATARIOS Y REPRESENTANTE LEGA Y TODOS LOS QUE RESULTEN RESPONSABLES, POR LOS ACTOS COMETIDOS EN PERJUICIO DEL SEÑOR NICHOLAS TUFFNEY.

HONORABLE Y AUGUSTO (A) SEÑOR (A) FISCAL, FISCAL DELEGADO, FISCAL ADJUNTO, AGENTE DE INSTRUCCIÓN DELEGADO, DE LA FISCALÍA METROPOLITANA, AGENCIA REGIONAL O SUB REGIONAL DEL MINISTERIO PÚBLICO DE LA REPÚBLICA DE PANAMÁ, E.S.D.:

As the Panamanian Government had ignored the judgement of the UN Rapporteur, Redress wrote and filed the petition themselves in the Human Rights Court, and it was accepted in Washington for process, the first stage in the court's proceedings. The filing date was October 2018, and it is expected to take several years to work its way through the court.

Organization of
American States

Inter-American Commission on Human Rights (IACHR)

Your petition before the Inter-American Commission on Human Rights has been received and preliminarily registered under the number indicated below:

Number: P-2012-18
Date Received: 09/10/2018
State: Panama

When submitting questions or information, you must include this number.

Once the Executive Secretariat has completed the initial review of the petition, it will inform you regarding its processing. The initial review is performed as established in Article 29(2) of the Rules of Procedure of the IACHR and, due to the large number of petitions received, the processing requires some time.

Panamá has ignored or stifled every complaint so far made by me and my attorneys. Yet the president of Panamá has stated, "Our country respects and complies with the judgements issued by (the UN), faithfully respecting its constitutive framework."

In that case, maybe I will yet receive compensation for my improper incarceration. Perhaps I'll also see some pigs fly.

Prior to lodging a formal complaint, Redress made every effort to settle. They did so through Daniel Fabréga, Panamá's ambassador to the United Kingdom. In a letter dated June 20, 2018, he stated that my complaint was 'being taken seriously by the Panamanian authorities, and that a true commitment does exist to resolve this matter.' If that were true, why did these same authorities, including the president, fail to respond to the UN High Commissioner back in October of 2015? Why did the government of Panamá ignore a criminal complaint, lodged against them within their own country in August of 2016? Why did the Procuraduria, the attorney general of Panamá, turn a deaf ear to my complaints about human rights violations, which I submitted through their own ombudsman, the Defensora del Pueblo, back in April of 2014?

I am still waiting for evidence of Panamá's 'true commitment'. In recent meetings between President Varela, the ambassador, the UK's foreign secretary and representatives from the Foreign Office, discussions of human rights issues were apparently avoided.

The Foreign and Commonwealth Office is responsible for the promotion of the UK's interests overseas. It supports British citizens and businesses around the world, through embassies and consular offices, and has discretionary powers to help those who are in need. In Panamá, representatives visited La Joya Penitentiary every three months in order to check the health and welfare of Brits being held there. The Embassy received numerous complaints, mostly health-related, from those inmates and did what it could despite local obstructiveness to obtain medical treatment for its citizens. My complaints, however, were much more complicated, as I was being held unable to obtain a court hearing. My hearing was cancelled seven times. I felt that the British and American consuls should have intervened to ensure fairer treatment and that they did not, therefore, behave responsibly towards me.

I applied through a Freedom of Information request for the consular notes about my case and found the following had been written about my condition after my stay in La Palma:

> 'Nick was handcuffed by his ankle to the hospital bed and appeared low in energy. He had an IV in his arm and they were giving medicine for his stomach... Nick was visibly depressed and would begin crying every so often... he had not eaten since he was arrested and kept repeating that he wanted to die. Nick will possibly need a follow up psychiatric evaluation due to depression.'

And, in the following month,

> 'Nick expressed suicidal feelings... And seemed very depressed.'

Yet in the mistreatment report covering the same time period, the FCO answered the questions, 'Is medical treatment required?' and, 'Are there any other vulnerabilities to be aware of?' with the answer, 'Not Applicable.' I was a UK citizen being held against my will and had been abused in Ancón by the national police, in front of officials. Yet to the question, 'Have we informed the detainee of any local complaint procedures?' the mistreatment report answered, 'We have not informed... about any local complaint procedures.'

One has to question the integrity of the officials involved. Part of the problem may have been that these British representatives were, in fact, Panamanian. UK government cutbacks lead to the embassy employing a Panamanian national as consul and many administrative posts were held by people with poor or no spoken English. The interpretation of human rights abuses is likely to differ widely between a British citizen and someone who was raised in Panamá.

I continued to complain about conditions and legal inconsistencies to the consular office, but got nowhere. When I then complained to the ambassador, I was told that the FCO policy was to not interfere with the internal laws and politics of host countries.

I felt I was treated as presumed guilty by both the government and Panamá's news media, and that my particular circumstances warranted attention and support. The UK consular office in Panamá, to its credit, had approached the Panamanian Ministry of Foreign Affairs back in August 2013 on my behalf, but two months later, the Ministry flatly denied any allegations of mistreatment or torture, a judgement made without consulting me or medical professionals. Our consul decided not to offer any rebuttal. This was a major disappointment. The embassy totally ignored a British citizen's complaint about torture and instead meekly sided with Panamá.

Back in the UK, Redress raised the matter with the parliamentary and health service ombudsmen in November

2017, by filing an extensive report on the limitations and inconsistencies of the British embassy from the time of my arrest to my eventual deportation. The result of this complaint will be important to me, but may also have wider implications. Redress has made a series of recommendations for the FCO to implement when British citizens are detained abroad.

On December 4, 2019, the FCO buckled when the parliamentary ombudsman upheld my complaint. The embassy had failed to address issues regarding my health, welfare and well-being.

THE TIMES | Monday November 25 2019   2GM

Diplomats left me to rot in foreign jail

Jonathan Ames Legal Editor

A businessman who spent more than a year in a Panamanian jail on charges including witchcraft and corruption was failed by Foreign Office officials, a watchdog has ruled.

Nicholas Tuffney, 55, was arrested after travelling in the Central American country in pursuit of his estranged wife who he claimed had taken their son from their home in Miami without his agreement.

He spent 16 months in jail in 2013-14 on charges including corruption, child

Nicholas Tuffney has been awarded compensation for his ordeal

sex abuse and witchcraft. All charges were dropped immediately when he finally faced a court, he said.

On Friday it emerged that the parliamentary ombudsman has upheld a complaint that British consular officials failed to provide adequate help for Mr Tuffney during his ordeal. It is only the sixth complaint over Foreign Office consular services that has been upheld in eight years.

Mr Tuffney told *The Times* that the experience had ruined his business and that he was now living on benefits in

Harrietsham, near Maidstone in Kent. He still has not seen his son.

Campaigners for Mr Tuffney, who owned a teak and mahogany plantation in Panama, said he was held in brutal conditions that did not meet international standards. He slept in a room with 150 other prisoners with only one, non-flushing lavatory. Guards forced him to strip naked and refused to let him wash his clothes.

Mr Tuffney said that British embassy staff saw him handcuffed to a hospital bed but failed to raise his treatment with Panamanian authorities. He also alleged that guards chained him to a wall in public view for about two days.

He said he was held for more than 16 months without being brought before a court. He told *The Times* that when a hearing was eventually held, it lasted just minutes before he was told that all charges had been dropped.

The parliamentary ombudsman found the British embassy guilty of "maladministration" in dealing with Mr Tuffney in Panama. It said Foreign Office officials should apologise and pay him nearly £3,000 in compensation.

Mr Tuffney said that he was grateful for the ombudsman's ruling but remained angry at the Foreign Office. "It doesn't speak up for Brits abroad," he said.

A Foreign Office spokesman said: "We note the parliamentary and health service ombudsman's report and will respond in due course."

British National who was ill-treated in Panamá has complained against the FCO, upheld by an Ombudsman, a report by Redress has found.

Redress.org: The Parliamentary Ombudsman has upheldthecomplaint of a British national against the Foreign and Commonwealth Office (FCO) for failing to offer him adequate consular assistance during his detention in Panamá, where he was ill-treated, at one point being chained to metal bars in full view of the passing public.

Nicholas Tuffney spent 16 months in several Panamánian detention facilities, between 2013 and 2014, on charges which he always contested and which were eventually dropped. He was held in very poor conditions that did not meet international standards, including being forced to sleep in a room with 150 other prisoners with only one, non-flushing toilet.

He was also forced to strip naked in front of other prisoners, and not allowed to walk, go to the bathroom or wash his soiled clothes. After feeling ill, he was hospitalised and was handcuffed to a hospital bed

— this was witnessed by embassy staff, but they failed to raise it with Panamánian authorities, despite it being possible ill-treatment.

On his return to the UK, Tuffney complained to the FCO, but was not satisfied by its response. REDRESS then helped him submit a complaint (through his MP, Helen Whately) to the ombudsman, which investigates complaints of poor or unfair service from government departments and other public organisations.

After investigating the complaint, the ombudsman's findings, released on 28 October 2019, upheld Tuffney's complaint and found multiple examples of maladministration by the FCO. They found that, contrary to their own internal guidance, embassy staff failed to promptly and adequately respond to his allegations of ill-treatment; could and should have done more to remedy other welfare concerns and failed to give him accurate information about what detainees might expect in Panamánian prisons.

Tuffney claimed that as a result of the FCO's failings, he has been caused "ongoing anxiety, frustration and increased feelings of isolation adding to an already very stressful and traumatic situation and has self-harmed." The ombudsman agreed with him, finding that the "FCO's lack of support would have added to his frustration" and "likely contributed to his beginning to self-harm".

The ombudsman recommended that the FCO apologise to Tuffney, and provide him and his family with financial compensation, recognising "a significant and/or lasting impact, so much so that to some extent it has affected their ability to live a relatively normal life" (see the ombudsman's scale of financial remedies). The ombudsman also suggested that the FCO explain what they intend to do to prevent a recurrence and update the information provided to British nationals detained in Panamá.

Between 2011-2018 only five out of 244 complaints were upheld by the ombudsman in relation to FCO's actions.

Reacting to the Ombudsman's findings, Tuffney said, "I am very pleased that the ombudsman has stepped in on my case and made recommendations for change which will benefit the public long-term. It will hopefully improve the way the FCO responds to other UK citizens who are detained abroad."

Earlier this month, the All-Party Parliamentary Group on Deaths Abroad, Consular Services and Assistance (APPG) recommended in its report 2019 that the FCO clarifies its guidance around consular assistance, and enshrines in UK law the right to consular assistance, echoing previous recommendations made by REDRESS.

REDRESS's legal advisor, Chris Esdaile, said, "We are delighted that the ombudsman has recognised the shortcomings in the assistance offered to Mr Tuffney. While we understand the difficult job which the FCO undertakes in providing consular protection, we will continue to argue that the FCO should be under a legal obligation to assist UK nationals, such as Mr Tuffney, who face such traumatic experiences."

Redress's report, *Beyond Discretion; The Protection of British Nationals Abroad*, lobbies for consular assistance and diplomatic protection to be enshrined in UK law, as the right of any citizen whose human rights are violated. At present, such protection is only a matter of policy and remains discretionary. My experience, along with that of several others, was used to demonstrate the need for such a law.

The United Nations has compiled a series of accords – among them the Universal Declaration on Human Rights and the International Covenant on Civil and Political Rights, which include the Convention Against Torture and Other Cruel, Inhuman or Degrading Treatment or Punishment and the Minimum Rules for Treatment of Prisoners. Between 1977 and 1987, Panamá ratified all these agreements, but for some reason its government feels no obligation to implement the rules. It talks a good game, though. President Varela, while hosting the Summit of the Americas in 2015, proudly offered Panamá as a shining example of respect for human rights in Central and South America. In the same year, the Permanent Mission of Panamá to the United Nations applied to the General Assembly for Panamá to join the Human Rights Council and the country was appointed membership between 2016 and 2018.

Their presentation to the secretary-general of the UN included Article (1), which is an institutional framework that upholds democracy and the protection of human rights, concepts rooted in its culture and enshrined in its constitution and legislation; Article (3): Its foreign policy is founded on the principle of promoting and supporting 'the rule of law in all its forms'; and Article (4): Panamá played a leading role in the drafting of the Universal Declaration of Human Rights in 1948. From 2006 to 2007, Panamá, through its Permanent Mission to the United Nations in New York, actively contributed to the establishment of the Human Rights Council.

However, during the period of its most recent appointment to this council, Panamá had at least two unanswered judgements against it by the Rapporteur on degrading treatment; mine and Arthur Porter's. A report from their Ministry of Foreign Affairs implied that they did not recognize such complaints, and would prefer concerns be brought before the Inter-American Court of Human Rights – a long and arduous process.

The contradiction is that the mission statement to the secretary-general claims something else. It states that Panamá commits to: Article (17e): Support the activities of the Human Rights Council and of its bodies, procedures and special mechanisms in the promotion and protection of human rights; Article (17l): Support the council's efforts to combat torture and cruel, inhuman and degrading treatment, including by strengthening of the work of the Special Rapporteur on Torture and other Cruel, Inhuman and Degrading Treatment or Punishment; and finally but not limited to Article (17o): Ensure that the council fulfils its mandate to strengthen the promotion and protection of human rights throughout the world and to address human rights violations.

The government's assault on my rights was matched by the attack on my reputation by TVN-2's internationally distributed film, *Terror en Darién*, a mash-up of sensational fake news reports that was packaged for international release two years after all charges were dropped. The production was a violation of International Principles of Professional Ethics in Journalism, which states:

> *'An integral part of the professional standards of the journalists is respect for the right of the individual to privacy and human dignity, in conformity with provisions of international and national law concerning protection of the rights and the reputation of others, prohibiting libel, calumny, slander and defamation.' (Ethics Net, Journalism Ethics)*

But now is the time to talk about what has happened to me since I was freed from La Joya.

My meetings with the Panamanian ambassador, Daniel Fabrega, were unproductive. He was a pleasant enough guy, but he had no teeth. He has now left the post in London and I hope his replacement, a woman, will make more of a difference.

In December 2019, a letter was drafted and sent to the president of Panamá to ask if he would grant me a pardon on humanitarian grounds, so that I can return to the country to find my son. Any updates will be posted on my site. As you have stuck with me this far, I am going to give you the key codes to access this amazing spin to my book:

1. Go to: www.buildingsixpanama.com.

2. Log in as a member using guest@buildingsixpanama. com. Your password is the ISBN of this book, which can be found above the barcode on the back cover.

Enjoy the ride.

In 2015, my lawyers submitted a Hague Convention application against international child abduction to Panamá, with the help of the UK government's Child Abduction Agency. The case, unfortunately, dragged on for nearly three years. Laura was initially living in Miami and could not be contacted, which caused a significant delay. By the time the first hearing was set, the case had been postponed because the results of a physiological evaluation carried out on Jason were not supplied. One year later, another hearing was cancelled because the judge would not accept my power of attorney, despite the fact that he had previously been accepted by the same judge.

Panamanian judges are not trained in the international Hague Convention or abduction cases, a shortcoming that worked against my application: they are only familiar with family courts. The standard practice with Hague Convention cases is to leave them open so that they can be modified as the child grows older. However, my case was closed without my knowledge and cannot now be re-opened.

The International Child Abduction Agency in London failed to pass on vital date- sensitive documents about my ex-wife's action in overturning the order and closing the case.

ICACU <ICACU@offsol.gsi.gov.uk>
Fri 13/04/2018 16:23

Dear Nick,

I have not heard back from Panamá to my previous request.

Your case was in my calendar for today to follow up with them. This I have done. I have also contacted the Foreign and Commonwealth Office in order to see if they are able to assist me in obtaining a substantive reply from Panamá. I am awaiting their reply.

I have asked Panamá if the mother has notified them of her relocation to the USA seeing as she was previously arranging some papers with them. If that is the case then we can transfer the matter to the USA. That said I am not sure what we do if the mother is in the USA and the child is in Panamá, I would need to seek guidance on this matter.

I will let you know as soon as I have any news.

Kind regards,

Clair Joslin

International Child Abduction Contact Unit (ICACU)

Official Solicitor & Public Trustee 8th Floor, Victory House

30-34 Kingsway London WC2B 6EX

In 2014, I auditioned for a series with Raw TV to expose Panamá's failures. We were given the green light by the National Geographic Channel and I spent three days filming in Acton studios. The project was pulled, however, because I didn't have enough evidence at the time to validate my story. It was a severe disappointment, and since then I have worked tirelessly to gather material, including extensive video footage, that verifies all parts of my story. This approach has led to the creation of my website and to this book. I am now confident that I have provided full documentation.

Once I had recovered sufficient strength back in the UK, I embarked on a letter writing campaign to support my 'right to a family life'. The list of recipients included Prime Minister Theresa May, former Prime Minister David Cameron, MP Helen Whately, ambassador to Panamá Irene Delgardo, ambassador to Panamá Daniel Fabrega, President of Panamá Juan Carlos Varela, US ambassador Woody Johnson, President of the US Donald Trump, HRH the Queen, and congresswoman Debbie Wasserman Shultz.

Only one replied in full and that was, with impeccable manners, the Queen. I received the following on October 7, 2019:

> *Dear Mr Tuffney,*
>
> *The Queen has asked me to thank you for your recent letter from which Her Majesty has taken careful note of the views you expressed regarding the appointment of a new Panamánian ambassador to the United Kingdom*
>
> *I must explain, however that as a constitutional Sovereign the Queen acts on the advice of her Ministers and remains strictly non-political at all times. This is therefore not a matter in which Her Majesty would intervene.*
>
> *Yours sincerely Miss Jennie Vine, MVO*

My mental health remains fragile and I have trouble focusing, but writing this book has been cathartic. The very acts of remembering and confronting the nightmare has helped me to heal.

My self-harming is slowly abating with time, as are the awful flashbacks that used to ambush and destabilise me. In 2018, my state of mind was so poor that I could not hold down my position as director of the family company and it was forced into foreclosure. As someone whose self-image was built on being successful businessman, I felt totally useless. I also worried that my children, to whom I had been a kind of hero, would lose their respect for me.

All my personal possessions and my investments were picked over and stolen by Panamanian buzzards. I now live on £60 a week, working as a carer looking after my elderly mother in Kent. It is not the most dynamic ending for someone who has enjoyed such a driven and colourful career, but I retain my strong faith that things will change for the better one day.

I have kept in touch with many of the people I met in Building Six. The ones who have managed to fly that hellhole are now dispersed around the world in Canada, Peru, Ecuador, Nicaragua and Colombia. All of them have added their compelling and emotionally charged video testimonies to my website, which can be found on pages 33 and 34.

Since my release, I have managed to meet two of the survivors in person: flying one from Canada and driving to see the other in the UK. The opportunity to talk about and share the experiences that we are all struggling to process in our different ways was helpful – and difficult, too. Tears were shed.

We agreed that the collateral damage inflicted on our families, especially our mothers, was immense. After the prolonged pain of separation, our homecomings caused complex issues of their own.

None of us who endured La Joya emerged unscathed but, for the ones lucky enough to be freed, there is now the chance to move towards a brighter, more hopeful future

The sordid, dirty, cruel reality of the prison and of Panamá's corruption still needs to be revealed. It is a reality that Panamá does not want people to see. My website's whole purpose is to spin you in your seat with shock at what this apparently civilised country feels is an acceptable interpretation of human rights. (Please note that the site's contents have been copyrighted, so any reproduction, regardless of the format, must be granted prior approval.)

There are some days, back home in the greenery of Kent, when it seems impossible that I was ever locked up with mass murderers and

375

drug lords, but the memories are still all too clear. If I cannot erase them, I prefer to travel back in my mind to happier times. I remember instead fishing in the Miami sunshine with Jason.

I wish to thank all my children and family. They played a major role in supporting me as I wrote this book. Without their love and their approval, I would never have been able to bring such an amazing story to you.

I would like, also, to thank everyone from Building Six who went the extra mile and trusted me enough to hand over their valuable pictures and video footage as evidence to strengthen my campaign.

There are three people who are also incredibly dear to me but who will be unable to read this book. They played a pivotal role in my life and will forever remain in my heart. I hope sincerely that they now rest in peace.

My job is done here. I can now work to move on, damaged but intact.

Printed in Great Britain
by Amazon

63134476R00211